1

THE WORD ALIVE

THE WORD ALIVE

Commentaries and Reflections on the Scripture Readings for all Sundays, Solemnities of the Lord, Holy Days, and Major Feasts for the three-year cycle.

by

Eugene H. Maly

ALBA · HOUSE   NEW · YORK

SOCIETY OF ST. PAUL, 2187 VICTORY BLVD., STATEN ISLAND, NEW YORK 10314

Library of Congress Cataloging in Publication Data

Maly, Eugene H.
 The word alive.

 1. Bible—Meditations. 2. Bible—Homiletical use.
3. Bible—Liturgical lessons, English. I. Sena,
Patrick J. II. Title.
BS491.5.M34   220.6   81-20571
ISBN 0-8189-0416-X   AACR2

Nihil Obstat:
Patrick Sena, C.PP.S.
Censor Deputatus

Nihil Obstat:
John J. Jennings
Censor Librorum

Imprimatur:
†Daniel E. Pilarczyk, V.G.
Auxiliary Bishop of Cincinnati
October 9, 1981

Designed, printed and bound in the United States of
America by the Fathers and Brothers of the
Society of St. Paul, 2187 Victory Boulevard,
Staten Island, New York 10314, as part of their
communications apostolate.

---

1 2 3 4 5 6 7 8 9 (Current Printing: first digit).

Additional Material

by Patrick J. Sena, C.PP.S.

Edited by

Thomas A. Lennon

TABLE OF CONTENTS

EDITOR'S INTRODUCTION

Late in August 1979, Father Eugene Maly arrived at the Seminary of St. Vincent de Paul, Boynton Beach, Florida. He was to be visiting professor of Scripture for the first semester. Then from January to March he would work on a major project: collecting and assembling into a book a selection of his commentaries on the Sunday Scripture readings for the three-year liturgical cycle. For more than a decade they had been published week by week in *The Catholic Telegraph* of Cincinnati and numerous other diocesan newspapers.

Prior to that time in Florida I had had only a few, brief conversations with Father Maly. But at the seminary we became good friends and had many long talks. He was intrigued by the idea of a layman teaching homiletics to seminarians, and he seemed particularly interested in the way I would edit the students' written homilies.

One chilly night in February 1980, Father Maly came to my room. In his hands was part of the manuscript of this book.

"I'm wondering if you would consider editing these 15 columns," he said. "And if I like what you do to them, would you consider editing all the columns for the book?"

I would. I went to work on the 15 columns he had given me and appreciated the fringe benefit of learning more about the Bible. A week later I returned the edited columns to him, and after examining them, he "hired" me.

But I heard no more about the work until July when I met Father Gene at his "home," Mount St. Mary's of the West, in Cincinnati. He was negotiating with a publisher but nothing was settled. And he was still planning to do about 20 more columns for a number of feasts and Sundays that he had never dealt with in his weekly columns. He wanted, for example, to have commentaries for all three of the Christmas Masses, rather than only one for the Midnight Mass. That meeting was the last time I saw Father Gene alive. His untimely death came near the end of July 1980.

Months later Father Gene's family asked me to continue work on the book.

Father Maly never did the additional columns he had planned to write. That task was taken up by his associate at Mount St. Mary's Seminary, professor of Scripture, Father Patrick Sena, C.PP.S. The columns he wrote are signed with his name.

Whether running the manuscript through the copying machine or explaining to me some point of biblical scholarship, Father Sena has been patient, hard-working, and always gracious.

A special word of thanks is extended to Father Maly's cousin, Frank Bill. Through the years Frank kept all of the articles, and as the manuscript was being assembled last winter, he supplied from his own file several that were missing.

When I first received the manuscript, I read it in its entirety. Most readers, I suspect, would enjoy doing the same, for I believe such a reading of the total book reveals more startlingly its treasures and pleasures. Afterward, readers can approach these commentaries on a week-by-week basis.

Father Maly's reflections are filled with wisdom, sanity, practicality, and scholarly information. He affirms the past, cherishes the present, and is hopeful about the future. He not only explains the ancient themes of our Scriptures but also relates them to the present spiritual concerns of a Church striving to improve itself. Consider some of the topics and questions he treats: Does structure stifle the Holy Spirit? Should we eliminate legalism by doing away with laws? Is love enough? Responsible openness. Orthopraxy versus orthodoxy. The good life. Communism. Should we refer to Christ as "king" in the 1980's? Amazing grace. Hell. The "I've Found-It" mentality. Reincarnation. And the cross.

The excellence of these weekly columns was attested to by the Catholic Press Association in 1979 when that organization gave one of its annual awards to Father Maly. The CPA judges commented that he "seems uniquely attuned to the spirit of the Gospels. His columns are very well written."

In working on this manuscript for the past six months I have sensed Father Gene's presence in my home. It has been the presence of a wise, happy, gentle friend who is also an apostle proclaiming the Gospel to me and urging me to holiness.

I suspect all readers of this book will welcome that presence into their lives over and over again. They may want to share and lend this book—but they'll also want to get it back to reread many times in the years to come. Likely this book will lead them to both the Old and the New Testaments with renewed interest and zeal, and to additional volumes that will shed still further light on the Bible. Such an outcome would please Father Maly immeasurably.

Thomas A. Lennon

Dayton, Ohio
Trinity Sunday 1981

PREFACE

For nine years I collaborated with Gene Maly in teaching Bible Studies here at Mount St. Mary's Seminary. I also worked with him on various writing projects: *The Good News Bible, Catholic Study Edition*, and articles in *The Bible Today*. Our collaboration was rooted in a close friendship. Now, almost a year has passed since his death, and with the publication of this work our collaboration comes to an end.

I am deeply grateful to Gene's family for having chosen me to complete this work. It has been a labor of love. For many years I and countless others urged Gene to gather his weekly reflections on the Sunday readings and put them into a book. He finally accepted our pleas and asked Tom Lennon to edit his manuscript. It has been a joy working with Tom as I wrote the unfinished columns and oversaw the theological aspects of the editing.

Sitting at my typewriter, I often remembered Gene sitting at his. He lived a highly disciplined life. A vacation for him was a time when he could write book reviews for *Catholic Biblical Quarterly* or some other professional journal. He always wrote his columns several weeks in advance and always on Saturday morning. Sometimes when he was hard pressed he would ask me to pinch-hit for him on some other Saturday project so that he could get his column mailed on time.

The picture of Gene I most enjoy came from seminarians who, like most students, have a talent for mimicking their teachers. Gene's students would often imitate his manner of saying the word, *eschatology*. When he said it, he would throw his head back and chuckle. The students did an expert job; they gave me a picture of him I shall always remember with pleasure.

Gene, on behalf of all your colleagues, students, friends, relatives, and readers everywhere, "Thank you for having made the Bible the word alive."

Patrick J. Sena, C.PP.S.

Norwood, Ohio
1 May 1981

AN ALLELUIA MAN
SUPREME

by

Joseph F. Beckman

On Wednesday evening, 30 July, Fr. Eugene Maly didn't come to the faculty room at Mt. St. Mary's Seminary for his usual bit of preprandial cheer and conversation. But it was summer vacation and no one really thought much about it. At noon, Thursday, Father Gene didn't keep a luncheon date with two of his nieces and their young babies. Father Gene was quite conscientious, and it wasn't like him to miss an appointment. His car was in the garage, and his office where he studied and wrote wasn't locked, but no one had seen him throughout the day.

Apprehension grew when Father Gene didn't appear for dinner Thursday, and after a brief search, his body was found in the seminary gym where he often went to jog or hit paddle balls against the wall. Apparently he had collapsed and died Wednesday afternoon.

A friend used to comment, "Fr. Gene Maly is the greatest thing to hit the Archdiocese of Cincinnati in the last thirty years." In his scholarly, but human and gentle manner, through his many classes at the seminary, his newspaper column, his books, lectures to Newman and parish groups, retreats, clergy conferences, and through countless personal contacts, Fr. Gene Maly brought the modern interpretation of Scripture to the people of God in Cincinnati.

Maly was also a national and international figure. On several occasions he lectured to Maryknoll missionaries in Guatemala. He was a peritus at two sessions of the Second Vatican Council and a

Reprinted, with permission of The Liturgical Press, from *The Bible Today* 18 (November 1980) 405-410, copyright 1980 by the Order of Saint Benedict, Collegeville, Minnesota.

member of U.S. Bishops' press panel for media representatives at the
Council. His writings in English, or in German, Spanish, and Italian
translations, found their way into rectories, libraries, and classrooms
throughout the world.

The affable Father Maly was especially close to his family: his two
brothers, his sister, his eighteen nieces and nephews, and twelve
great-nieces and nephews. His father had died in 1965 and his
mother in 1970. "From my earliest memories," his nephew Jerry said
recently, "I'll always picture Uncle Gene as a happy man, a man who
appreciated the gift of life and lived it to the full." Nephew Mark
considered his uncle "a constant reminder of the goodness and joy
that come from a life in the presence of God." Father Maly was loved
by his nieces and nephews because, in the words of Mary Beth, "He
made each of us feel special in our own different ways." Nephew
Tom declared, "He viewed all persons as equals." This learned
Scripture scholar often sang lullabies in Hebrew, Greek or Latin to
the babies in the family. "That's how I'll remember him," niece
Joanne said, "singing, smiling and loving."

On 18 December 1975, on the thirty-second anniversary of
Father Maly's ordination, a tragedy occurred in the Maly family.
Father Gene's 11-year-old nephew, named after him, Eugene H.
Maly, died suddenly of a mysterious heart ailment in the parish
gymnasium, across the street from the Maly home, where Father
Gene himself had been born. How odd that the two Gene Malys died
of heart failure in a gymnasium.

Father Maly's nephews and nieces made three banners for dis-
play at his wake and during his funeral Mass at St. Peter in Chains
Cathedral. One proclaimed, "We Are An Alleluia People," a favorite
Maly slogan, and another, "Father Gene—Set Apart For the Gospel."
The third, inscribed, "We love You Uncle Gene," was buried with
him.

Fr. Eugene Harry Maly was born in Cincinnati, 6 September
1920. He attended Holy Family parish school, St. Lawrence Latin
school and St. Gregory and Mt. St. Mary Seminaries in Cincinnati. He
was a good student, especially in languages, and skipped two years
in the course of his studies. He was ordained 18 December 1943, at
the age of twenty-three.

After ordination he studied languages at the University of Cincinnati and later at the Hebrew Union College in Cincinnati. At this same time he served at several parishes, was a hospital chaplain, and on weekends ministered to some Mexican railroad workers—this was World War II time—for whom he sometimes offered Mass in a boxcar. In October 1946, he went to the Angelicum University in Rome where he was awarded a doctorate in sacred theology in 1948. In 1950 he was named a faculty member at Mt. St. Mary's Seminary in Cincinnati, a position he held until his death. In 1957 Father Maly returned to Rome where he studied at the Pontifical Biblical Institute for a doctorate in Sacred Scripture, which he was awarded in 1959. In 1971 Father Maly was appointed dean of theology at Mt. St. Mary's, and later that same year he also assumed the position of vice-rector. During his years at the seminary Father Maly offered Masses on Sundays at several parishes near his family home.

Father Maly's principal work was in the classroom. His students respected him not only for his knowledge, but also for the care he showed for each of them. According to Fr. Norman Langenbrunner, a former student, "Father Maly imparted much more to us than the historical facts and exegetical criticism of the books of the Bible. He gave us a love for the Scriptures, an awareness that in these writings we could come in touch with the patriarchs and Moses and the prophets as they pursued their centuries-long journey to and with the Lord. He reminded us often that the primary purpose for studying the Bible was to encounter the God who made it all possible."

On many occasions Maly warned his students against trying to tie God down, to capture him in some neat capsule or concept. "When you can explain God," he said, "then you can be sure you've got the wrong god, that you've created your own."

Father Maly was a demanding teacher, but highly respected. In one of the classic stories told of him as a new teacher at Mt. St. Mary's, he failed a good percentage of his class in a Scripture exam. When one student went in for his grade, Maly told him, "Of all the students who failed, you got the highest mark."

At. St. Vincent Seminary, Boynton Beach, Florida, where he sometimes served as a guest professor, some of the students were tardy in coming to class. Maly merely locked the doors at class time, and late comers couldn't get in. The students' reaction to Maly's locked doors showed up in a student impromptu play some weeks later with a parody to the tune of "I'm Getting Married in the Morning." It went:

> I've got Maly in the morning.
>> Ding! Dong! the bells are gonna chime.
> Please help me wake up.
>> Please help me wake up.
> For Pete's sake get me to the class on time.

Maly taught many summer courses and seminars throughout the country. His team-taught courses on "Sin" and "Love" at Mt. St. Mary's with psychologist Fr. James McWilliam and moralist Fr. John Civille were extremely popular. Maly was offered a position as a seminary rector shortly before his death, but he wasn't greatly interested in administration. He was relieved when the job didn't materialize. He wanted to teach for the rest of his life.

Maly's work as a writer was another main phase of his life. Through most of the years since 1950 he wrote a column on Scripture, or, for a time, on the Second Vatican Council, for *The Catholic Telegraph*, diocesan newspaper of Cincinnati. Through most of these years his column was syndicated in as many as fifteen other diocesan papers.

He was chairman of the editorial board of *The Bible Today* since it began in October 1962. He wrote 103 *Haggadah* columns and a score of articles on different topics for this popular publication of biblical truth. Father Maly was always excited about *The Bible Today* and deeply interested in increasing its quality and circulation. His most difficult job as editor was rejecting articles. He always tried to soften the blow by sending a personal note along.

Father Maly produced books of biblical theology and history, too—"clear," "excellent," and "lively" volumes, to quote the reviewers. He wrote *The World of David and Solomon* (1966), *Prophets of Salvation (1967), Sin: Biblical Perspectives* (1973), and *Romans* (1979). For the Liturgical Press' New Testament Reading Guide he did *The Epistles of Saint James, Jude, Peter,* and for the Old Testament Reading Guide he did commentaries on *The First Book of*

Samuel and The Second Book of Samuel. He also wrote The Book of Wisdom in the Paulist Pamphlet Bible Series.

He contributed articles to the New Catholic Encyclopedia, Concilium, the Jerome Biblical Commentary, and the other collections of scholarly essays. He was general editor of the introductory material of the Sadlier edition of the Good News Bible and at the time of his death was editor of a new edition of The Liturgical Press' New Testament Reading Guide. He also edited The Priest and Sacred Scripture, commissioned by the National Conference of Catholic Bishops in 1972.

Father Maly wrote articles for more than twenty-five different national publications, from HiTime, a magazine for high school students, to scholarly periodicals like the Catholic Biblical Quarterly. He wrote book reviews for popular magazines and for Theological Studies. For the last five years he contributed a weekly exegesis on the New Testament Sunday reading for Homily Helps published by St. Anthony Messenger Press. Many of his lectures and talks throughout the nation are available from at least four different cassette companies.

Gene Maly was a deeply spiritual man. He was an early riser, and one friend reported that Maly made a holy hour before the Blessed Sacrament from six to seven each morning, often with his Hebrew Bible open before him. This fact wasn't generally known at the seminary. He was an open man, liberal in thought and not afraid of new ideas. Some years ago in at least one diocese he wasn't welcome as a speaker. But how odd! Father Gene Maly was always prudent, respectful, and totally loyal to the Church.

Father Maly served in any capacity he could. He was a member of the priests' senate in Cincinnati for eight years. He was president of the Catholic Biblical Society from 1962 to 1963. But he also spent hours answering letters and talking to people, personally or on the phone, about Scripture or problems in the changing Church. He was as much at home with the kitchen staff at the seminary as with high Church dignitaries. His impromptu homilies on the Scripture readings at small vacation-time Masses were beautiful.

He had a touch of St. Francis in him. He loved animals and was always ready for a trip to the zoo. He loved the out-of-doors, the beaches in Florida, or a cabin in the Ohio woods.

He was a disciplined worker. He had many writing deadlines, and he labored faithfully each evening until ten o'clock. He was very conscientious, but also knew how to relax. He liked TV and occasionally played bridge or poker. One criterion for the success of any faculty party was the fervor with which Father Maly sang the "Whiffenpoof Song." His brother even half suggested it as a song for his wake, which was an informal but respectful ceremony conducted mainly by his family in the seminary chapel.

Maly loved to read in many fields. He once said he hoped it was possible to read in heaven. There were so many wonderful books he hadn't got around to yet. He also loved gadgets. He had an automatic telephone dialing attachment, a cruise control on his car, a TV recorder to catch programs which came on during his working hours, a micro-wave oven—he ordinarily ate lunch alone in his room—and even a fictitious "left-handed cigar-making machine" which he told his nephews and nieces about for many years.

Fr. Eugene Maly was an Alleluia man supreme. "We are an Easter people, and 'Alleluia' is our song," he repeated constantly. But he also added that the tension between the "already" and the "not yet" of Christ's Kingdom meant that we must also say, "We are a Good Friday people, and 'Miserere' is our song too."

Archbishop Edward A. McCarthy of Miami in his homily at the funeral of his classmate, lamented: "Troubled in spirit, we come to mourn, to comfort each other in this moment of painful realizations, that a warm, loving, cheerful, dedicated, pure, priestly heart is no longer beating. The chuckle is stilled, the tongue that eagerly proclaimed the Word and the praises of the Lord is silent.

"The professor's chair is now empty. The writer's pen is lifeless. Yet Father Maly's rostrum will be his memory and his writings his bequest. He will continue to speak to us of life and death with his passion for the truth and his vision into the mystery of the Good News of the Lord. . . ."

(Journalist and photographer, Father Joseph F. Beckman of Cincinnati was a student of Father Maly when he began teaching in 1950—and later a good friend when both priests resided at Mount St. Mary's.)

TABLE OF YEARS AND CYCLES

The Christian liturgical year begins on the First Sunday of Advent. Hence the cycle of Scripture Readings for a given calendar year begins on the First Sunday of Advent in the preceding calendar year. For example, the use of Cycle C in the year 1983 begins with the First Sunday of Advent in 1982.

YEAR	LECTIONARY SUNDAY CYCLE
1982	B
1983	C
1984	A
1985	B
1986	C
1987	A
1988	B
1989	C
1990	A
1991	B
1992	C
1993	A
1994	B
1995	C
1996	A
1997	B
1998	C
1999	A
2000	B

THE WORD ALIVE

THE WORD ALIVE

Cycle A

First Sunday of Advent (A)
Isaiah 2:1-5; Romans 13:11-14; Matthew 24:37-44

"Its time has come." This expression suggests that a new product or project has been lying in the womb of time waiting for the right moment to be revealed.

In the sense that the expression suggests some kind of continuity in history between past, present, and future, it is similar to the biblical view of time. But there are also major differences between our view of time and the biblical view. Two of them will help us appreciate the Church's celebration of the Advent season.

The first difference: In the modern, Western view, time is seen as a kind of clothesline stretching from creation to the end. On this line the events of history are hung like various items of clothing. Thus, time would be conceived of as separable from history and events, although it is the necessary support for them.

In the biblical view time and event are intimately associated. In a sense, time *is* the event. If there were no event, there would be no time. When the Bible speaks of time, it is always speaking of an event.

The second difference: Since the event of which the Bible speaks is always intended by God (salvation or judgment, depending on the human response to God's free offer of love), history attains its continuity from God himself. That is why there is always and necessarily a connection between past and future event. To put it another way, the present event anticipates the future event, the latter far exceeding the former in intensity.

This is why we, the Church, celebrate *Advent*. Latin in origin, this word means "coming." The coming is that of the Lord, but it can be and is a manifold coming, each one preparing for the next, and anticipating the final climactic one.

The first reading for this Sunday, from Isaiah, anticipates the Lord's coming, not in itself, but in its effects. That is, it speaks of the future conversion of the nations and the reign of peace when the Lord does come. The passage is famous for the reference to beating swords into plowshares and spears into pruning hooks.

Because of the necessary continuity in history and events, the prophet was not just writing of a future that was unconnected with the past. There must have been some other saving event of which Isaiah knew and which he saw as sign of the future. Perhaps it was the deliverance of Jerusalem from complete destruction by Sennacherib in 701 B.C. That would have provided the background for the reference to the (pagan) nations and to the instruments of war. In any case, there was an initial "advent" of the Lord.

Paul, in his letter to the Romans, speaks of the "day," which is technical language for the time when the Lord will come at the end of time, the second coming of Jesus Christ. It is another "advent" to which he looks forward, anticipated, of course, in the Word's coming in the flesh.

It is the same second coming of which Jesus speaks in the Gospel (v. 44), although the emphasis here is on the need for watchfulness, for being prepared. That is the "particular" side of Advent.

The coming of the Lord at Christmas, in the Eucharist, at the end of time—all these we celebrate in Advent. All these together make our Christian history and are our Christian time.

Second Sunday of Advent (A)
Isaiah 11:1-10; Romans 15:4-9; Matthew 3:1-12

Discord in a community is evil. Those who experience it, whether in a parish or a neighborhood, a diocese or a city, know how discord drains energy and raises many barriers. In alienating themselves from one another, people become less human, more prone to irrational acts.

It is suggested that a better understanding of and more active participation in the Advent season can help restore harmony. This should be clear simply on the basis of the meaning of Advent. It is a season of anticipation, of looking forward to a common goal.

The goal of the Christian Advent is transcendent—the coming of the Lord. Reflection on such a goal will lead to a deeper faith and stronger hope; this will inevitably weaken the virulence of less significant differences. Advent provides a unity of purpose.

An idyllic picture of the goal is given in the first reading for this Sunday. It is one of Isaiah's messianic prophecies. Here he speaks of a coming David's son ("the stump of Jesse," David's father) on whom the empowering spirit of the Lord would rest and who would bring justice and peace to the land.

That the prophet has in mind a transcendent goal (that is, one far surpassing the possibilities of creation as we know them) is evident from the descriptions of animals and children and their activities. However literally this is to be understood, we can be sure that the prophet was serious in what he was saying. And what he was saying is that there is a future glory for those who believe.

The Gospel reading shatters the idyllic character of that first reading, or so it seems. Here we have a rampaging John the Baptizer telling a "brood of vipers" about "the wrath to come." He speaks of the axe being laid to the root of the tree, of the tree being thrown into the fire, and of the chaff being eternally burned.

Isaiah and the Baptizer are really not working at odds with one another. The first is looking at the final enduring results of the coming, while the second has his eyes on the preparation that is needed. The way has to be made ready; the straight path has to be cleared. Then the One who is to come can come.

This aspect of Advent can be conducive to reducing friction in a community. If each member can work at removing the obnoxious, the offensive, the insensitive from his or her life, that chaff will be burned and the way made ready. The Christ is worthy of the best in all of us. That was the Baptizer's conviction.

Paul's words in the reading from Romans speak even more directly to the point. The whole tenor of this section of the letter has to do with establishing harmony among the Christians of Rome. Specifically, Paul is concerned that those who are strong in faith not scandalize by their actions those who are weak in faith.

To this end he speaks of the "lessons of patience" that are found in the Scriptures. In the Greek world patience was a form of inner tranquility that refused to be touched by the concerns of the world. But for Paul here, as for the Greek Old Testament, patience is almost the same as hoping, or even waiting for the Lord. "I have waited, waited for the Lord . . . " (Ps 40:2, where the same root word is used in the Greek).

Then Paul goes on to say that this patience, whose source is God, will enable them to "live in perfect harmony with one another. . . ." The kind of patient expectation that Advent means will look with charity on the weaknesses of others and encourage a peaceful working together "for the glory of God."

Third Sunday of Advent (A)
Isaiah 35:1-6.10; James 5:7-10; Matthew 11:2-11

John came for the sake of the One to come. This description of the Baptizer puts him in a position of inferiority with regard to Jesus. At the same time, because of the One for whose sake he came, it confers on him a dignity greater, at least in one respect, than any other man's.

The Gospel reading is divided into two main parts. The first concerns John's delegation to Jesus and the latter's reply about his identity. The second deals almost exclusively with the Baptizer, as described by Jesus to the crowds.

When asked by John's disciples whether he was "He who is to come," Jesus simply referred to his deeds and message. By his deeds he had brought relief to the afflicted and by his message he had brought good news to the poor. John would rightly understand this as an affirmative reply to the questioning of Jesus' identity as the One to come.

He would understand it because he knew the Scriptures. There are many references in the Old Testament to the coming day of salvation when the world of nature will be transformed. Isaiah 29:18 says that "the deaf shall hear" and "the eyes of the blind shall see." And Isaiah 26:19 says the people are told that "your dead shall live."

But it is probably Isaiah 35:4-6 that John would have thought of first, the passage that forms part of our first reading for this Sunday.

The whole reading presupposes the conditions of the Babylonian Exile and so was written much later than the historical Isaiah.

The author is exuberant in his description, not only of the cure of the handicapped, but also of the transformation of the desert. The unknown prophet is clearly thinking of a new exodus that will take place on the release of the Jews from captivity. It is a new exodus, but exceeds the old one in the manifestation of God's glory. In doing so it signals still another more perfect exodus to come.

It is likely that the Baptizer, and certain that Matthew, would have understood Jesus' words in the context of that exodus. In doing and preaching what he does, Jesus brings perfect salvation to the world. The One who is to come has come. John need wait no longer.

The second part of the reading is devoted almost exclusively to Jesus' description of the Baptizer. He is not a swaying reed, a term used for the untrustworthy in the Old Testament (Is 36:6). He is not luxuriously dressed as they thought the Messiah would be. All of this is typical Semitic imagery designed to heighten the tension and lead to a dramatic resolution.

Is John a prophet, a spokesman for God and one of the figures most highly esteemed by the Jews? Yes, but he is more than that. He is the Lord's messenger who was predicted by Malachi (3:1) and who would prepare the way for the Lord, the "One who is to come." In this respect, Jesus can say that John is the greatest man born of woman.

This extolling of John by Jesus was deliberate and sincere. But many of the Baptizer's disciples apparently misunderstood it and John's own preaching and promoted his cult long after his death (cf. Ac 19:1-5). There is some evidence that the early Church was concerned with a sectarian movement associated with John the Baptizer (Ac 19:3).

But in the New Testament there is never any doubt. John's greatness comes from Jesus and is totally dependent on him. The Baptizer truly came for the sake of the One to come. That is his glory. That is why Jesus could say that "the least born into the kingdom of God is greater than he."

Fourth Sunday of Advent (A)
Isaiah 7:10-14; Romans 1:1-7; Matthew 1:18-24

One scholar estimates that verse 14 of the passage from Isaiah for this Sunday has been commented on more than any other verse in the Old Testament. It contains the well known sign that the prophet gave to King Ahaz: "... the virgin shall be with child, and bear a son, and shall name him Immanuel."

One of the reasons scholars comment on it so often is that the verse is used in Matthew's Gospel where it refers to the coming birth of Jesus from the Virgin Mary. The passage containing it is our third reading. This use of the verse by Matthew not only makes it better known; it also contributes to the complexity of the original meaning.

The historical context of Isaiah's use of the verse will help to clear up the mystery, and, perhaps also, to intensify the mystery. The year was about 735 B.C. Ahaz, king of Judah, was being pressured by two other kings (those of Israel and Damascus) to join an alliance against the superpower, Assyria.

The prophet met the king and told him that he must not join any alliance but must put his faith absolutely in the Lord. "Unless your faith is firm, you shall not be firm" (v. 9b). Then when Ahaz hypocritically refuses a sign that God would be with him, Isaiah gives him the sign contained in our disputed verse.

The sign was primarily for Ahaz. It was the promise of a son, a royal heir, a Davidide, to be born in his own time. This is clear from the verse immediately following our verse where it says that before the child reaches the use of reason the land of the two attacking kings would be deserted. And we know that they were, indeed, invaded and ravaged by Assyria in 732 B.C.

Who was the "virgin" (strictly, a "young maid" according to the Hebrew)? Probably one of the women in the king's harem. And the child to be born would be a royal son, a fulfillment of an ancient promise made to David (2 S 7:12-16) that his house would last forever, and a much more immediate fulfillment of Isaiah's prophecy.

Why did Matthew say that it applies to Mary and Jesus? It may be that the inspired evangelist simply recognized that the words had their complete meaning only in these two. Jesus, Son of God, really is "God with us." It may be, too, that God intended this meaning from the beginning, thus providentially letting Isaiah choose words that would admirably suit the fuller divine purpose.

Finally, it may well be that Isaiah himself, after having delivered this oracle, and others about a special child (cf. 9:1-6; 11:1-5), gradually realized that this son of Ahaz was only a foreshadowing, an anticipation of a greater wonder to come. He would have seen in Ahaz's royal child a type of a perfect Davidide who would come in the end-time. Matthew makes it perfectly clear who it is.

In any or all of the above cases there are two convictions that must be stressed as important for us now. The first point is the real continuity in history because of the divine Word. History is not a meaningless chain of events. It is, rather, as Paul would put it, a mystery that is gradually unravelled for those who believe. God's Word in the past has an inherent power that releases itself only in the time of perfect fulfillment.

The second point is the necessity of faith to live in a history so charged with the divine Word. Ahaz could not bear it because he did not believe, and his plans, in the end, came to naught. Those who do have faith, who do trust in the Lord in total surrender to him, can live in that history knowing that the fulfillment will inevitably come. They know that what "Immanuel" means is true.

Christmas: Mass of the Vigil (ABC), December 25
Isaiah 62:1-5; Acts 13:16-17, 22-25; Matthew 1:1-25

A genealogy is more than a list of names. It also points out the path that has led to the present moment. Isaiah and Acts both find fulfillment in Matthew's genealogy. Acts reminds us that David was to have a descendant far greater than himself; Isaiah recalls the promise made to Abraham that he would be the father of a great nation and have many descendants.

A genealogy suggests birthdays, and these are usually happy occasions. At least from the fourth century Christians have celebrated the birthay of Christ on December 25 in the West and some on January 6 in the East.

This Christmas Eve celebration is filled with the wonder of God's marvelous ways with his people. In Jesus Christ we have the presence of God in our midst; he is the Emmanuel—God who is with us. And it is this presence that we celebrate this evening.

In his presentation of the genealogy of Jesus, Matthew heightens this sense of wonder by dividing the preceding history into three groupings of fourteen generations. But are there really fourteen generations in each group? Not really; the last group is composed of *names* that are for the most part unknown to history. The list has fourteen names, but not fourteen generations. Matthew has a motive for this arrangement.

He seems to be underlining the Davidic sonship of Jesus. At the time of Christ the Hebrew language did not contain numbers as separate entities. Like the Roman numerals of Latin, which are letters that stand for numbers, so too certain Hebrew letters stood for numbers. *David* in Hebrew is the number fourteen.

All of history has been schematized into three periods. From creation to David's rule as king—considered the highpoint of the monarchy. From David to the deportation to Babylon in 586 B.C.— the low point in Jewish history and a time of degradation. From the return from Babylon to the birth of Christ—the greatest event in all history.

In each of these historical periods, the names seek to click with a certain rhythm and style. On occasion an interruption occurs to point out a special moment in the cycles; this is especially true when women are mentioned—Tamar, Rahab, Ruth, the unnamed wife of Uriah—Bathsheba, and above all Mary.

The motherhood of all these women was special, each in its own way. Certainly the motherhood of Mary was the most exceptional of all.

But who are all of these people mentioned in the genealogy and why are they important? They serve as the background by which we can appreciate Jesus himself. The four women in the earlier part of the genealogy are not Jews; each is a foreigner. Matthew takes pains to inform us that Jesus' background includes Jewish and Gentile blood; Jesus came for all people regardless of race. No single race has an undue claim upon him. Jesus is the Emmanuel, God who is with us. The *us* is all people.

Matthew's genealogy is ostensibly Joseph's through the Davidic ancestry. Generally people married within the same tribe. What we have, however, is to be understood as theologized history to point out how Jesus, conceived by the Holy Spirit in Mary, has fulfilled the longings of God's people by completing the promises that have been made to them.

The whole account emphasizes the name Jesus. He is the Savior who has delivered us from sin. He is God's Son, and he is Mary's son. He is Joseph's foster son. Tonight we wish him, "Happy Birthday!"

P.J.S.

Christmas: Mass at Midnight (ABC), December 25
Isaiah 9:1-6; Titus 2:11-14; Luke 2:1-14

The practice of celebrating three distinct Masses on Christmas, each with its own readings, is based on a symbolic meaning given to them. Mass at midnight symbolizes Christ's eternal birth in the bosom of the Father, the Mass at dawn his birth from the womb of Mary, and the Mass of the day his mystical birth in the hearts of the faithful.

The earliest mention of the celebration of Christ's birth on December 25 comes from the year 336. The celebration then spread rapidly and, within a century, was observed almost everywhere. This is understandable since the Scriptures made much of the birth of great persons, including that of Jesus, as our reading from Luke's Gospel illustrates.

Luke, of course, had Old Testament precedents for noting such a joyous event. The first reading, from Isaiah, is one of the more significant. The prophet has in mind, primarily, the birth of a royal son in Jerusalem. The period is that of the Assyrian threat. It would have been about 730 B.C. Isaiah sees in the birth of the child a sign of the ultimate victory of God over the enemy.

But he also saw more than the defeat of this particular enemy, which did not occur in his lifetime in any case. The extraordinary names given to the child and the eternal peace and justice that will be the effect of his reign lead scholars to conclude that Isaiah envisioned also an end-time ruler who would usher in God's kingdom. Only such a One could truly be called "Wonder-Counselor, God-Hero, Father-Forever, Prince of Peace."

Luke knew of this prophecy. He has alluded to it in the annunciation scene (1:32). Also, many see in the reference to the infant Jesus as Savior and Messiah born in David's city (Bethlehem was the birthplace of David) another allusion to Isaiah's prophecy. The "God-Hero" had come.

But what a contrast! The birth of a royal child in Isaiah's time would have been celebrated with feverish joy throughout the mountain fortress of Jerusalem and throughout the land. The nobles of the court, the priests and wise men, and all the people would have joined in the festive event.

But for Jesus "there was no room" in Bethlehem. He was born in an out-of-the-way place and laid in a manger. The attendants at his manger-throne were Mary and Joseph and the lowly shepherds. His birth could not have been less conspicuous than this. Whoever saw a God-Hero" here could do so only with the eyes of faith.

The evangelist had that faith. The angel's proclamation of this Jesus as "Messiah and Lord" and the heavenly host singing "Glory to God in high heaven" are testimonials to that faith. Angels, shepherds, and a convert Gentile share a common secret.

But it will not always be a secret. Luke knew that what had occurred in this obscure corner of the world, would, in time, change the whole of that world as the evangelist knew it. Subtly he indicates this when he mentions Caesar Augustus, emperor "of the whole world," and Quirinius, "governor of Syria," under whose jurisdiction Palestine fell. Luke puts the story in its proper context.

The ultimate effects of this birth are less subtly indicated in the second reading, from the letter to Titus. "The grace of God has appeared, offering salvation to all men." The same Greek word ("appeared") is used here as later in the "appearing" (literally, "epiphany") of our Savior Christ Jesus. Thereby the author tells us that the coming of Christ is an epiphany of grace, of God's love.

In one sense Christ's birth came nowhere close to fulfilling the vision of Isaiah. His lowly birth hardly resembled that of a royal child. But in another and far more real sense for us, this birth went far beyond the prophecy. Jesus Christ is the "God-Hero" who would save the world.

Christmas: Mass at Dawn (ABC), December 25
Isaiah 62:11-12; Titus 3:4-7; Luke 2:15-20

In the art of the Middle Ages the rooster, the bird of dawn, was an important image, nearly always appearing on the highest weather-vane, on cathedral towers and domes. It was a symbol of vigilance, urging the Christian to be wakeful and to greet the Sun, Christ, even before he rises in the East. In such a spirit, Shakespeare, in *Hamlet*, had the officer Marcellus speak these lovely words: "Some say that ever 'gainst that season comes/ Wherein our Savior's birth is celebrated,/ The bird of dawning singeth all night long."

This morning the bird of dawning seems to urge us in a special way to look to the East and greet the divine Sun, Jesus, who by his birth proclaims the great love God has for his people. At this momentous hour the Church celebrates the dawning of a new hope for humankind, a dawn symbolic of rebirth, fresh attitudes, and new beginnings.

The theme of this Mass at Dawn is one of exuberant joy—the joy of Isaiah's proclamation, the joy expressed in Titus' "eternal life," and the joy of the shepherds. The joyful shepherds were among the lowly of Israel. Among the poorest of the poor who could still find some type of work were numbered the common laborers and the shepherds. Luke has no magi or kings in attendance at the birth of Christ; only shepherds, a widow, a devout old priest, Mary and Joseph—all of whom count for little in the world's eyes.

At the end of the Babylonian Exile, Deutero—Isaiah spoke of salvation coming to the people of Israel—"your savior comes." The people had been redeemed from the bondage of Babylon; they were liberated and set free. Isaiah called them a "holy people," separated from among the other nations of the world because they were God's possession. Yet Isaiah longed for something greater than physical release from exile. Today's celebration speaks about that fulfillment. In the shepherds' proclamation the prophecy of Isaiah has been fulfilled; true liberation has come about by one who is indeed the Savior of the world, "the baby lying in the manger."

This celebration is called the Shepherds' Mass, and the emphasis of the scriptures is on proclamation of the good news. The joy of the shepherds knew no bounds; they glorified and praised God. To whomever would listen they spread the good news of the birth of the Messiah. The shepherds are the first Christian evangelists giving good news about Jesus and echoing the words of Isaiah: "your savior comes."

The content of the shepherds' good news is found in our second reading. In Titus, Jesus is proclaimed the Savior. He has come. The Christian filled with the Holy Spirit is baptized into the Body of Christ, the Church, and continues the work of proclamation (cf. 1 P 2:9-10). From the time of Isaiah until the coming of Christ the people of God had longed for liberation, for the champion of the people, for a savior. With the coming of Christ a new dawn has occurred for the human race; salvation is obtainable through baptism and the Holy Spirit (cf. Ep 5:26).

Now the good news comes that the Savior has been born and lies in a manger in Bethlehem. The goodness of God has appeared— Jesus Christ. Titus presents Jesus as God's gift to us. The word, *appeared*, in Greek usage means the visible manifestation of a hidden divinity. Thus Jesus is God made flesh; the hidden, transcendent God has become incarnate, God who is with us (Mt 1:23). His gift is to make us "heirs, in hope, of eternal life."

The dawn of new hope is a dawn of wonder. Isaiah stood in awe of God, Mary ponders in her heart the events of her son's birth, and the shepherds proclaim the glory of God.

The Christian stands in awe this morning, astonished at God's love and amazed at the way in which he has worked out his plan for our salvation.

P.J.S.

Christmas: Mass during the Day (ABC), December 25
Isaiah 52:7-10; Hebrews 1:1-6; John 1:1-18

During this Christmas celebration we have already heard from

Matthew (Vigil) and Luke (Midnight and Dawn); now it is John's turn to speak in the Gospel of Christmas Day. Our third reading is the prologue to John's Gospel. The event of the Word become flesh, Christ's birth, is put into parallel with the other great act of God, creation. "In the beginning" is the same phrase found in Genesis 1:1, but in our text there is a difference. John's "In the beginning" is outside of time because it is treating of the preexistence of God's Word before becoming incarnate. The phrase in Genesis is dealing with the first moment in time.

Throughout his Gospel, John emphasizes the divinity of Christ. The "Word was God" is in a parallel with the words of Thomas, who doubted the resurrection. At the end of the Gospel he will acclaim Jesus with the words, "My Lord and my God" (20:28).

Many of the themes to be found in the Fourth Gospel are already brought to the fore in this prologue: the need to witness, the meaning of truth, the importance of light, and the necessity of belief. The world for John is not merely the created universe, but also and more importantly it is understood as the community of men and women who do not accept Christ. It was through the Word that the world was made, but his own did not receive him.

The Baptizer prepared the way for the revelation of the Word made flesh, the one who came to give "grace and truth." Our text clearly points out the inferior position of John the Baptizer to Jesus. Our second reading, Hebrews, points out the inferior position of the angels as regards Jesus. God's Son is supreme. The Baptizer prepared the way, just as Isaiah speaks in the first reading of a way prepared for the one who was to bring peace, comfort, and redemption to God's people. Isaiah's prophecy had been fulfilled in the Word made flesh.

A joyful preparation has been made for the advent of the Messiah; one herald had proclaimed, "Your God is King" (Is). Glad tidings were forthcoming.

In Hebrews the author focuses upon the role of Jesus as Son of God and his relationship to the plan of salvation. This second reading too is a prologue to what is contained in the rest of the work; the author treats of essential themes: the sonship of Jesus, the priesthood of Jesus (cleansing), and the glory of the enthroned Jesus.

For the unknown author of the second reading, the Word made

flesh is unique; God has uttered a word that is different from the past. Now God speaks through *one* person, a Son, and not *many*, the prophets. The "final age" has come upon us; the last days are already here in the birth of Jesus. They began with the Incarnation, and, in every generation since, Christians have been living in the last days.

This Son, for the Hebrews' author, was present in creation and works at sustaining the universe. This same Son is the "reflection of the Father's glory" and the "exact representation of the Father's being." Later Christian teaching would use our text from Hebrews to substantiate the fact that Jesus has the same nature as God; he is God's Son and at the same time that he is God, he is also man (Heb 2:14).

On Christmas Day the Church celebrates a unique and wondrous event—the Word was born in time. Jesus is begotten of God the Father, he is above every angel and every human being, and he is the fulfillment of the good news, prepared for in the remote past by Isaiah, immediately preached by John the Baptizer, and made flesh in Jesus Christ on this astonishing day.

P.J.S.

Holy Family (A)
Sirach 3:2-6.12-14; Colossians 3:12-21; Matthew 2:13-15.19-23

Often when we conjure up a picture of family life, we see a happy occasion with family members gathered peacefully around the dining room table or before a cozy fire in the family room. This is an ideal picture. But we know that family life can be beset by dissensions and disorder, and leave much to be desired.

The three readings for today make a plea for a Christian lifestyle in families. The Holy Family is the ideal. Perhaps Paul says it best in Colossians: "Christ's peace must reign in your hearts." Only when Christ's peace is accepted by all the members of a family can they live together in harmony.

A thirteen-year-old was asked by her counselor: "What is peace?" Her swift response was. "Peace is having friends." Another way to say it: peace is founded upon proper relationships among husbands and wives, brothers and sisters, parents and children.

Paul admonishes the Christians of Colossae to lead lives of virtue "with heartfelt mercy, with kindness, humility, meekness, and patience." All of these virtues are to be put into the proper order with one another through the bond of perfection, love. The word, *bond*, refers to a union of separate items into a whole. Love is the virtue that unites all others. Elsewhere Paul tells us that it is the greatest virtue of all (1 Cor 13:13).

To love as a Christian must is difficult. Matthew sets the tone for Christian love when he speaks of the necessity of loving one's enemies (5:44). If loving one's enemies is Christ's command, how much more love must the Christian lavish upon members of his household?

The Christian family's life must be characterized by a love giving peace, a love that each member can offer only because each member understands his or her proper relationship among the members. Parents exercise authority because they accept their authority from above. Children acknowledge the role of parents in their lives. Husbands and wives accept positions of coresponsibility and still acknowledge one another's gifts and personhood. Children live together in an atmosphere that is conducive to growth and not to strife.

Sirach points out the diverse roles of family members. He comments on Exodus 20:12, which treats of the fourth commandment: honor your father and your mother. Such treatment of one's parents will bring countless blessings upon the children, and no one is ever excused from showing honor to his or her parents. At the same time Paul joins Sirach in warning fathers especially not to abuse their children, but to treat them with respect. Children, too, have dignity as persons.

In these three readings the family is presented as a unit—diverse members who are nevertheless in harmony with one another. Matthew presents us with the ideal family unit: Joseph, the father-figure and protector, his wife Mary, and Jesus. At God's behest Joseph leads them into exile in Egypt and again at God's behest returns with them to the land of promise. What is important to note on this feast day is that the peace of family living does not exclude hardship and strife originating from outside the family. Matthew speaks of forces beyond the control of the Holy Family, but God's peace remained with them. After all, Mary and Joseph had in their midst the Prince of Peace, Jesus Christ.

If today a Christian family does not experience peace, might it not be because the Prince of Peace does not rule the heart of each member?

P.J.S.

Mary, Mother of God (ABC)
Numbers 6:22-27; Galatians 4:4-7; Luke 2:16-21

In the Christmas celebration the emphasis was on the glory of God in the human birth of his Son. Isaiah, Paul, and Luke marvelled at the appearance of this "God-Hero." In this Sunday's celebration the emphasis is on the effects of this birth on us. In Catholic tradition Mary plays an important role in both. When we acknowledge her as Mother of God, we implicitly acknowledge her as Mother of the Church, inasmuch as the Church is the Body of Christ, her Son.

The reading from the Book of Numbers contains one of the most beautiful prayers in the Scriptures. It is called the "Priestly Blessing," assigned by God to Aaron and his priestly descendants to be conferred on God's people.

Notable is the triple repetition of "the Lord" in the threefold blessing. It is the name by which God was known by his people Israel. This invocation of his name was the invocation of his person, of his power, of his love and peace. In Hebrew thought the name *is* the person and all that the person is and stands for. For that reason God could say, "So shall they invoke my name upon the Israelites, and I will bless them."

By placing this reading here the Church is inviting us to see this blessing in its Christian context, and specifically in the context of Christmas. Now it is the name of Jesus that will be invoked in blessing. He is the "Lord" who is gracious to us and gives us peace.

There is no connection here with the feast of Mary. All that can be said is that the blessing was given in the Jerusalem temple and in the synagogues each day at the morning service. Mary must have heard it many times. She could have seen it fulfilled marvelously in her own motherhood.

In the reading from Paul's letter to the Galatians we see explicitly the effects of Christ's coming. The reading was chosen primarily for its reference to Mary (though not by name), the only time Paul refers to her in his letters. But the reference is an important one. Paul "needs" Mary, as indeed God himself "needed" her, to show the manner of our redemption. Jesus Christ was, by divine necessity, "born of a woman."

In the Old Testament the mother was given much respect. We glimpse this already in the first mother whose prestigious name of Eve meant "mother of all the living" (Gn 3:20). The queen-mother had a special place in the royal court, seated on a throne at the right of her king-son (1 K 2:19). Both Isaiah (7:14) and Micah (5:2) mention the Messiah's mother, not the father. This high regard for the king's mother may have been in Paul's mind as he wrote those words.

He is, however, mainly concerned with the final outcome of the birth of the Son: "that we might receive our status as adopted sons." The proof of this status is the presence of the Spirit in our hearts, the Spirit who cries out and makes it possible for us to cry out, "Abba!" ("Father!") All three Persons of the Trinity have an active role in the redemptive word.

The Gospel reading is the conclusion of Luke's narrative of the shepherds. The Christmas reading had included only the angelic announcement to the shepherds and the heavenly host's song of praise to God. Now the stress is on the shepherds' reaction. They go in haste to find Mary and Joseph with the baby. The "astonishment" of all who heard the report is a typically Lukan expression for the effect that Jesus has on people.

Toward the end of the account Luke notes that "Mary treasured all these things and reflected on them in her heart." Later on Luke would record the parable of the sower and the seed and would add the saying of Jesus in which he identifies his mother as one who hears the word of God and acts on it (8:4-21). Did Luke have that in mind as he wrote these words about Mary at the manger?

Today is Mary's feast, not because she initiated salvation, but because she was the willing virgin who gave birth to God's Son.

Epiphany of the Lord (ABC)
Isaiah 60:1-6; Ephesians 3:2-3, 5-6; Matthew 2:1-12

Few American Catholics know that Epiphany is an older feast than Christmas. Or that many Catholic countries still celebrate it more solemnly than they do Christmas. Or that it is liturgically more significant.

Since the last statement is the most basic, we will devote this column to exploring the reason for it. And we will begin with the name itself. The word, of Greek origin, means manifestation or disclosure. In the ancient Greek mystery religions an epiphany occurred when one of the gods appeared and manifested himself to someone.

But the Bible does not use the word at all, probably to avoid any association with pagan religions. The closest it comes to it is the reference to the Hellenistic king, Antiochus Epiphanes (1 Mc 1:10). This pagan king took the name because he considered himself to be "god manifest." No wonder the Scriptures avoided the term.

By the third century when the term was first applied to Jesus Christ the danger of any pagan association had disappeared. In fact, now it could be given its truest meaning. For Jesus Christ is, indeed, "God manifest" in a way that no pagan king could ever have dreamed.

When the feast of Epiphany was first celebrated, in the Eastern Church, it was in the context of Jesus' baptism by John in the Jordan. As our readers will recall, it was then that the voice from heaven proclaimed, "You are my beloved Son" (Mark 1:11). The Father here makes "manifest" for the first time who Jesus really is, the Son of God.

When the Western Church adopted the celebration of Epiphany about a hundred years later, it was the visit of the magi, as recorded in our Gospel reading, that became the focus of attention. This is understandable. The magi represent a non-Jewish or Gentile people and so prefigure the acceptance of Jesus by all the world.

We could quibble about this and argue that the magi story reflects more a human acceptance than a divine manifestation. But there are elements of the latter in the theme of the guiding star and in the prophecy pointing to Bethlehem. The magi (representing all of us) could not have found the infant Savior, Matthew is saying, unless God had "manifested" him to them.

The reading from Isaiah provides us with the imagery appropriate for such an event: the "splendor" and "light" and "glory" of the Lord, sons and daughters "coming from afar," "the riches of the seas" and "the wealth of nations," "caravans of camels" and "dromedaries from Midian bearing gold and frankincense, and proclaiming the praises of the Lord." This is language fit for an epiphany!

But the second reading gets to the heart of it. The reading speaks of "God's secret plan" now "revealed," a plan, we learn elsewhere, that God had intended from the beginning. It was a plan that the prophets of the Old Testament had hinted at but whose full meaning even they did not know. Only with Jesus Christ was it fully revealed. Epiphany, God manifest in Jesus Christ, is the whole message of the Scriptures.

One last important point. The Christian Epiphany took place not as an act of divine self-satisfaction, but for us. God hoped that we would be amazed at it all, that we would react like the magi and give him ourselves as gifts, that we would be awestruck by this supreme act of love and begin to love in return. Will he be disappointed?

Baptism of the Lord (A), Sunday after January 6
Isaiah 42:1-4, 6-7; Acts 10:34-38; Matthew 3:13-17

In the TV film by Franco Zefferelli, *Jesus of Nazareth*, the baptism of the Lord has been captured in a splendid way. The words of Matthew 3:17, "This is my beloved Son. My favor rests on him," are not boomed out of the heavens. Instead, they are put on the lips of the Baptizer, who looks up to heaven as he utters them. John the Baptizer is the last of the Old Testament prophets. A prophet is not primarily one who speaks about future events, though he may; a prophet is God's mouthpiece for the current generation. He speaks in God's behalf. By putting the words in the mouth of the Baptizer, Zefferelli is quite faithful to the biblical tradition. God most often speaks to us through other people.

Although Matthew mentions the Baptizer several times later on in the Gospel, nevertheless, with the baptism of Jesus, John's prophetic mission comes to an end. God's revelation rests solely in the person of Jesus. Jesus speaks to us in human fashion and with words that we can understand. He is fittingly called "the man for others."

Later on, John, in prison, will send messengers to Jesus to find out if he is the one who was foretold (Mt 11:2-6). Jesus will reply that the messengers should announce to John that "the blind recover their sight." The words spoken by Isaiah 42:7 have been fulfilled.

Today's reading from Isaiah contains the words, "My chosen one with whom I am pleased" (42:1). It is this verse that the Gospel reiterates in God's oracle, "my beloved Son" (3:17). The application of the Isaian passage to Jesus places the emphasis upon Christ as servant, not Christ as king. Isaiah speaks eloquently about the release of God's people from the slavery of Babylon; that bondage is ended. A new era is about to begin.

All three readings remind us that God's word comes through his chosen messengers, Isaiah, Peter, the Baptizer. The people of God had expected a kingly Messiah, but Isaiah underscores the point that the one who will come will be a servant. In the second part of Isaiah, Deutero-Isaiah, four Servant-of-the-Lord hymns occur: 42:1-4; 49:1-7; 50:4-11; 52:13-53:12. In the last of these oracles we find that the servant is to bear our sufferings.

There appears to have been an early cult dedicated to following John the Baptizer. This is alluded to in Acts 19:3 where the apostles found individuals who had not yet received the revelation about Jesus, but had received only the baptism of repentance from the Baptizer. Matthew's theological position in today's Gospel shows John in a subordinate position to Jesus for he does not wish to baptize Jesus. Indeed he protests. But Jesus as the servant asks that John fulfill "all of God's demands." Then (according to Zefferelli) John graciously speaks in God's behalf.

The second reading shows a reluctant Peter speaking freely in God's behalf. Earlier in the chapter (Ac 10) Peter was reluctant to go to the home of the pagan Cornelius. Only after a revelation from God in a dream did he come to realize the necessity of going to preach to "foreigners" about Jesus Christ. Peter opens his preaching with the beginning of the public life of Jesus, his baptism. In the early Christian communities the baptism of Jesus signified the end of preparation for the ministry and the beginning of the saving activity. In many of the speeches in Acts, the baptism of the Lord is part of the early preaching of the apostles. The end of that ministry will be noted when blood flows forth from Christ's side at his death (Jn 19:34).

With this feast, the Christmas season comes to an end. Ordinary Time begins tomorrow. The emphasis will be not on feasts of the Lord, but on the daily ministry of Jesus to the people of his day in New Testament times and to the people who liturgically celebrate that ministry in our times.

P.J.S.

First Sunday of Lent (A)
Genesis 2:7-9; 3:1-7; Romans 5:12-19; Matthew 4:1-11

This Sunday's Gospel scene raises significant questions: Why was Jesus tempted? Even if we might understand a first temptation, why the second and the third? If Jesus truly was God's Son, why did he not banish the tempter immediately? John has no temptation scene at all in his Gospel. Was it too embarrassing for him?

The answers tell us something radically important about Jesus and even the whole human condition. Whoever would deny the importance of the temptations does not know the meaning of Christianity. But first, let us discuss some preliminary questions.

Why doesn't John have a temptation scene? We really aren't sure. It is known that John's tradition about Jesus is different from that of the other three evangelists. We would conclude that his tradition did not have that story in it. And he does not appear to have known about the other three accounts.

But—and this is essential—John does portray Jesus as tempted several times during his ministry. One instance is found in John 6:14-15. When Jesus multiplies the loaves for the crowd, the latter became so overwhelmed that they want to carry him off and make him king. Aware of this, Jesus flees "back to the mountain alone."

This was clearly a temptation to political messiahship. It is at root the same kind of temptation as the third one in this Sunday's reading, where the devil offers Jesus the kingdoms of the world. Hence, it has been suggested that the several temptations that Jesus experienced during his ministry and that are recorded in John's Gospel were brought together by Matthew and Luke and placed at the beginning of the ministry. They provide a theological introduction to his mission: he must and will overcome the power of evil.

This is a powerful insight. No doubt both Matthew and Luke had in mind here the portrayal of a Savior who vanquished truly transcendent powers. As one author puts it, the temptation scene is "an anticipation of the victory which was to be consummated on the Cross." Necessarily, we share in that victory. If it were otherwise, the Gospels would never have been written.

So John was not too embarrassed to record Jesus as being tempted. He seems to recognize temptation as much a part of Jesus' earthly existence as do the others. But the question remains: why was Jesus tempted?

To respond adequately, we must go all the way back to the beginning of human history, as the Church does in the first reading, from Genesis. It tells of the creation of man, of the trees in the garden, of God's command to the first parents, of the devil's temptation, and of the first sin.

To put it briefly, Jesus has to be tempted because, as Genesis tells us, from the very beginning men and women have been tempted—to undue power, wealth, pleasure—and have succumbed. On the one hand, how could Jesus have known what it was to be human if he was not tempted? On the other hand, how could he have been our Savior if he had not overcome the tempter?

The author of Hebrews says the same thing when he writes that only in this way could Jesus be "a merciful and faithful high priest before God. . . . Since he was himself tested through what he suffered, he is able to help those who are tempted" (2:16-18).

One question remains. Why was mankind tempted from the beginning? Only one answer is possible. God wanted free people, not puppets. The possibility of refusing evil when offered (temptation) enhances and intensifies our freedom. Jesus has done this in an eminent way.

Second Sunday of Lent (A)
Genesis 12:1-4; 2 Timothy 1:8-10; Matthew 17:1-9

Is biblical religion concerned primarily with the worship of God or with the salvation of mankind? Different passages of the Scriptures could easily be cited in favor of either position. But considering the practical nature of the biblical approach to reality, human salvation would seem to be primary. In almost every line we can find the *pro nobis* ("for us" or "for our sake") element present.

The first reading for this Lenten Sunday is no exception. It is the call of Abraham to leave his country and to go to a new land. There the Lord would do great things for him.

This call, while it comes in a sense as a surprise, by that reason takes on greater meaning for our understanding of God's purpose. The first eleven chapters of Genesis showed how the tragedy of sin had wreaked its havoc on mankind. Murder, vengeance, flood, drunkenness, worldwide dispersion of peoples—all were recorded in those chapters. The direction that humankind was taking was all downhill and could only end in annihilation. Then came the call.

Those opening chapters are obviously intended as introductory. They were placed there by the final editor of the book to prepare the reader for what he considered the major theme of the whole. As book after book was added to this book to form *the* Book, these eleven chapters retained their introductory position.

The nature of the chapters suggests, or rather, shouts that the human person can achieve nothing apart from God. That is what makes the call of Abraham so dramatic. The situation will be changed; the direction of the human story will be reversed. Instead of damnation there will be salvation.

In the Bible salvation always means that God takes the initiative in bringing about a wholeness of being in his creatures. This does not mean that no human response is required. God's grace is a gift but it must be used.

The divine initiative is abundantly clear in God's blessing of Abraham: "I will make you a great nation, and I will bless you; I will make your name great. . . ." Only God could speak words like that effectively. Some men had tried to speak them before (Gn 11:4) but had failed miserably.

The object of each individual blessing is some form of salvation, or wholeness of being. Greatness of nation, of name (which, in biblical thought, means greatness of the person), and divine blessing are all salvific. Thus does the reading speak predominantly of human salvation.

The Gospel reading, describing Jesus' transfiguration, seems to be in another world. Here the glory of Christ, Son of God, is emphasized. Moses and Elijah, representing the Law and the Prophets, are there because they had prepared the way for the Christ. The booths mentioned by Peter are a probable allusion to a harvest feast in which God was worshipped as king. And the falling of the disciples to the ground is a symbol of awesome adoration. God's glory is Christ's glory; both are the object of worship.

How, then, are we to answer our initial question? The true biblical response would be that it is not a valid question. Divine worship and human salvation are not two separate realities. When we worship God we are aleady partaking in salvation. When God saves us he is already manifesting his glory, so worthy of worship.

Jesus transfigured announces a future glory that will be his because he saved us through death and resurrection. The *pro nobis* is as inseparable a part of the transfiguration as is the acknowledgment of divine glory.

Third Sunday of Lent (A)
Exodus 17:3-7; Romans 5:1-2, 5-8; John 4:5-42

A suggestion: let each reader go over the three Scripture passages for this Sunday and propose the theme that is common to them. It should not be difficult. But then see if another, more radical, theme can be detected. This can be an enriching experience.

The first reading, from Exodus, narrates the story of the Israelites murmuring about the lack of water in the wilderness. At the command of God, Moses strikes a rock and water gushes forth. This is a sign of God's presence in their midst.

The water theme is obvious in the Gospel reading. Jesus asks the Samaritan woman for water and goes on to speak of water that he would give, a fountain "leaping up to provide eternal life." Paul, in

Romans, doesn't mention water, but he does speak of God's love being "poured out" in our hearts. This is similar to the spiritual water of which Jesus had spoken.

Throughout Israel's history water was always recognized as of basic importance. From the earliest times villages were invariably located near some water supply. Disputes over wells or incidents involving people coming to the wells mark the patriarchal narratives in Genesis. Israel's desert wandering, as we have just seen, brought its own experience with the basic need for water.

Because of this it is not surprising that water took on a symbolic meaning. The Hebrew word is used 570 times in the Old Testament and a majority of these usages are symbolic or later given a symbolic meaning. Thus, in the Exodus reading the water from the rock symbolizes God's saving presence even while it slakes their physical thirst.

Other passages in the Scriptures indicate the strictly spiritual meaning intended by the use of the word. For example, God tells the Babylonian exiles that he will "sprinkle clean water" upon them and cleanse them from their impurities and their false gods (Ez 36:25). In his grand dream of the end-time, the same prophet envisions a wonderful stream flowing from the Temple in Jerusalem all the way to the Dead Sea (47:1-12).

In these and other passages water symbolizes the richness of God's blessings, his saving and refreshing presence in the midst of his people. That is why Paul, in our second reading, when he speaks of God's love, almost instinctively says that it is "poured out" in our hearts. And that is why, in the Gospel reading, Jesus could pass so easily from the physical water of Jacob's well to the spiritual water of eternal life.

All this richness of meaning in the water symbol should make us more appreciative of the use of water in our own faith life. Just as the waters of the flood held aloft the ark of Noah and so meant salvation for that family, so do the waters of Baptism signify and effect the new life of the Christian (cf. 1 P 3:20-21). When the *Asperges* is used at the beginning of Mass, it symbolizes God's cleansing power over our sins. Each time we enter the church we remind ourselves of our baptismal cleansing by signing ourselves with holy water.

All this is one more reminder of God's gift to us, and each reading proclaims it. But there is a still more radical theme present. It involves the recipients of this gift. In no case are they presented as persons who deserve the gift. The grumbling Israelites and the calculating Samaritan woman can be gifted only by a gracious God.

Paul says it most clearly: ". . . when we were still powerless, Christ died for us sinful men. . . .It is precisely in this that God proves his love for us: that while we were still sinners, Christ died for us." That kind of love is not trapped in a well; it must be a free-flowing stream.

Fourth Sunday of Lent (A)
1 Samuel 16:1, 6-7, 10-13; Ephesians 5:8-14; John 9:1-41

"Not as man sees does God see, because man sees the appearance but the Lord looks into the heart." That statement is made in the course of the first reading from 1 Samuel. It provides the basic theme for our reflections for this Sunday.

The story is the choosing by Samuel of a successor for King Saul, who had been rejected by the Lord for his disobedience. Samuel goes to Bethlehem where a man named Jesse lives with his eight sons. One of the sons is to be the future king.

After the seven eldest sons of Jesse are brought before Samuel and each rejected in turn, the prophet asks if any others remain. One, the youngest, David, is outside tending sheep. He is brought before Samuel who recognizes him as God's choice and anoints him in anticipation of his future role.

The story would only have been fully appreciated later on when David not only became king but even carved out a mini-empire for himself in the surrounding lands. Shepherd becomes emperor! Our story is only the beginning of a drama that unfolds over many centuries until it reaches its climax in a son of David, born in Bethlehem a thousand years later.

In the light of that whole revelation we can understand the depth of the statement, "Not as man sees does God see. . . ." The Old Testament author did not know how profoundly true that statement was.

Anyone who believes in God would have to believe that he does indeed see as no human person can see. But to accept that in our lives is the great challenge. To accept the reality of a divine providence that mysteriously works out its will is the beginning of wisdom. To allow God the guidance of one's life is, in effect, to see as God sees.

The whole drama of the Johannine narrative revolves around this same theme of seeing. A blind man is cured by Jesus and a major controversy breaks out between the cured man and Pharisees. Just under the surface of the whole story is the struggle between the sight of belief and the blindness of disbelief. Only at the end of the story, in vv. 39-41, does it clearly surface.

The story may well have been told at this particular time because in the preceding chapter Jesus says, "I am the light of the world. No follower of mine shall ever walk in darkness; no, he shall possess the light of life" (8:12). The blind man is a powerful illustration of this truth. He possesses "the light of life" in the fullest sense, both physically and spiritually. He sees and believes.

It is true that the blind man does not immediately recognize who Jesus is. Even after he is cured, he does not show in his disputes with the Pharisees that he is aware of Jesus' identity. It comes to clear expression only at the end (vv. 35-38).

But the blind man *allowed* Jesus to enter his life. He willingly followed his directions. In doing so he "came back able to see." He permitted this unknown providence to guide him, and he was able to see as God sees.

The Pharisees refuse entrance to this "light of the world." Their overly prescriptive interpretation of God's will makes them judge even a miracle as an evil act. They refuse to see as God sees, and they remain blind in a manner far worse than the cured man ever experienced.

The second reading states that Christians are "light in the Lord." We have said "yes" to him. We share his light and his seeing. Our lives must reflect that.

Fifth Sunday of Lent (A)
Ezekiel 37:12-14; Romans 8:8-11; John 11:1-45

The Scriptures ring with one startling proclamation after another. But perhaps, like Chesterton's man who was so tall he couldn't be seen, these are so startling they fail to register on our consciousness. Or, repeated so often, they fail to make an impression any more. Then the only solution is to read the Scriptures as though for the first time and to let their full force fall upon our open minds and hearts.

Several statements in our readings have the power to move us if we let them. But surely the most startling is Jesus' proclamation in the Gospel: "I am the resurrection and the life!" No ordinary person would say anything like that. It is as though a doctor were to say, "I am the operation that will save you." One who heard a doctor say that to a patient would surely advise the patient to change doctors.

Yet Jesus made that statement. For close to two thousand years people have been hearing it. Some have laughed it off as ludicrous. Others have found it too profound to think about. But others have reflected on it, discovered a meaning, and believed in him.

In all of the so-called "I am" statements in John's Gospel where Jesus identifies himself with some other reality, such as "the light of the world" (8:12), "the sheepgate" (10:7), "the good shepherd" (10:11), "the true vine" (15:1), there is intended a salvific relationship to others. In other words, that other reality symbolizes or expresses some saving effect Jesus will have on believers.

Thus when Jesus says "I am the resurrection and the life," he is not referring simply to his own resurrection from the dead. He is talking about resurrection and life that he will bring to those who believe in him. Such people will be raised from the dead; they will have life.

But there is more. He does not mean only the resurrection to life on the last day. (That is implied in V. 24 where Martha expresses belief in such a resurrection.) He means, also and especially, a new kind of life that is already shared here and now. This is indicated by another remarkable statement, ". . . whoever is alive and believes in me will never die."

This kind of life is what has traditionally been called the "life of grace." It is a life that puts one in intimate relationship with the Father, Son and Spirit. And it is a relationship that may never cease. Thus, even though physical death will intervene, the union with God will continue.

When Jesus, therefore, says that he is the resurrection and the life, he is saying that those who believe in him, who surrender in faith to his Lordship, not only will be raised from physical death on the last day but also will enjoy a special kind of life here and now. The author of 2 Peter said the same thing, though somewhat more philosophically, when he wrote that we are made "sharers of the divine nature" (1:4).

Scripture has this preoccupation with life. God is known as "the living God" (Dt 5:26) and the God "of the living" (Lk 20:38). As such he wills life for all things and especially for his people. All he asks is that they accept him and the life he offers. That is why Jesus asks Martha if she believes before he restores her brother to physical life.

The Ezekiel reading also speaks of resurrection to life. Here the prophet means the restoration to national life after the ignominy of exile. That, too, is life. But Paul, in the Romans reading, is speaking of life in that fuller sense when he writes of the life of the Spirit in Christ.

"I came that they might have life and have it to the full" (Jn 10:10) That is Jesus' amazing offer. What is our response?

Passion Sunday (A)
Isaiah 50:4-7; Philippians 2:6-11; Matthew 26:14—27:66

At the beginning of Lent we asked, Why was Jesus tempted? Now, at the season's close we ask, Why did he suffer? The early Church knew that he *did* suffer and die. She also knew that this had to be in accord with God's plan, or, as St. Paul calls it, with his mystery.

One hint is found in an enigmatic figure described in the Old Testament. In the second part of the book of Isaiah (cc. 40-55), written during the exile in Babylon, there appears in four distinct poems one who is called the Servant of Yahweh. In the third, and especially in the fourth, the servant is said to suffer at the hands of others.

The first of this Sunday's readings is the third of these "Suffering Servant" poems. Monday of this Holy Week will offer the first poem, Tuesday the second, Wednesday the third again, and Good Friday the fourth and climactic one. In this last one the Servant is said to suffer and die for the sins of others. ". . . he gives his life as an offering for sin."

It is clear from this liturgical usage that the Church considers Jesus to be the fulfillment of the ancient oracles. They provide the answer, at least partially, to our question. Jesus suffered and died for the sins of mankind. His passion and death become our means of salvation.

This identification of Jesus as the Suffering Servant is not a recent one. It was made from the beginning. Matthew, for example, refers at least twice to the Isaian poems in speaking of Jesus (cf. 8:17; 12:18-21). What is more important, Jesus probably saw himself as fulfilling that role.

But there remains a profound question. Why did the Old Testament prophet think of suffering as a means of doing away with sin? And even more to the point, how *did* Jesus' passion and death bring this about?

With regard to the Isaian author, he was certainly moved by the suffering of his people in exile. He would have seen that, in some way, those sufferings were accepted by God as atoning for the sins of others. What is that "some way"?

The New Testament authors use a number of terms to express the relationship between Jesus' suffering and the forgiveness of sins. We find words like salvation, redemption, expiation, justification, reconciliation. Each of these has a richness of meaning that cannot be explored in this limited space. What we can and must say about them is that they do not mean that Jesus paid a price to the Father that sinners might be bought back, or that his blood appeased a vengeful God. These are crass notions often found in primitive religions but completely contrary to the biblical notion of God.

What is basic to that notion is that God has first loved us with an inexhaustible and unmerited love and that he expects a response of love from us. Suffering (obviously not self-inflicted) that is borne as an expression of obedient love is just such a response. It is a surrender of self that the self might be filled with God's love. When this is abundantly realized, that love brims over and touches the lives of others.

This is what is expressed in better words in the hymn of the second reading. Jesus Christ, though equal to God, so emptied himself of divine glory that he became a slave (or servant, the "suffering Servant"). This obedient self-emptying led to death on a cross. And *because of that* he was exalted on high and given the name of "Lord"—a saving Lord for us.

Suffering, obedient love, and divine love that forgives sins—all of these are intimately connected. Only in the context of love can suffering have any meaning. But then it means reconciliation of God and sinner.

Easter Sunday (A)
Acts 10:34, 37-43; Colossians 3:1-4; John 20:1-9

The resurrection of Jesus Christ is so overwhelming for the Church that she has all three readings for this Sunday and for the days following speak of this event. Although no Old Testament passages speak directly of a risen Messiah, several texts can be seen as preparing for this belief. Still, the Church finds more than enough for her purpose in the New Testament.

The first reading shows Peter at the home of the Roman centurion, Cornelius. He is given an occasion to preach. His sermon consists of a brief summary of Jesus' life, with some emphasis on his crucifixion, and with greater emphasis on his resurrection and present status "as judge of the living and the dead."

It is clear that Peter is in a hurry to get to this climactic and almost unbelievable conclusion. After all, as one of the Twelve, and the most frequently mentioned one at that, he could have told all kinds of stories about the things that Jesus said, about his miracles, about his confrontations with opponents, about those last fateful days in Jerusalem. Instead, we have but three and a half verses on all of this. It is the risen Jesus that Peter must proclaim.

In one sense this first reading is the most directly relevant one for us. This is so not because it is the clearest presentation of the resurrection. The Gospel reading does that service. Rather, it is because Peter speaks of the effect of the resurrection on all people, especially on those who believe.

Jesus is designated "judge of the living and the dead." This is a divine title since only God could so act with regard to the whole human race. The title usually given to Jesus in this regard is that of *Kyrios*, Lord. In his Philippian hymn (2:6-11) Paul says that in his resurrection-exaltation Jesus is solemnly declared Lord. In Romans he says that through his resurrection Jesus was made Son of God in power (1:4), that is, able to exercise his lordship over all.

This is why we are Christians. Like Peter, we believe that Jesus was raised from the dead and that, because he was, he is our Lord and judge of all peoples. Moreover, we believe, as Peter does, that precisely as believers we have "forgiveness of sins through his name." We can see in what sense this reading is the most relevant *for us.*

Even so, that first reading doesn't say all there is to be said about being a Christian. It does tell us how it is possible, by believing in Jesus Christ. But there must also be a response in our lives to his forgiveness. We can't simply say "I've found it!" We must use the treasure that we've found.

This is what St. Paul is concerned with in the second reading. He says not only that Jesus is our Lord but also that we have been raised up with him. By that he means that our status as Christians is different from what it would have been as pagans. Therefore we must act differently. Our hearts must be filled with the concerns of Christ, not with our selfish concerns.

In a sense, John's Gospel reading is a climax. It records for us the discovery by Peter and his friend of the empty tomb. The disciple "saw and believed." Here was the origin of it all. What Peter and Paul say in the other two readings, what the whole New Testament is about, what the meaning of our lives is depends, not on an empty tomb, but on a risen Lord. The first can be seen; the second must be believed. When it is, astounding things happen. Ask Peter and Paul and that disciple.

Second Sunday of Easter (A)
Acts 2:42-47; 1 Peter 1:3-9; John 20:19-31

Easter is chocolate eggs and Jesus risen. According to C.S. Lewis, such was the response of a young boy when asked the meaning of the feast. The response was more profound than he probably realized.

Like every Christian feast, Easter is a celebration of both the sacred and the secular. It was the Incarnation of the God-man that so intimately united the two. All other feasts reflect the same mysterious union.

The reading from John's Gospel emphasizes the sacred element of the celebration. There is the appearance of the risen Jesus, the offer of the kingdom peace, the investing with the Spirit, and Thomas' expression of belief in this utterly transcendent event. The world of the disciples has been caught up in the world of God.

But it is not an unreal world. There is the *pro nobis* effect here, just as in every other feast. The reality of "down-to-earth" sins is faced; they are to be forgiven. And a fullness of life is promised to those who believe. The sacred does not destroy the secular; it ennobles and consecrates it.

In the second reading, from 1 Peter, we find the same mixture of the sacred and the secular, but again with the emphasis on the sacred. A number of scholars are convinced that much of the first two chapters, including our reading, is part of an ancient baptismal homily. At least it is certain that we do have here profound insights into the meaning of that great sacrament.

Baptism is described as a new birth, similar to what Jesus says in John's Gospel (3:3-8). It is a birth into the resurrection world described in the Gospel reading. This is implied when the author calls it a "birth unto hope which draws its life from the resurrection of Jesus Christ from the dead." It is not only the first disciples who share that world; it is all of us who are baptized into his resurrection.

Baptism is also "a birth to an imperishable inheritance." We may recall that ancient Israel looked upon the promised land as their "inheritance," the inheritance based on a divine promise. The Christian inheritance, unlike Canaan, "cannot be ravaged by war, defiled by enemies, or faded by time. It is heavenly" (J. Fitzmyer).

Finally, Baptism is "a birth to a salvation" to be perfectly fulfilled in the end-time. While these are all highly transcendent, or sacred, realities, the author says that through Baptism we are born into them *now*. Our secular world is inwardly transformed by them and made sacred.

This is why the author can speak so confidently of those aspects of our world that we would more readily recognize as secular. He speaks of "the distress of many trials" and "the passing splendor of fire-tried gold."These we can feel and touch. But now, in the light of Baptism, we experience them in a new way. Because of that new vision we have "cause for rejoicing here."

The first reading, from Acts, is filled with secular elements: the communal life, sharing, selling of property and goods, caring for each one's needs, and meals together. But it is all suffused with the Easter faith, as the reading abundantly testifies. It is a life for "those who believed."

Easter faith is a new vision that makes even chocolate eggs a gift of the risen Lord. How we use and share that gift, Luke would tell us, is the sign of the depth of our faith.

Third Sunday of Easter (A)
Acts 2:14, 22-28; 1 Peter 1:17-21; Luke 24:13-35

"Were not our hearts burning inside us as he talked to us on the road and explained the Scriptures to us?" The two disciples said that after experiencing the risen Jesus and hearing his explanation of the startling events that had so recently occurred. The words are part of the third reading for this Sunday of Easter.

The events were the passion and death of Jesus and his resurrection from the dead. The two disciples must have been among his closest followers during the public ministry. They would have been utterly dismayed by his arrest, trial, and crucifixion. Now the news of the empty tomb and of his being alive puzzles them even more.

The events, however, are not our primary interest here. We are concerned with their significance and especially with the communication of that significance to others. If such things did happen (and we are accepting the fact that they did), how in the world are others made aware of them?

In the case of the two disciples we have a unique experience. The risen Jesus himself explains the events. Spiritual writers through the ages have remarked how privileged the disciples were and how great it would be if all had that same experience. But would it? In last week's Gospel Jesus noted that Thomas had believed because he had seen him, but he then blessed those who believed without seeing. We are in that latter group.

But perhaps the two disciples also are in that group. A number of scholars maintain that St. Luke has taken a typical story of an itinerant Christian preacher, reworked it to present Jesus himself as the model preacher, woven into it an account of Eucharistic celebration (the blessing, breaking, and distribution of the bread) and presented it as a story of the communication of the Easter message.

If this interpretation is correct, it has exciting significance for all of us. First, it means that the official preacher of the Word truly represents Christ. When he proclaims the Good News of resurrection, it is the risen Jesus speaking through him. The power of his words is in truth the power of Christ's Word. And the events that puzzled the two disciples are made present in the proclamation.

Moreover, it means that you, the reader, must experience your heart burning within you "as he talked to us on the road. . . ." No doubt, the human element in the preacher is often an obstacle to effective communication. But even more than that, it is the absence of open hearts that keeps the Word from entering that it might do its burning. Jesus can overcome a faltering voice more readily than a hardened heart.

Finally, the Paschal events and their power are communicated in the Eucharist. This has been the Christian understanding of the Mass since the beginning. In our Gospel it is presented in the statement that the disciples, on receiving Communion, had their eyes opened, "and they recognized him."

Our Gospel story, then is an accurate picture of the liturgy of the Word and the liturgy of the Eucharist. In every Sunday Mass the Emmaus experience is repeated.

Fourth Sunday of Easter (A)
Acts 2:14, 36-41; 1 Peter 2:20-25; John 10:1-10

We offer this week a variety of reflections on the three readings. The first reading continues and concludes Peter's first address on Pentecost Sunday to a group of Jewish pilgrims to Jerusalem. Probably Luke, in recording this whole scene, has incorporated elements from the missionary life of the chief apostle. But what he wants to do, and does effectively, is to dramatize the action of the Holy Spirit, the meaning of the resurrection for Jesus, and, especially in our reading, the effect of all this on people when they hear the Word with open hearts.

The reading begins with what seems to be a strange statement by Peter. He says that Jesus, on the occasion of his resurrection (cf. the preceding verse), was made Lord and Messiah by God. This would suggest that he was not this from the moment of his birth. Some theologians in the past concluded that Jesus was only the adopted Son of God, a heresy the Church condemned.

What Peter says here is perfectly in accord with orthodox teaching and with the Semitic mentality. According to the latter, the meaning is that Jesus was *manifested as exercising* his lordship only after his resurrection. St. Paul says the same thing about Jesus as Son of God in Romans 1:4.

This effective manifestation is made evident in the response of the audience. "Deeply shaken," they realize they must do something. Peter says two things are necessary: reform and baptism. Reform means a reversal of one's life goals, a radical change of heart and of one's way of life. In its most profound sense, as here, it assumes that one is a sinner whose sole life purpose has been self-seeking satisfaction. The change must be the love of God and service of others.

Baptism is the sacrament of initiation. By introducing the sinner into the life of the Trinity, it effects the forgiveness of sins and the gift of the Spirit. The Spirit makes it possible to carry out the reform in one's life.

A pastoral note about reform (or repentance) is appropriate here. While it can be understood in the radical sense just described, it is also used, especially in Luke's Gospel, to describe a continuing movement of the Christian toward the Lord. Reform in this sense should be the effect of *every* homily (not just Peter's) and of every Eucharistic celebration.

The reading from Peter's letter is part of an admonition to household slaves. Since they suffer unjustly, they remind the author of Jesus' own suffering, which he describes in some detail. What he wants to emphasize is that Jesus' sufferings were salvific. Hence, no matter what our sufferings might be, we can be assured that in our life with God we have been healed.

Peter concludes by saying that they have "returned" to Jesus Christ. For Luke the Greek word has much the same meaning as "reform." In both cases it is a "movement toward the Lord." The Lord here is called both shepherd and guardian. The latter word can also be translated as bishop. This reference to Jesus as both shepherd and bishop is the origin of the combined usage in the history of the Church.

In John's Gospel we have a mixture of figures. In the first part (vv. 1-5) Jesus sees himself as a shepherd. As such he cares for his flock who in turn trust him completely. In the second part (vv. 7-10) Jesus is a sheepgate that both allows the flock to go out to pasture and keeps them protected from wild animals.

To summarize our three readings, we say that they tell us about Jesus and the remarkable effect he has on us. We are no longer the same. We belong to him who is shepherd and guardian of our lives.

Fifth Sunday of Easter (A)
Acts 6:1-7; 1 Peter 2:4-9; John 14:1-12

Service of others is one of the principal themes of our three readings. A more technical term for this is ministry. While once associated almost exclusively with the clergy and Religious, ministry in some form is now recognized as incumbent upon all who follow the Lord. Stressed by the Second Vatican Council, ministry by all the faithful has its roots deep in the Scriptures.

The first reading doesn't make the point we just enunciated, since it speaks of a special group called for a particular ministry and for whom an ordination rite is exercised. Still, it does show how important the early church considered the office of ministry. It doesn't say it here, but it suggests that ministry to others flows from being a Christian.

Our passage deals with a particular situation where a special group of people was in need of help. Seven specifically chosen men were brought before the apostles for this purpose. The apostles "prayed over them and then imposed hands on them."

Traditionally this passage has been seen as the biblical basis for the ordination of deacons as special ministers in the Church. And it can be so understood. However, Luke doesn't use the Greek word for "deacon" here. It may be that the word was just not part of his vocabulary, as it doesn't appear anywhere in his writings. Certainly we have in the account an ordination rite for a special ministry of service.

The second reading, from the letter of Peter, contains explicit reference to a universal call to ministry. The author may well be using an ancient baptismal liturgy here. If true, that adds to the significance of our point, for it means that what is said of Christian flows from the very sacrament of Baptism whereby they were initiated into the Church. And what is said to them certainly includes ministry.

First, Peter speaks of living stones and a cornerstone. The latter, of course, is Christ himself, who is a firm foundation for those who believe in him but a stumbling block for those who reject him. By their faith Christians become living stones of the new spiritual edifice, the Church.

He then goes on to proclaim them "a chosen race, a royal priesthood, a holy nation, a people he claims for his own. . . ." The figures are taken from Exodus 19:6 where they were once applied to Israel. And in the figure of priesthood, referred to also earlier in our passage, we have a clear indication of a ministry to others. Again, it is a ministry that flows from Baptism.

But the author completes the sentence by saying that they have been claimed (by God) "to proclaim the glorious works of the One who called you. . . ." Christians cannot rest on their divinely gifted laurels. They must be a witness to their gifts. To evangelize, even by suffering, is to be a Christian.

In the Gospel reading, too long to comment on in detail, Jesus also says that the one who believes in him "will do the works I do. . ." And Jesus came, not to seek his own glory, but to glorify the Father by serving others. This service of others constitutes the "works" that he does.

The notion of election is not a popular one today. To some it suggests elitism, a holier or better-than-thou attitude. But in the Scriptures election is never intended as a source of self-glory, because election does not rest on merits or goodness. Rather, election finds its fullest meaning in service of others. Christians are chosen to serve.

Sixth Sunday of Easter (A)
Acts 8:5-8, 14-17; 1 Peter 3:15-18; John 14:15-21

The first and third readings for this Sunday anticipate Pentecost. In the first the Holy Spirit is active in the missionary work of Peter and John. In the Gospel Jesus promises the disciples that "another Paraclete" (one of John's ways of designating the Spirit) will be given to them. In all three readings we can almost feel the intensity of the Father's loving action through the Son and Spirit.

Luke conveys this sense of intensity in his report of Philip's preaching and healing by noting that "The rejoicing in that town rose to fever pitch." The Greek text reads literally, "And there was much joy in that town." But the way in which St. Luke uses the Greek word for joy justifies the "fever pitch" translation. For him it is a climactic, superabundant joy that is evoked when the Lord is fully at work.

The second part of the story tells how Peter and John, representing the "official" Church in Jerusalem went "down" to Samaria. (They really went north, but anywhere from the holy hill of Jerusalem is "down" in the Bible). There they imposed hands on those baptized by Philip, and the new converts received the Holy Spirit. This is one of the root passages for our sacrament of Confirmation.

In this section of Acts St. Luke is beginning his narrative of the spread of Christianity to the whole of the civilized world. He had just recounted the story of Stephen's martyrdom and then noted that a general persecution broke out in Jerusalem. It prompted the scattering of the disciples to other lands. As our reading shows, this scattering was to have its fruit in the conversion of the Gentiles.

In Peter's letter we see again the intensity of the Lord's saving action, but now made manifest in the wholehearted response of Christians. The opening verse sets the tone, "Venerate the Lord, that is, Christ in your hearts." In the preceding verse he had told them to cast out fear. In the light of that we can paraphrase the present verse in this way: "Let the Lord Christ and his holiness, his sanctifying majesty, fill your hearts so that there will be no room for fear."

Peter then goes on to say that Christians should be able to explain their faith (here expressed as "the reason for this hope of yours"). The context speaks of suffering, which may suggest persecution and so the need to defend one's religious stance. But it must be done "gently and respectfully." The second word refers to the Lord who is in their hearts. It is out of respect for him that they speak.

The underlying ground for this Christian response is always the saving work of God. That is why Peter cannot help but mention again the death and resurrection of Jesus Christ. If he "was given life in the realm of the spirit," it was that we might walk in that same life and act in that same spirit.

In John's Gospel we can detect an alternation between the saving work of the Father and the Christian's response. Again the intensity of Jesus' words is there and is explained by the depth of his vision into the Father's plan.

On the part of the Christian there is the need to keep the commandments or "words" of Jesus and to love him. The two are inseparable, and the first only confirms the second. If there is love of Jesus, there will be the kind of obedience he asks.

But there is more emphasis on what the Father will do and the Spirit whom he will send. They will make possible a fullness of life and a mutual indwelling of Christ and the Christian.

We can understand why the Church would use these readings for a Sunday in Eastertime. They reveal the intensity of resurrection life.

Ascension (A)
Acts 1:1-11; Ephesians 1:17-23; Matthew 28:16-20

No one can go it alone. A wife needs the support of a trusting husband; a teacher needs encouragement from students; a public speaker becomes better when she receives a warm reception from her audience. And so it is with the Christian—who never goes it alone; with Christ's presence the quality of living becomes richer.

At the beginning of Matthew's Gospel (1:23), we learn that Jesus is the Emmanuel, God with us. Now at the end we have the words of Jesus, "I am with you always." The Ascension is not a time to commemorate Christ's departure from us, but rather a time to recall Christ's presence in our midst. This presence is made manifest in the work of the people of God, the Church.

On this Ascension Day the Scriptures are forceful in showing the demands of Christian discipleship, which finds meaning in the fact that Christ remains with his people. The eleven disciples are told to go forth and make still more disciples, to baptize, and to teach, knowing that their strength comes from the power of Jesus. Jesus, who possesses all authority from his Father, now transmits that same authority to his disciples.

Christian discipling is the process whereby individuals are educated and inaugurated into a new way of life; it is part of the process of evangelization. This is the charge given to the associates of Jesus at the time of his ascension; "do what I have been doing" and "continue my ministry" are other ways of recounting the words left us by Matthew.

In a society in which religion has low priority and in a world in which secularism reigns supreme, the words of today's celebration are vastly important. In them is power to move the Christian into a deeper communication with the Lord and power to assist that same Christian to go forth and proclaim the good news message: Jesus lives.

Jesus' ascension has conferred power upon all those who follow him and find strength in that most powerful of all names, Lord Jesus Christ (Ephesians). He desires to remain close to his people; that is why he says, "I am with you always." He is no absentee leader leaving his disciples to go it alone. His words of presence have provided comforting strength for the multitudes from the time when they were uttered until the present day: for those in concentration camps, for those seriously ill, for those who have lost loved ones, for those who doubt, for those who want to give up.

On this day we are called to accept the headship of Jesus Christ over his Body, the Church (Ephesians). It is the feast on which we are called to acknowledge that Jesus in whom we believe did ascend to the right hand of his Father. He is glorified and possesses power. And he will come again with that same power (Acts).

Pope Paul VI in *"Evangelization in the Modern World"* reminded us that the sign of true evangelization is this: the truly evangelized individual must eventually go out to evangelize others. Such a person cannot keep his faith to himself. The power that Jesus has given to us so that we might indeed lead the victorious life of grace must eventually become vocal. The way of life must lead to a proclamation of the word of life.

The same holds true for the Church herself; through the power of the word of God the entire Church must be evangelized and evangelizing. The Church and each member need not only be faithful and dedicated to the glorified Christ, but must also be seen and heard by those who do not yet know Christ. The ascending Christ has given us this charge.

P.J.S.

Seventh Sunday of Easter (A)
Acts 1:12-14; 1 Peter 4:13-16; John 17:1-11

The glory of God is man alive; the glory of man is the praise of God. This is a reconstruction of an ancient patristic saying. It sums up well the theme for this Sunday. Especially in the Gospel reading does the saying find a remarkable resonance.

"Glory" is a word and concept that runs throughout biblical literature. We say it primarily and almost exclusively of God. Only when understood of him can it be seen to have any other relative application. Glory is the external manifestation of an ineffable majesty that is God's always and which now appears in mighty saving actions for others. In this sense it is an exclusively divine attribute.

The notion of glory presupposes someone who can recognize it. That, of course, is the world. The whole of creation acknowledges God's majesty in the mighty acts that he has performed and that glorify him. "All the nations you have made shall come and worship you, O Lord, and glorify your name. For you are great, and you do wondrous deeds; you alone are God" (Ps 86:9).

In the New Testament John develops the theme of divine glory more than any other author. The second part of his Gospel, chapters 13 to 20, is called the Book of Glory. Here Jesus speaks of the glory that he gives the Father and which the Father in turn will give to him. (This notion that Jesus can be glorified is, as suggested in our definition, an implicit acknowledgment of his divinity.)

At the beginning of the reading Jesus says that his hour has come. At least ten times before this he had spoken of it as coming. This "hour" is the time of his glorification. And that glorification takes place, in John's theology, in Jesus' death and resurrection. In both these actions, the raising up on the cross and in resurrection, God's mighty acts are revealed and glory is given to both the Son and the Father.

In this farewell address of Jesus John sees the beginning of the end. That is why Jesus speaks of his hour having come. It is the beginning of the end of his public ministry. But it is also the beginning of his entrance into glory. It is, therefore, *the hour* par excellence. This is why Jesus can say to the Father, "Give glory to your Son that your Son may give glory to you. . . ." Father and Son mutually recognize the majesty of the other.

But we said this glory is revealed in saving actions for others. This is abundantly clear in the remainder of the reading. Jesus speaks of bestowing eternal life on those whom the Father has given to him. He says that he has given the Father glory by "finishing the work" given him, which is the work of salvation. The passage abounds with references to all the good things that Jesus has done for others in order that his glory might be acknowledged.

From all that is said about God's actions for us we can understand why that ancient writer said the glory of God is man alive. We are alive with the eternal life of the Son. We are walking images of his majesty revealed, of his glory.

Further, if there is any glory that we can share, as the ancient saying indicates, it can only come through our recognition of the prior and constitutive glory of God. That alone is why it can be said that our glory is the praise of God. "O Father most holy, protect them with your name which you have given me. . . ." That name is "glory," majesty made visible in our praise of the Lord.

Pentecost: Vigil Mass (ABC)
Ezekiel 37:1-14; Romans 8:22-27; John 7:37-39

The celebration of Pentecost has begun! A vigil, which is a watch in the night anticipating what the new day will bring, is already the beginning of the celebration of the new dawn. For people of old, a day really began at sunset and continued to the following sunset— from the beginning of night until the end of day. On this Saturday evening the Church anticipates the beginning of the Pentecost celebration.

And the Church shows us first Ezekiel, standing in the center of the plain outside Babylon, lamenting the fate of his captive country-men, and hurling curses upon the foes of God's people, Israel (viz. 21:1-37). In tonight's reading he prophesies the rebirth of Israel; a devastated land and its inhabitants will be made to live by the powerful breath (spirit) of God.

It is easy to visualize the dried bones of the defeated Israelites strewn over the countryside after the violent destruction of Jerusalem in 586 B.C. But our reading is one filled with hope in the power of the Lord to restore to life that which appears dead. Man became a living being when God breathed upon him (Gn 2:7); now by God's breath a nation returns to life.

What Ezekiel had prophesied in this evening's reading did come to pass when Cyrus freed the Israelites from their Babylonian bondage and allowed them to return to the land of their ancestors in 538 B.C. Hope in that dream of the prophet was realized in the near future.

In the second reading Paul too emphasizes hope; he speaks of the successive stages of redemption. (Redemption is liberation; it is freedom won by the saving, life-giving blood of Jesus). Although creation has suffered because of sin (v. 20), nonetheless, there is hope within creation. Creation, too, longs for the fulfillment of its hope. Creation is depicted as going through labor pains; just as the wom-an's suffering will eventually lead to the joy of new life, so too creation's present groaning will be transformed into glory.

Humanity still hopes for the final liberation—the transformed "redemption of our bodies." "In hope we were saved" is the basis for our seeking and yearning for the glorified state of our beings. Having been saved by the redeeming blood of Jesus we have the rightful expectation of future glory.

We groan inwardly (v. 23), but it is the Spirit who "makes intercession for us with groanings." The Spirit makes our inward groanings and longings his own and so intercedes for us with God the Father. With the Spirit as life-giver, we have the right to hope. This vigil that we celebrate tonight is hope-filled in anticipation of the bestowal of the Spirit of Pentecost.

Our Gospel passage focuses on the last day of the Feast of Tabernacles. Water was an important element in the celebration in the Temple; each day water was drawn from the Gihon fountain, which supplied the water to the pool of Siloam (John 9:7). The water was then poured upon the altar of holocausts as a liberation offering. Now Jesus rises and informs his hearers that he is the source of living water.

Jesus is also the source of life. It is his testimony that gives life, and after his resurrection it will be the Spirit who will bear testimony to him. At the time of his death Jesus gives up his spirit (John 19:30). In tonight's Gospel we are told that the Spirit had not yet been given because Jesus had not yet been glorified.

Yet already the celebration of Pentecost has begun. We wait this evening in joyful anticipation of the full celebration of the bestowal of the Spirit upon the Church on the morrow. Only then will the disciples begin to preach and to share the good news that Jesus Christ is the glorified Lord.

P.J.S.

Pentecost Sunday (ABC)
Acts 2:1-11; 1 Corinthians 12:3-7, 12-13; John 20:19-23

What role does the Holy Spirit play in your life? Or, better, what role do you understand him to play in your life? He's there, and he's active. But do you recognize his presence at all?

One of the reasons for this feast of Pentecost is to enhance our understanding and appreciation of the Holy Spirit. This Sunday's

Word is ideally suited for that. Each of the readings gives us a rich insight into the meaning of the Spirit for us.

One of the general purposes for which Luke wrote his Gospel and the Acts of the Apostles was to show the universal nature of Christianity. It's offer of God's saving love is for everyone everywhere and in every age. The agent of its worldwide expansion is the Holy Spirit.

There are intimations of this in Luke's Gospel. But it is in his history of the young church that he shows clearly the Spirit's power at work, the power to evangelize all kinds of peoples. This Sunday's reading from that book is the most striking text in that regard. In his inaugural appearance to the whole community of believers he brings the good news to peoples "of every nation under heaven."

Luke understands this experience as the official beginning of the Church and of her commitment to evangelize the world through the Spirit's power. But, as Peter will bring out in his first discourse, the Spirit is given in this saving way because of the prior saving activity of Jesus (2:32-33). The Spirit brings Christ's saving love to us.

To us. To all of us who believe. If you can truthfully say that you believe in Jesus Christ, then you know that the Holy Spirit has been at work in you. For, as Paul says in the second reading, ". . . no one can say; 'Jesus is Lord,' except in the Holy Spirit." Your being a Christian is a determined part of the Spirit's goal to spread the faith. Pentecost has happened to you.

In the reading from Paul's letter to the church at Corinth we note two characteristics of the Spirit's work. The first is the bestowing of special gifts on the believer. In later passages Paul gives lists of them. Some are "extraordinary," such as speaking in tongues, but many are the ordinary tasks of everyday life, such as teaching, assisting others, and engaging in administration.

The point is that anything we do as Christians to help one another is the Spirit's power working in us; it is his gift. The one major criterion for recognizing the possession of a gift is if it helps others, or, as Paul puts it, if it is "for the common good." The Spirit's gifts are not for a chosen elite; they are for all who believe and who act on their belief. That is why Paul says that the greatest gift is love (c. 13).

The other characteristic of the Spirit's work mentioned here is his unifying power. He makes the most disparate peoples one. That means that "in one spirit" all of us "were baptized into one body." While every Christian around the world has his or her own special gifts, they all form one body of Christ. The Holy Spirit is the unifying principle.

Finally, our Gospel reading brings still another insight. Here the Holy Spirit is directly associated with the forgiveness of sins. While the passage no doubt refers to a special power to forgive sins on the part of the apostles, the New Testament would surely testify that every time we forgive one another we are acting in the power of the Spirit.

The Holy Spirit and you? Your faith, your gifts of service no matter how menial, your oneness with others all over the world, your ability to say "I forgive" to one who has hurt you—all of these are the proof of the Spirit dwelling and acting in you.

Trinity Sunday (A)
Exodus 34:4-6, 8-9; 2 Corinthians 13:11-13; John 3:16-18

The Feast of God! That is one way of describing our liturgical celebration this Sunday. Holy Trinity is simply (hardly the correct word) the Christian expression of our belief in one God. Father, Son, and Spirit are one God. If the word "God" is a human attempt to speak the inexpressible, the term "Trinity" is no improvement from a rational point of view.

While the nature of Trinity, three distinct Persons in one God, is ultimately beyond human comprehension, theologians throughout the ages have grappled with the problem of understanding it in at least a limited way. The clearest attempt this writer has found among recent works is Joseph Ratzinger's *Introduction to Christianity* (Herder and Herder, 1970). But let the reader be wary; this is not pool side reading.

Our Scripture readings, happily, are not concerned with this philosophical problem. They are chosen, rather, to emphasize the significance of the triune God *for us* (once again, the *pro nobis* aspect of the Scriptures). In the Exodus reading we see the face of the Father turned toward his children. In the Gospel that face is visibly manifested in the incarnate Son. In the letter of Paul all three Persons are invoked at once in a blessing on the readers and hearers of the Word.

The context of the first reading is important for an appreciation of the words about God. While Moses was on Sinai's mount, the people, grown weary, had fashioned themselves an idol and stooped to revel in their idolatry. Enraged at such perfidy, Moses hurled the tablets of the Law to the ground, indicating the rapture of the covenant between God and people.

But then, on Moses' plea, the tablets were renewed and God again turned toward his people in mercy and love. "The Lord, the Lord, a merciful and gracious God, slow to anger and rich in kindness and fidelity." The first word from God at Israel's choice as a people had been creative love; the last word from God is now merciful and forgiving love. Four Hebrew words that defy adequate translation are used here. The first, translated "merciful," implies compassion, tenderness, the heart of a father moved by unmerited love. The second, "gracious," means the favor or benevolence of one who has gifts to give and wills to give them. The third, "kindness," is the love that marks the covenant bond between two parties. The fourth, "fidelity," connotes rock-likeness, constancy, the inability to be turned from the will to love.

This is our God. He knows anger because of sin and lets his servant Moses express it. But, in the end, he wants only merciful and faithful love to be known.

While the Exodus passage describes the true heart of God, the Gospel reading tells us how far that heart can go to reveal its true nature. "God so loved the world that he gave his only Son." Some say this is the most frequently quoted passage in the Scriptures. There is good reason for the frequency. But the passage's exquisite beauty and unrestrained power became a sentence of death to the unresponding heart (v. 18).

In his valedictory blessing, Paul gathers together the characteristics of the God who has revealed himself in history. The characteristics are really those of the one God, and so of all three Persons. But in a way they are seen in our worldview as appropriated by the three in a distinctive manner.

To God the Father belongs love, the principle of all he wills and does. The result of this love for us is the gift, the grace, that is the

Father's Son, Jesus Christ. That love and grace, through the power of the Spirit, bring us together in fellowship and union.

This is the feast of God we celebrate, the feast of love and grace and fellowship. They are Holy Trinity.

The Body and Blood of Christ (A)
Deuteronomy 8:2-3, 14-16; 1 Corinthians 10:16-17; John 6:51-58

As the Christian sees it, death is both dissolution and transformation. As dissolution it is the cessation of physical life and the deterioration of the body no longer sustained by life-giving blood. As transformation it is the ushering of the human spirit into a new kind of life that had been prepared for in the previous existence.

In the earlier Catholic services for the dead the emphasis was on death as dissolution. At least this was true in many of its external trappings. The black vestments, the plaintive *Dies Irae* ("Day of Wrath"), and often the homily accentuated this note of loss and sorrow.

In the renewed liturgical rites the emphasis is clearly on death as transformation. The white vestments, the repeated *Alleluias*, and, again, the homily all express the joy that a new and better existence is now shared by the deceased faithful believer.

It may sound strange to be speaking of death on the feast of The Body and Blood of Christ. I am doing so only that I might speak all the more forcefully about life.

The medical doctor would tell us that, while death does in a certain way mark a dissolution, in reality the dissolution had already begun before the actual moment of death. As some have pointed out, the seeds of dissolution are sown at the moment of conception.

Having said all that, we now can concentrate on our real subject, but with greater appreciation in the light of what has been said. In the Gospel reading for this feast Jesus says, "He who feeds on my flesh and drinks my blood has life eternal. . . ." There is no question of Jesus' meaning, the verb is in the present tense, the communion with Christ in the Eucharist means a sharing here and now in eternal life.

What is meant by "eternal life" in the Fourth Gospel? It does not mean, primarily, everlasting life, even though that is a feature of it.

Later on in our Sunday reading Jesus says, ". . . the man who feeds on this bread shall live for ever." Death, therefore, does not destroy this kind of life.

But seeing it only as everlasting is seeing it from a purely quantitative view. In this view eternal life is the same as natural life except that it lasts longer. It is evident that Jesus meant more than that. Receiving his body and blood in Communion must mean more than just keeping the human heart beating longer.

Rather, for John "eternal life" is the kind of life that is proper to the Father and which he shares with the Son. That is what our reading says about it. Eternal life, then, is God's life. And the most frequently mentioned quality of this kind of life is that it is shared. This is at the basis of the Christian doctrine of Trinity. That is why the real enemy of eternal life is not natural death, which affects only natural life, but sin, which destroys the union with God and, accordingly, eternal life.

When we receive the Eucharistic body and blood of Christ, we are united to him and to the Father. This is sharing in eternal life that is a life of union with God. But so central to the concept of eternal life is this note of sharing life that it also means union with others who receive Christ's body and blood. Paul says that in the second reading: ". . . we, many though we are, are one body, for we all partake of the one loaf."

There is the miracle of this great feast. We share Christ's life. We are already living eternally!

Second Sunday in Ordinary Time (A)
Isaiah 49:3, 5-6; 1 Corinthians 1:1-3; John 1:29-34

In recent weeks we have been celebrating radiant mysteries: the birth of Jesus, the motherhood of the Virgin Mary, the epiphany of Christ. Now we continue the cycle of liturgical readings as we celebrate the beginning of Jesus' public ministry.

The word "cycle" is the term used for the three groups of Scripture readings selected for three consecutive years. We are now in Cycle A when Matthew's Gospel will be used most frequently for the third reading.

The word "cycle" could be misleading. It might suggest that liturgical celebration is simply a repetition over and over of the saving act of God, without any change or progress being made. It is true and obvious that we do celebrate the same feasts year after year. But the celebration must be accompanied by a constant growth in our love of God and in our concern for justice, mercy, and peace in the world. If that was not present, the celebration would be tinsel.

This view is important. We believe in a history that is moving toward the moment when the Lord will appear in all his glory and saving power. That is why St. Paul said that we celebrate in the Eucharist "the death of the Lord until he comes!" (1 Corinthians 11:26). Our future is open to all kinds of possibilities for growth, for the building up of the Body of Christ. And the Eucharist, as all liturgical prayer, is the catalyst for that.

That is why I used the word "mystery" in the opening paragraph. In the Scriptures, mystery is not an impenetrable problem. Rather, it is God's saving plan that is gradually unfolded in the course of time and history. While the fullness of its meaning was revealed in Jesus Christ, we still celebrate the "mystery" because it has not been fully appropriated by us in our lives.

I have dwelt on this notion of liturgy and growth, because as we proceed in this new year of grace, it is imperative that we continue to slough off the "old man" of sin and self-seeking and put on the "new man" of self-sacrifice for others.

That idea is an excellent introduction to our first reading, which is part of one of the famed "Servant Songs." The identity of the Servant is not known, but one aspect of him is constant: he exists *for others*; he is a servant. In fact, in the fourth song (Is 52:13—53:12) he is described as suffering and dying for the sins of others. The early Church saw Jesus as fulfilling this role.

In our reading the Servant's role is described not only as restoring "the survivors of Israel," i.e., at the end of the Babylonian exile, but also as being "a light for the nations, that my salvation may reach to the ends of the earth." There is a remarkable universalism here that does great credit to the Jewish author.

The Gospel reading for this Sunday is from John. It records the Baptist's recognition of Jesus as "God's chosen one." One of the more startling statements in the passage is John's declaration that Jesus "is the Lamb of God who takes away the sin of the world." Why "Lamb of God?" Possibly there is a reference to the Pascal lamb that is slaughtered on the eve of Passover. Or the Church may have thought of the "Servant of Yahweh" who is described in the fourth song as "a lamb led to the slaughter." This could be the reason why we have a Servant song in the first reading.

In any case, what we have in Jesus is not some "Superstar" come to amaze the populace and win plaudits for the Father. Rather, we have incarnate God's own love that the sins of all might be forgiven and that we might love one another.

That alone is the reason why Paul can say what he says in the second reading. He—and we—can wish "grace and peace" to others that they might continue to grow in the mystery of God's salvation.

Third Sunday in Ordinary Time (A)
Isaiah 8:23—9:3; 1 Corinthians 1:10-13, 17; Matthew 4:12-23

If we consider the three readings for this Sunday in the order of Isaiah, Matthew, and Corinthians, we can see clearly the movement from anticipation to fulfillment to further development. The Isaian passage foresees "a great light," Matthew announces Jesus as the "great light," and Paul must contend with those who would dim the light by factions in the Christian community.

About 732 B.C. the Assyrian conqueror, Tiglath-Pileser, had devastated the upper territory of Israel, "the land of Zebulon and the land of Naphtali." But Isaiah the prophet knew that God would not forget his people and so confidently predicted that a restoration was to come. Darkness would give way to light, sorrow to rejoicing.

The future jubilation is compared with two of the greatest occasions of joy for the people of the ancient Near East. One is seasonal, the time of harvesting (which can have another symbolic meaning in the light of the Gospel reading). The other is episodic, the time of sharing the spoils of victory in war.

Isaiah probably foresaw this moment of joy coming on the occasion of the birth of a royal child (who is described in the verses following our reading). He would bring victory and peace. But Isaiah, or his disciples who recorded the oracle, would have seen a still more perfect fulfillment in the end-time. For them history was always pregnant with a richness of meaning because it was God's history.

What Isaiah could have foreseen only dimly Matthew was able to identify clearly. Jesus, who began his ministry in a town that was within the territory mentioned by the prophet, must be the "great light" and source of joy predicted long ago. Matthew, of course, could never have written that in the time of Jesus' early ministry, but in the light of his Easter faith he had no doubt about Jesus.

So the prophecy is fulfilled in the very appearance of Jesus in the land, proclaiming the gospel. But, by including the following section, the call of the first disciples, in this same Sunday reading the Church seems to suggest that that event also participates in the fulfillment.

The very simplicity of the call narrative is dramatic. Jesus sees the men and calls them; they abandon all and follow him. There is no questioning, no hesitation on the part of either Jesus or the men. Matthew had a purpose in such a presentation. On the part of Jesus, there is absolute authority. On the part of the men, there is absolute trust and the surrender of faith. And throughout his Gospel Matthew stresses both Jesus' authority and the disciples' faith. Both are present from the beginning.

The Church seems to suggest here that vocation and response are part of the fulfillment of the prophetic announcement of a great light and of rejoicing. And it is that because through the miracle of vocation to ministry, these men are rendered worthy of bringing the gospel, the "good news," to all people. As "the light of the world" (Mt 5:14), they share in the "great light," who is Jesus alone.

In the Isaian passage the joy was likened to that of harvesting time. Jesus himself uses the figure of a harvest to indicate the great need for vocations to ministry (Mt 9:36-38). Thus we can see another likeness between the first reading and the third where disciples are called to be fishers of men.

Nothing can take away from the fulfillment that Jesus brought. Unfortunately we Christians do not let the fullness of his light shine upon us. We attempt to make lesser lights the "great light" and wonder why we see so dimly.

That is the difficulty Paul encountered in Corinth. Distinct groups were following Paul and Peter and Apollos as they would follow Christ. What Paul says in effect is that only when Jesus Christ and he alone is the "great light" will there be a united community.

Fourth Sunday in Ordinary Time (A)
Zephaniah 2:3; 3:12-13; 1 Corinthians 1:26-31; Matthew 5:1-12

This Sunday an obvious theme threads its way through all three readings. It is that of the "humble and lowly" (first reading), the "weak and lowborn" (second reading), the "poor in spirit and the lowly" (third reading). The Hebrew Bible developed a technical term for those people; it called them the *anawim* (ah-nah-weem). They are the ones to whom the Messiah would bring *shalom* (peace).

The prophet Zephaniah lived in the seventh century B.C., perhaps toward the end of that century and so not too long before the total collapse of Judah and the destruction of Jerusalem. Like Amos and Hosea in the northern kingdom a century before him, he witnessed the bankruptcy of the policies of kings and princes, of the wealthy and powerful. Their materialism and lack of social concern could only lead to disaster.

Against that background what Zephaniah has to say in the first reading makes perfect sense, at least for believers. There will be a day of "the Lord's anger," but the *anawim* will be a remnant preserved. They recognize the ultimate source of all strength, wisdom, and wealth. It is the Lord and in him they take their refuge.

St. Paul would have studied his prophets well as a student under Gamaliel and would have been acquainted with Zephaniah. His basic thought in our reading is one that could have been borrowed from that prophet. But it is such a common biblical theme that it would be wrong to link Paul here too exclusively with Zephaniah.

Paul comes through with a power that is even greater than the prophet's. It's not just the weak and despised who are God's elect; the chosen are "those who count for nothing," the "nobodies" (the Greek suggests an even stronger notion: "the nonbeings," or things that don't exist). The apparent absurdity of Christ's death, which Paul came to realize was a victory, had completely reshaped his thinking.

The actual occasion for Paul's powerful words was the situation in the church at Corinth. Most of the Christian converts were of the lower class, probably about as close to being "nobodies" as any group in the city. But Paul detected a kind of elitism growing among them, a shuffling for favored positions. For Paul that is much worse than being "nobodies." Indeed, real "nobodies" are "somebodies" compared to falsely ambitious ones.

No one can read the Gospel passage without recognizing our theme immediately. The poor in spirit, the sorrowing, the lowly, the hungry and thirsty, the merciful and singlehearted, the peacemakers and persecuted—these people are the objects of Jesus' blessing just by being what they are.

The difficulty in writing about this controversial theme is that even when it is explained, it still won't make sense to one who does not believe. Faith is a necessary part of the explanation, and faith, by definition, is not rational proof.

The Hebrew people always had a positive attitude toward creation. They appreciated and enjoyed the "good life." But their origins as a semi-nomadic people also led them to realize that a purely material "good life" was frequently not at hand. Moreover, their experience of those who sought such a life exclusively, whether through war or politics or business, showed that they are not the happy ones.

It was, above all, their conviction of the Lord's presence that transformed life. His presence did not make created things less good or less desirable; rather, it enhanced them. But that presence also made the absence or scarcity of those goods less noticed, less an affliction. For the *anawim* the "good life" consists most radically in the possession of the Lord. In that possession there comes trust, confidence, and security. If our three readings do not say that, they say nothing.

Fifth Sunday in Ordinary Time (A)
Isaiah 58:7-10; 1 Corinthians 2:1-5; Matthew 5:13-16

Long ago, people considered the basic elements of the universe to be earth, fire, air, and water. Behind this designation, no doubt, was the conviction that these were absolutely necessary for human life. A certain pragmatism (does it work?) lay behind their choice.

Biblical religion contains a similar pragmatism. In other words, religion is not just a matter of worshipping a holy God no matter how deeply rooted that act is in human nature. It is also a matter of relating to others. Does religion affect my life? Does it work?

When we consider how ingrained in the Israelite spirit was the offering of sacrifice to Yahweh, it is remarkable that the prophets could condemn such offering in any fashion whatsoever. And yet they did—at times with such ferocity that some commentators thought they were against cultic worship itself.

They were not. They were only against its abuse. They were against the use of worship as an escape from life's responsibilities. And they were against its use as a means of manipulating God, of making him happy, and of leading him to forget their crimes. In effect, the prophets asked the people, Does your religion work?

This is what is behind the first reading for this Sunday. In the preceding section the people were pictured as asking God why he didn't hear their prayers. They were doing much fasting and nothing happened. Then the prophet tells them that their fasting should include feeding the hungry, sheltering the homeless, and clothing the naked.

He then moves on to another, apparently quite distinct theme, that of light. He says, in a marvelous phrase, "Your light shall break forth like the dawn. . . ." This could mean that in doing these things for others, they manifest a light to the world. In that case it would be quite in accord with the light theme in the Gospel reading.

But the author apparently sees the light as an *effect* of the charitable actions. This is especially clear in verses 9 and 10 where the prophet explicitly states that if they remove oppression and help the poor, "*Then* light shall rise for you in the darkness."

Light is a rich theme in the Bible. It is intimately associated with God and was the first product of his creative word. Light has its origin in God and the one who shares light shares in the divine life. This is the extraordinary meaning behind the prophet's words. Those who care for the poor will, in the end-time, experience "the glory of the

Lord." Their darkness will become light, their gloom "like midday." They will be God-like.

The Gospel reading has a similar theme, although somewhat nuanced. But again we can say of this passage as we did of the first that it reflects the religious pragmatism of Jesus. Does it work? Does it have any effect on other lives?

This is painfully clear in the words about salt. Flat or tasteless salt has no meaning. It neither seasons nor preserves food. Technology has yet to discover a profitable use for flat salt. And such is a Christian who does not affect the lives of others for the better.

In the light saying the pragmatism is again clear. This differs from the prophetic saying inasmuch as light is associated with the Christian not as a result of his or her activity but as being identified with that activity. To shed light as a Christian is to help others.

In the previous chapter Matthew has identified Jesus as the "great light" come to the people living in darkness (4:13-16). Because he is that, those who follow him can also become "the light of the world."

An awesome event. . . .

Sixth Sunday in Ordinary Time (A)
Sirach 15:15-20; 1 Corinthians 2:6-10; Matthew 5:17-37

One of the most vexing problems the early Church had to contend with was what to do with "law." Is there a place for law in Christianity? Do the Ten Commandments still have their validity? As is clear, the problem of the ancient Church is also our problem.

The answer is not simple. Anyone who has studied the question or anyone who has tried seriously to live the Christian way realizes there is no facile solution.

The root cause of the problem is the radical nature of Jesus' message. He said things that hadn't been said before and with an authority never experienced before. The beatitudes are one example. Reading the Gospels, you can discover others for yourself.

And yet Jesus was a Jew who followed Jewish customs and obeyed Jewish laws, except when a person's dignity was endangered by doing so. He knew the Decalogue and respected it (cf. Mark

10:19). Certainly he envisioned some continuity between the "Law and the Prophets" and his message.

But the radicality of that message also established a discontinuity. It was, in fact, the discontinuity that so shocked his contemporaries. He was looked upon as a rebel against the old, as one who ignored the law of his ancestors. In part it led to his rejection and death.

Paul saw this discontinuity between the message of Jesus and the Old Testament. He expressed it forcefully when he stated that "If you are guided by the spirit, you are not under the law" (Gal 5:18). In other words, Christians are freed of the law. And still Paul himself laid down laws for his churches and expected them to be obeyed.

This apparent ambiguity concerning the Christian's approach to law colors the Gospel reading. Here the evangelist tried to summarize the teachings of Jesus in such a way as to remove the ambiguity. He was possibly addressing himself to a situation in his own community where some Christians were living lawless lives and claiming that such was "Gospel."

The reading insists that Jesus did not destroy the law. Rather, he fulfilled it. The word "fulfill" is the operative word. The Greek-writing evangelists intended it not in the sense of literal compliance, so as to suggest that Jesus kept the letter of all the laws of old.

Rather, "fulfill" means to comply with and go beyond the law. It means to radicalize the meaning of the law, to intensify its motivation. Note the examples Jesus gives of this radicalization and intensification in the rest of the reading.

What, then, does this do to the law of old and to any human law? It means that the convinced Christian sees the value of law but, at the same time, that his Christian values allow him to go beyond what the law commands.

At times, the letter of the law may be violated by the need to express a Christian value. Jesus did this a number of times. But this is still "fulfilling" the law, since the underlying spirit or purpose of the law is now brought out more clearly.

This is why, as Christians, we can read the words of Sirach, in the first reading, and accept them without hesitation. We must choose to keep the Lord's commandments. But we see them now with the eyes of Christian faith.

This gives no simple answer to every question that will arise about "law and order." But it should provide some guide to understanding the nature of the problem.

Seventh Sunday in Ordinary Time (A)
Leviticus 19:1-2, 17-18; 1 Corinthians 3:16-23; Matthew 5:38-48

Holiness is wholeness. The follower of Jesus must strive for a harmonious wholeness of body, mind, soul, and emotions, a wholeness that rules out vengeance, anger, and lack of charity. Indeed the Christian must always bear in his heart these words of Jesus, "You must be made perfect as your heavenly Father is perfect." To some these words may seem perplexing, and one may ask, "How can I be perfect when only God is *that* good?" But Matthew is not speaking about absolute perfection, for only God is perfect in that sense. Rather the evangelist is stressing the necessity of the wholeness that is holiness.

Alone of the world's religions, Christianity makes the demand that practitioners love their enemies. Some religions and philosophies oppose violence and advocate nonresistance; others urge acceptance of whatever abuse enemies inflict. Only Christianity demands love toward those who do us harm.

Our reading from Leviticus is in the Legal Code of Holiness (cc. 17-26). All the rules and regulations of this Legal Code, although disparate, are grouped together under the rubric, "Be holy, for I, the Lord, your God, am holy." The devout Israelite is instructed to love relatives, coreligionists, and neighbors, and to hold no grudge against such people. Where punishments are mentioned in the Legal Code, the severity is mitigated as against the more severe punishment meted out in similar pagan codes. Israel was to be different from pagans; Israel was to be holy.

So often our idea of holiness is linked to the image of hands folded in prayer. Nevertheless, although piety is associated with holiness, it is not the outstanding mark of holiness. Difference or separation is the most distinguishing characteristic.

The Israelites appreciated the fact that God was different from them. He was unique—far greater than any gods that their pagan neighbors worshipped. He was separated from other gods by his holiness just as he was separated from the people whom he had created.

The Israelites, through their holiness, were called upon to be different from the non-Israelites; they were called upon to live in a different manner and worship in a different way, at the same time exhibiting harmony among themselves.

In the Gospel Jesus emphasizes this difference even more; Christians are to be different from non-Christians not only by their beliefs, life style, and worship, but also by their outer-directedness, exhibiting love, care, and concern for others without any expectation of personal gain. Christian love is tough love.

Paul reminds us that Christianity is not founded on human wisdom. And so to one who has no faith, the following of Jesus crucified makes no sense. God's wisdom is found in the great Christian paradox: authentic life can only come about because Christ died and arose from the dead. That is God's wisdom—life which springs forth from death.

The faction ridden church at Corinth was afflicted with controversy and problems. Some members had been following the teaching of Paul, others that of Cephas or Apollos. Many had forgotten that through baptism they had been made into a holy temple, that God's Spirit was the interior principle of their lives, and that they were to be different from the general pagan population of Corinth. Their religion was not another Greek philosophy among the many to be found in that part of the world. In the past all things were said to belong to the wise individual in this world; he had dominion over them. Now Paul tells the Corinthians they are truly wise for they belong to Christ, who has done the will of his heavenly Father. There is no room for dissension, factions, and hero-worship in God's holy temple; such behavior breaks down wholeness. When all is said and done, we arrive at the point at which we started—holiness is wholeness.

P.J.S.

Eighth Sunday in Ordinary Time (A)
Isaiah 49:14-15; 1 Corinthians 4:1-5; Matthew 6:24-34

Deutero-Isaiah reminds the Israelites that God had always been faithful to his people; he had never forgotten them. Our first reading presents God under the tender image of a mother, and the people of God under the image of a nursing infant. Isaiah makes it clear that God's love is even greater than the image presented.

In 612 B.C. the Assyrian monarchy had collapsed only to be succeeded by the Neo-Babylonian empire of Nebuchadnezzar. He destroyed Jerusalem in 586 B.C. and took its inhabitants into exile in Babylon. The Jews were to remain there until that empire fell at the hands of Cyrus the Great, who in 538 B.C. authorized all exiles held in bondage to return to their native lands.

At the time of this return Deutero-Isaiah reminded the people of God that even while they were in exile in Babylon, God still loved them; their release was a sign of compassion. He had never abandoned them, and they had no reason to lament. Their ancestors had refused to listen to the prophet Jeremiah, who had spoken for God in warning Israel that if she did not repent and submit to Nebuchadnezzar she would be punished (c. 27).

All through their punishment God had remembered them and had now liberated them from bondage. Isaiah's message is that we are to trust God even when the days are darkest, for God does not abandon his people.

Today's Gospel proposes the same message. Matthew shows us Jesus preaching to people who toiled under the hot Mediterranean sun day after day. Jesus reminds them and us of the necessity of trust. We must work, but we cannot rely on our own means for all of our needs; it is necessary to trust God and his Son Jesus Christ. At the same time such trust does not mean that we are to sit back and do nothing. The peasants who heard Jesus knew this, and we know it too. The Israelites in bondage had attempted to rely on their own help and their own means; they had been punished. In speaking to workers Jesus has to remind them to take one day at a time and let the rest to God. He takes care of his own. What is demanded of workers for the Lord is that they remain steadfast in their resolve to serve him and not to be governed by the things of this world.

Paul addresses this problem of the need both to trust in God and to work. Paul had been attacked verbally by the Corinthians who claimed that by his absence he had shown a lack of loving care for them. In Sunday's reading he replies by describing his ministry as an apostle. He and those associated with him are to be regarded as "servants of Christ" and "administrators of the mysteries of God." This is his solution to the dilemma of trust versus work.

"Servants" is the term used of those who sat in the lowest rank of the triremes, the ancient galley ships of the Romans that contained three tiers of oarsmen. Such ships were propelled by manpower in the strictest sense of that word. Those who labor for Christ must do so in a similar way; they must accept the lowest job, the hardest one, the most despicable and most tiresome one. The servanthood of those who follow Christ entails an exhausting effort.

"Administrators of the mysteries of God" designates those in a trusted and trusting position. Such a one is a steward who works in behalf of his master; the master trusts him, and he the master. And in that trusting relationship the "administrator" exercises a great deal of freedom.

A steward both preserves and dispenses that over which he is steward. Today's stewardship focuses upon God's revelation, and that revelation is Jesus Christ. Thus in trusting the Lord one is called upon to proclaim God's mysteries in life and word so that Jesus is recognized and acclaimed as Lord. That is the steward's work.

P.J.S.

Ninth Sunday in Ordinary Time (A)
Deuteronomy 11:18.26-28; Romans 3:21-25.28; Matthew 7:21-27

This Sunday's readings present an apparent contradiction whose resolution is at the heart of Christian faith. In his letter to the Romans Paul says our justification is a gift that is not dependent on our works. "All men are now undeservedly justified by the gift of God. . . .apart from observance of the law." In the Gospel Jesus says that "only the one who does the will of my Father in heaven" will enter God's kingdom.

We can add that the first reading, from Deuteronomy, seems closer to Jesus' statement than to Paul's. God is said to place before the Israelites two alternatives, a blessing and a curse. The blessing falls on those who obey the commandments, the curse on those who do not.

Note that Paul was not a follower of the historical Jesus and so did not hear him speaking the words found in the Gospel. Note also that Matthew's Gospel was written about fifteen years after Paul had died, so he did not have that as a source either. Despite that, we say that there is no contradiction between Paul and Jesus.

We must realize, first of all, that Paul had been converted from one strong religious conviction to another. A profound change had taken place in his soul as a result of his experience on the road to Damascus. Whereas he had been trained in the belief that salvation could be achieved only by the strictest kind of adherence to the laws of Moses, he now was convinced that it came through faith in Jesus Christ.

Paul uses the word "faith" almost one hundred times in his epistles and the word "believe" just under fifty times. The concept clearly played a major role in his theology. By it he means a radical surrender of the whole self to the person of Jesus Christ. This is sometimes expressed as accepting Jesus as our personal Lord and Savior. While that is not a false expression, it does not really say all that "faith in Jesus Christ" means for St. Paul. It doesn't convey the profound interior change that has taken place.

This interior conversion, this radical change, this faith in Jesus Christ is not the product of works of the law, or of any human effort. It is a gift of God. Paul was well aware of this as a result of his experience on that trip to Damascus. That explains his strong emphasis on faith as gift in his epistles.

Through the centuries people have experienced this same kind of conversion, this same faith in Jesus Christ. The discovery can, unfortunately, lead to a false complacency that seems to be expressed in the slogan, "I've found it!" It is a mistaken complacency if it leads to the conviction that I need do nothing now, that I've won the race. The race is not won until the last breath.

That is where Jesus' words are so telling. He knew that there were those who had experienced the basic conversion he had preached. And Matthew, clearly, is writing for Christians who had already accepted Jesus as their Lord and Savior. But to these very ones Jesus says that it isn't those who say "Lord, Lord" who enter God's kingdom. They must respond to God's salvation. Thy must now do "the will of my Father in heaven."

Good works *are* important, not works that command or merit God's saving love, but works that are our response to that saving love, works that are done *in Christ Jesus*. That is why Jesus talks about *doing* the Father's will. And Paul says equivalently the same when he writes to the Philippian Christians, " . . . work with anxious concern to achieve your salvation." There is no real difference between Paul and Jesus on this point.

God's grace, his love, is free, but it isn't cheap. We must accept it and let it "work" in our lives.

Tenth Sunday in Ordinary Time (A)
Hosea 6:3-6; Romans 4:18-25; Matthew 9:9-13

To know God, to love him, to follow him in singlehearted devotion— these are the basic "building blocks" of biblical religion. Such undivided attention presupposes the prior and empowering love of God for us. That is the one principle the biblical authors take for granted when they do not make express mention of it. This Sunday's reading, however, stresses the response that we are to make to his love. That response is the complete surrender of love.

The first reading begins as though Israel really did want to get to know the Lord and follow him. But then it continues with God wondering what he is going to do with Israel because her "piety" (that is, her love of God) is as passing as the morning dew. Her protestations of wanting to turn to him are feigned; they do not ring true.

Hosea leaves no doubt about what he is asking of these people.

All the ritual sacrifices in the world mean nothing if they are not offered in love. In typical Semitic form he quotes God as saying, "For it is love that I desire, not sacrifice, and knowledge of God rather than holocausts." The verse is quoted by Jesus in the Gospel reading; he saw it as the heart of Israel's faith.

The two words used here are filled with meaning. "Love," in its Hebrew form, is a special attachment to God. This love seals the relationship between two covenant partners. Therefore, it is a loyal and steadfast love, a love that can be counted on.

The closest image to this love of God is the love of husband and wife, an image the prophet had made use of in the first three chapters of his book. God is Israel's Baal, her husband, and his initiating and all consuming love for her is seeking a response.

The other word is "knowledge" of God. This word, too, in its Hebrew form is rich in meaning. It doesn't mean simply the kind of knowledge that comes from reading a book or attending a lecture. While he would not exclude that, Hosea would certainly put it rather low in his list of things that "knowledge" means.

Above all it means a total, personal experience of the one who is known. So while that would mean intellectual understanding, it also and especially means the attachment of the will, the affections, the whole person. To know God in this way is the singlehearted devotion we spoke of in the opening sentence.

This kind of total response as the hallmark of biblical religion is repeated in the second reading, from Paul's letter to the Romans. The term that Paul uses here to express complete attachment to God is faith. The faith of Abraham is used as the illustration.

As Paul understands it here, the object of faith is not a truth that is believed but a Person on whom one is dependent. Abraham was so radically attached to God in the surrender of faith that nothing could make him waver in his hope. This kind of faith is the foundation for all hope.

The Gospel reading provides still another remarkable picture of this exclusive kind of following of the Lord. The first part recounts the call of Matthew. It is simply told, but it is staggering in its implications. Matthew was busy collecting tax money, happily no doubt. Jesus comes to him and says, "Follow me." And then we read,

"Matthew got up and followed him." It is as simple, as total, as revolutionary as that.

To know the Lord, to love him, to believe in him, to follow him without question—those are the lifelong tasks of the people whom the Lord has first loved.

Eleventh Sunday in Ordinary Time (A)
Exodus 19:2-6; Romans 5:6-11; Matthew 9:36—10:8

The combination of lessons in the Old Testament and Gospel readings for this Sunday is unusually interesting. Both have to do with a special call by God and with a call to ministry in some sense. But in Exodus the whole people is the object, while in Matthew a special group within the people is the concern.

The Exodus reading speaks of Israel, under the leadership of Moses, coming to Sinai after having left Egypt, the land of bondage. Here the Lord was to establish a special relationship between himself and them; it was to be called a covenant, meaning a treaty or pact. Our passage indicates how God looked upon his new covenant partner.

But first there is recorded what God had done for Israel. This is always a presupposition in the biblical concept of any vocation. God acts first and acts out of love. Here he is said to have borne his people to Sinai "on eagle wings" to himself. Eagles are referred to often enough in the Hebrew Scriptures to suggest that the people were greatly impressed by their strength, speed, and concern for their young. Thus they are an apt figure for the Lord's action on behalf of his own.

More important for our purpose is the manner in which God identifies his "special possession." They are "a kingdom of priests" and "a holy nation." The latter expression is clear enough. "Holiness" is a special characteristic of God (cf. Is 6:3) and describes his freedom from contamination by anything created. Applied to Israel it means that she is to show forth by her life her separation from anything defiled or unclean. The covenant laws that follow would show her how she was to achieve that.

Authors differ somewhat in their understanding of "a kingdom of priests." Some would see in it an allusion to the participation by the whole people in the official liturgy, where the anointed priests play a more specific role. Others see it as a recognition of a ministry to the rest of the world, being the priestly mediators of God's love to them.

In either case (and both may be true) Israel is said to have, by reason of her call to be a covenant people, a "priestly" role. This concept of a priesthood of all the people is taken over also in the New Testament by the author of 1 Peter where he defines all Christians in the very same terms (2:5.9).

This universal priesthood, conferred at the time of Baptism, is being emphasized anew in our time. This is necessary if the Church is to allow all the rich potential in the laity to be expressed. It should not be at all a threat to the "ordained priesthood," which still has its own special vocation and special ministry.

That special vocation within the larger vocation of the people of God is presented in the Gospel reading. Jesus chooses "the Twelve" from among his disciples for a special task. Some have tried to argue that "the Twelve" were invented by the later Church and then retrojected back into the life of Jesus. But their arguments have convinced few. *Jesus really did choose a special group for a special task.*

Matthew uses the term "apostles" here for the Twelve. That is proper enough. The word means literally one who is sent and, in its usage, includes the idea that the one sent has all the authority of the one sending. Thus, just as Jesus is the apostle of the Father, so the Twelve are the apostles of Jesus.

Which lesson should we emphasize, the priesthood of all Christians or the ordained priesthood of the specially called? Both emphases are needed in our day. If we were to emphasize one to the detriment of the other, we would be false to the Scriptures. A "priestly nation" needs its special apostles as much as they need a "kingdom of priests."

Twelfth Sunday in Ordinary Time (A)
Jeremiah 20:10-13; Romans 5:12-15; Matthew 10:26-33

In Matthew's Gospel Jesus' public ministry is marked by five major discourses, each preceded by an account of various activities of the

Lord, including his miracles. The purpose of these discourses is to enunciate some aspect of the Kingdom of God, which was central to Jesus' message.

First, a word about that Kingdom. The phrase is used to describe God's loving reign among his people, a reign marked by profound peace and fullness of blessings, unmixed with evil. In the New Testament the Kingdom of God is always seen in the eschatological sense, that is, in a final, fully realized form. When Jesus proclaimed at the beginning of his ministry, "The kingdom of God is at hand!" (Mk 1:15), he was speaking of this climactic manifestation of the Father's reign.

The early Christians, after Jesus' resurrection, recognized that the Kingdom had arrived in Jesus' person and in his message. But it was clear that the world had not accepted that Kingdom; evil still existed in many forms. Hence they looked forward to a final inward breaking of the Kingdom at the time of the Lord's second coming.

But between that first and second manifestation of the Kingdom much had to be done. A seed had been planted. Workers were needed to prepare for the final harvest. The kingdom message, proclaimed once by Jesus, must be repeated to every generation.

Matthew sees this being done through the Church. He has arranged his five discourses in a way that shows the relationship between the Kingdom of God and the Church. In the first discourse, the Sermon on the Mount (cc. 5-7), we have the message of the Kingdom, a kind of *magna carta* for those who wish to enter the Kingdom through the Church.

The reading for this Sunday is part of the second discourse (9:35—11:1). This missionary discourse deals with the mission of the Twelve and how they are to conduct themselves as they take the message of the Kingdom from land to land. A profoundly stirring account, it has been the ideal of missionaries in the Church for centuries.

Our particular passage deals with persecution and how they are to respond to it. They must have no fear, and they must have complete confidence in the Master. While the directives contained here, as we have said, are intended primarily for missionaries, Jesus would surely expect everyone of his followers to be formed by them in some way.

What do they tell us? First, that the Kingdom message is explosive. It will make people rise up and try to stop those who preach it. It is a message that, once understood, people either accept wholeheartedly or reject violently.

The Lord tells us to speak out our Kingdom convictions in public. Jesus was able to reach only a tiny part of the Near Eastern world. His followers must be his voices down through the ages and throughout the world.

Despite the risk, our confidence and assurance lie, not in the acceptance of what we stand for by others (this may happen, but our experience may also be that of Jeremiah in the first reading), but solely in the Lord's concern for us. He takes care of his own. That, too, is a feature part of the Kingdom message. It is what makes the whole missionary task possible.

Thirteenth Sunday in Ordinary Time (A)
2 Kings 4:8-11.14-16; Romans 6:3-4.8-11; Matthew 10:37-42

Elijah and Elisha were two non-writing prophets active in the northern kingdom of Israel in the latter part of the ninth century B.C. Both were extraordinary characters who struck a responsive chord in Israel's imagination. Stories about them abounded and were early developed into narrative cycles.

One reason why their stories would have been preserved, especially by our biblical editors, was that they were true believers who were responsible for weakening the hold of paganism on the people. Elijah especially is credited by some scholars with having preserved the Yahwistic faith in the north.

Of the two men Elisha, the subject of our first reading, was surely the more bizarre. Some of the legends about him are grotesque, even unsavory by our standards. But Yahweh was considered capable of achieving his ends by all sorts of means. He begins his work in us where we are, not where we might ideally be.

The story in the first reading recounts an act of hospitality shown to Elisha by a wealthy woman and his later promise that she and her husband would have a child. The act of hospitality is motivated by her recognition of the prophet as "a holy man of God." It is a forceful affirmation of Israels' regard for him.

In the Semitic mentality, a "man of God" represents God and is thus worthy of special respect. Also, as a "man of God" Elisha is able to make the promise about a future child since his prophetic vision shares in that of God's. As a "holy man" Elisha would have a special share in the order of the sacred, the transcendent.

We have emphasized this act of hospitality shown to a holy man because that seems to be the theme the Church wishes to propose. The Gospel reading contains a saying of Jesus in which he is, almost certainly, referring to the Elisha story. Jesus says, "he who welcomes a holy man because he is known to be holy receives a holy man's reward." The Shunammite woman had said of the prophet, "I know that he is a holy man of God."

Our Gospel text is actually the conclusion of a missionary discourse (9:35-11:1) that had begun with the mission of the Twelve. Throughout the sermon Jesus is telling these first missionaries how they are to conduct themselves and what they are to expect. The opening verses of our reading, about divisions in family life caused by the Gospel, apply as well to the ministers as to the people to whom they minister.

This broader context helps us to appreciate all the more the words concerning the welcome extended to the preachers, prophets, and holy men. The words are ostensibly directed by Jesus to the Twelve, giving them some assurance of a hospitable welcome in their work. But certainly Matthew intends these words for his own people who are expected to extend the hospitality.

Again, the motivation for the hospitality is the identification of the prophet-holy man with Christ himself, a frequent theme. "He who welcomes you welcomes me. . . ." The sent one *is* the sender. The people can rightly identify Jesus in the apostle sent to them.

This is hardly a clarion call for a new clericalism. It is, however, a strong statement on respect for ministry. In the end, it is the Father, the ultimate Sender, who is being honored in his ministers.

Fourteenth Sunday in Ordinary Time (A)
Zechariah 9:9-10; Romans 8:9.11-13; Matthew 11:25-30

The first reading for Sundays is always chosen because of some theme that it contains which is also found in the Gospel reading. In the liturgical context, then, the first reading can help us to interpret the third. It may help to bring out a richness there not otherwise immediately apparent.

This Sunday the Gospel text is the well-known and highly revered passage about the Father's revelation of his wisdom to the Son. It goes on to speak of the mutual knowledge of Father and Son, and concludes with Jesus' invitation to the weary to come to him for refreshment.

The passage is incredibly rich in content, but only a few insights can be mentioned here. The Dead Sea Scrolls tell of the great Essene Teacher (living more than 150 years before Christ) who also praised God for the revelation given to him. The wording in both cases is similar. The great difference, however, is that Jesus praises God for revelation granted to "the merest children." Not to the learned and clever, but to "children," that is, to the disciples of Jesus, does God make himself known. But also, as is clearly implied from the context, Jesus is the medium of the revelation. The Father speaks to us through his Son. No Essene Teacher ever made that claim.

When Jesus says that all has been given him by the Father, he was probably thinking of the craftsman, such as a carpenter, who sees to it that his son receives all the knowledge and skill that he has gained over the years. Thus does Jesus have all the Father's wisdom, making possible the mutual and unique knowledge of Father and Son.

A wisdom theme is also found in the invitation to the weary. Thus, personified Wisdom is said to cry out, "Come to me, all you that yearn for me . . ." (Si 24:18). And the "untutored" are encouraged to "submit your neck to her (Wisdom's) yoke . . ." (51:23.26). These passages seem to be behind Jesus' words. He identifies himself as Wisdom incarnate.

The "yoke" that Jesus offers is probably being contrasted with the yoke of the Law that, for many of the ordinary people, was difficult if not impossible to bear. Commentators suggest that Jesus' yoke is acceptance of God's reign. This is quite probable in the context of Matthew's Gospel. But it would not be false to Jesus' teaching to see his yoke as that of love. Love makes the difficult easy and the burdensome light.

Jesus' invitation to learn from him is based on the conviction that he is "gentle and humble of heart." In the Greek there is not much difference between the two adjectives. They describe an attitude or disposition that is not overbearing but considerate of others.

The older translation of "gentle" was "meek," which was probably abandoned because of the "milk toast" connotations it has today. But "meek" is still the word used in the first reading to describe the king entering the royal city. That is why this reading was chosen for this Sunday.

The prophet describes a new kind of king, a "just warrior," one who, riding on an ass, banishes the war's chariots and the warrior's bow. He brings peace to all nations and reigns "from sea to sea."

This royal figure, the Church tells us in putting these readings together, is Jesus. He, too, is meek and humble. But he reigns over all by the light of his wisdom and by the yoke of his love. Those who accept that dominion experience the peace the prophet proclaimed.

Fifteenth Sunday in Ordinary Time (A)
Isaiah 55:10-11; Romans 8:18-23; Matthew 13:1-23

Ancient Israel had a fascinating conviction about the power of the word, about what a spoken or written word could do. It was looked upon almost as a surrogate, or substitute, for the one who uttered it. If the latter was a strong willed, strong souled person, then the word had all the greater effect. Once uttered, it went out into the world and did its work.

If such was the power of the human word, we can easily imagine what they thought of God's word. Its efficacy was limited, not in itself, but only by the human refusal to hear it, by the closed ear and hardened heart. But if there was openness, then wonderful things happened, lives were changed, miracles occurred.

This is the conviction that lies behind the first reading. God's word goes forth, like the rain and the snow, and achieves the end for which it was sent. To the parched but open heart it provides nourishment and new life.

Chapters 40 to 55 of the book of Isaiah (our reading is taken from this last chapter) are referred to as the work of "Second Isaiah," because his oracles are preserved with those of the historical Isaiah. This anonymous prophet wrote during the Babylonian exile (587-538 B.C.). His words speak of comfort and hope to refugees in a strange land. He was convinced that what he wrote, God's words, would achieve their goal.

In the beginning of his work, in chapter 40, we see how often he mentions or suggests the presence of the word. ". . . says your God." "A voice cries out. . . ." ". . . the mouth of the Lord has spoken." "A voice says. . . ." "Cry out at the top of your voice. . . ." The words are all words of encouragement, of good news, of freedom from exile. Now, at the end of his book, in our reading, he reminds his readers that these words of God will be fulfilled.

That is a helpful background for a deeper appreciation of the Gospel reading. It contains the famous parable of the sower and the seed. The seed falls in turn on a footpath, on rocky ground, among thorns and, finally, on good soil. In the first three cases nothing occurs. In the last case an abundant harvest results.

Scholars say that, when Jesus told the story, the only point he wanted to make was that of the great harvest. The other details, about the varying fate of the sown seed, were there only for dramatic effect. This is because the heart of Jesus' message was the coming of God's reign. And that reign would mean the abundance of all good.

But when the Church experienced the delay in the Lord's coming, when she experienced the different ways in which men and women responded to the Gospel, she realized that those details of Jesus' parable had a meaning too. They spoke clearly to her of the hiddenness of the Kingdom and the reality of evil.

The seed is the message or the word. It is God's word as preached by Jesus. Jesus knew the Old Testament well. He would have known of passages like our first reading that speak of the power of God's word. He knew, then, that his word (which was the Father's) would eventually have its effect. He could speak confidently and convincingly of a great harvest.

We mentioned above that God's word is limited only by the closed ear and hardened heart. If we are not open to the word, how will it have its effect? It must find a resting place deep within us so that it can do its work. If we are like the hardened footpath, or the patch of rock, or the unfriendly briers, the word remains a stranger to us.

To help us be more open to God's word we should reflect often on its power. If we don't really believe in the word's power, then it is powerless to help us. But if we believe, we will become, with increasing fruitfulness, the good soil. We will have the conviction and the confidence of Jesus himself.

Sixteenth Sunday in Ordinary Time (A)
Wisdom 12:13, 16-19; Romans 8:26-27; Matthew 13:24-43

Has Christianity failed? That question has been asked many times throughout the Church's history. When we realize that it was almost two thousand years ago that Jesus Christ, through his death and resurrection, redeemed the world, we might wonder what that redemption meant. Wars, crimes, poverty, diseases, and disasters continue to plague the human race. Where *is* the Kingdom of God that Jesus preached? This is no idle question.

Many responses have been offered. Perhaps the most quoted is that of G.K. Chesterton, who said that Christianity hasn't failed; it just has never been tried. He meant that if enough people lived the Gospel message in its fullness, the difference would be clear for all to see.

If that *is* the answer—and it must surely be involved in the final response—then it means that it is up to each of us to live the Gospel more fully. We must reflect on the Jesus Torah of the Sermon on the Mount (Mt 5-7) and ask how completely it is reflected in our lives. God's grace and strength are there; they only need acceptance.

Another response to the question is that we can never know what the world would be like without Christianity. If its powerful call to love had not drawn so many men and women throughout history to break down walls of hatred, fear, and selfishness, what image would the human race be reflecting today?

Still others say that no matter how powerful, how revolutionary, how radical the message of Christianity is, it will never force the human heart. God wants freedom above all, and that means freedom even to reject his greatest offer of freedom, the freedom of the children of God. If everyone were *forced* by God's grace to be another Mother Teresa of Calcutta, there would soon be no one to whom a free and authentic Mother Teresa could minister.

There is truth in all these responses, and one or the other is reflected in our Gospel reading. But that reading also tells us something else about our question, something that only a person of faith can accept. It requires no faith to conclude that, if everyone loved everyone else, we would have a hate-less, war-less, poverty-less world. What Jesus says does require faith.

He is telling us in these parables of the Kingdom—the parables of the wheat mixed with weeds, of the mustard seed, of the leaven—that the Kingdom works in a mysterious way, in a way that the human mind cannot comprehend. Still, it is there, even if as difficult to see, as a mustard seed. But in the end, it will be seen. "Then the saints will shine like the sun in their Father's kingdom."

We would like more evidence; we want our reasons to rest on more solid ground. At times, we, like Job, want God to defend himself, to prove his case. Like the Father, Jesus simply tells us that the Kingdom is there and is working its way. Only the vision of faith can see it. Because Jesus is who he is, we accept it.

Is this a "cop-out"? The nonbeliever is convinced that it is, but can never be really sure. Only the person of faith can have the certainty of faith. It is precisely because of the certainty of that faith that the believer knows what the human response must be.

Seventeenth Sunday in Ordinary Time (A)
1 Kings 3:5, 7-12; Romans 8:28-30; Matthew 13:44-52

The heart of Jesus' message was the coming of God's Kingdom. Mark indicates this by placing the following summary of his message at the beginning of his ministry: "This is the time of fulfillment. The reign of

God is at hand! Reform your lives and believe in the Gospel!" (1:15).
The core of Matthew's Gospel is structured around five major discourses of Jesus, each dealing with aspects of the Kingdom of God.

This Kingdom means God's presence as saving Lord among his
people. Because it is an active presence, some translations prefer
"reign" to "kingdom." In any case it is a situation of complete unity
among all people brought about by God to whom they surrender in
faith.

In its fullest sense the Kingdom has not yet been realized. The
parables in last Sunday's Gospel emphasized the hiddenness of the
Kingdom and its working in a mysterious way in our midst. What they
told us was that Jesus did inaugurate the Kingdom through his life,
death, and resurrection, but it would be fully realized only on "the
day of the Lord."

The parables in this Sunday's Gospel concern the Kingdom's
potential members, how they act, who they are. In the two instances
of the treasure and the pearl the one who finds rejoices and sells
everything to buy them.

There are at least three possible major points being made here.
One is the supreme value of the Kingdom; no other possession can
compare with it. Another is the willingness to renounce all for the
sake of the Kingdom. Still a third is the eschatological joy of the one
who finds the Kingdom.

The third seems hardly the major point, especially since it is
referred to only in the first parable. But commentators suggest that the
Greek word used here (chara) can have the meaning of a joy that only
God can instill. It is, for example, the joy that the magi experienced
on seeing the star (Mt 2:10). Certainly it is a point worthy of our
reflection. Do we think of God's reign with joyful anticipation?

Which of the other two points is more important is also disputed.
The second is clearly dependent on the first. That is, the willingness
to renounce all is possible, precisely because the Kingdom is what it
is. Its supreme value is the reason for any human reaction.

Perhaps in Jesus' mind the Kingdom's supreme value would have
been the foremost point. By the time that Matthew wrote his Gospel
that value was a presupposition. He would have been more concerned about the response, about the renunciation.

But again, both points should be our concern. Do we reflect on the Kingdom, on the thought of peaceful community with all, the presence of the Lord? What value would we give to that condition? Do our lives reflect *in any way* a spirit of renunciation for the sake of the Kingdom?

Then comes the parable of the net cast into the sea; the net collects all sorts of things. Necessarily a sorting process is undertaken, with the worthwhile being preserved and the worthless being discarded. Jesus harldy had to give us the interpretation, it seems so obvious. Our question is, in which group will we be?

These stories of Jesus are rich in wisdom. A wise Christian will think on them and act on his or her reflections. Perhaps that is what Jesus had in mind when he spoke about the Christian scribe who is learned in the things of the Kingdom and is able to draw out both the old and the new. That is true wisdom. It was only dimly anticipated in Solomon's prayer for wisdom in the first reading.

Eighteenth Sunday in Ordinary Time (A)
Isaiah 55:1-3; Romans 8:35, 37-39; Matthew 14:13-21

The reading from Isaiah beautifully introduces the theme of this Sunday, the banquet of the Lord. This part of the prophet's book was probably written in exile in Babylon, but after the Persian king, Cyrus, had signed the edict allowing the captive Jews to return home.

His are words of comfort and encouragement intended for the exiles who had returned to Judah and found the situation less than desirable. He invites them to eat and drink without cost, to "eat well' and "delight in rich fare." God would renew his covenant of love with them, a covenant apparently broken when the city and temple were destroyed.

But what is the prophet really offering the people? How can he, in Babylon, invite them, in Judah, to a banquet? Even if he were with them in the same country he could hardly have issued such a general invitation as this to the whole people. He must have had something else in mind.

To appreciate what he is saying it is important to realize that the prophets were captivated by the faith conviction of the end-time. The end-time was that period when history would come to its climax through the intervention of God and when the conditions of peace and happiness, thought to have prevailed at the beginning, would once again be realized. The prophets looked forward to the end-time with eager longing.

They used many images, taken from secular life, to describe this end-time. One was the banquet. It is not surprising that such a common and pleasurable experience should provide the basis for a higher reality. It would be understood by all and evoke in them a keen sense of anticipation.

How can the people prepare for this end-time of fulfillment? While it will be an act of God, they can prepare for it by putting themselves right with God. "Come to me heedfully, listen, that you may have life."

In his use of the banquet as a symbol of the end-time, the author is using a long and rich tradition. We need only recall the Passover meal, recorded in Exodus 12, celebrating God's liberation of Israel from Egypt. That act of God was seen as anticipating his final climactic act of salvation, and the meal was its sign.

The tradition carried over into the New Testament where we find numerous allusions to meals or banquets as signs of a special life with God. The most significant of these, of course, is the Eucharist, the Lord's Supper, which gives eternal life to those who share it. And in the Gospels, non-Eucharistic meals are often given Eucharistic meaning.

This is what has occurred in the story of the feeding by Jesus of the five thousand. Matthew's account of it is the Gospel reading for this Sunday. The evangelist does not belittle the event itself in which so many hungry people were fed. But he also sees it as a sign of something more.

This is evident in the words that are used to describe Jesus' action of blessing, breaking, and giving the loaves to the disciples to distribute. They are the same words used in the account of the Last Supper. The Eucharistic symbolism is in the account to give it a higher meaning. The feeding now becomes a sign of Jesus' feeding the people with his body and blood.

The Eucharistic meal is the end-time banquet in a real sense. No closer union with the Lord can be imagined except that eternal union with him in heaven.

The Old Testament prophet had issued the invitation to come to a banquet, to eat and delight in rich fare. Jesus, the end-time prophet, not only issues the invitation but also provides the fare himself. He has done what others could only point to. We Christians can share in this banquet now; the end-time has been inaugurated in our midst.

Nineteenth Sunday in Ordinary Time (A)
1 Kings 19:9, 11-13 Romans 9:1-5; Matthew 14:22-33

Wearied by his confrontations with the pagan elements in his homeland Israel, harried by persecutors who would have his life, Elijah, the prophet, fled to the south, to the land of Sinai. In his discouragement he asked the Lord to take his life. But the Lord had other plans and brought Elijah, finally, to the mount where God, through Moses, had first sealed the covenant with his people some four hundred years earlier.

The first reading for this Sunday records Elijah's experience on this mount. It is the experience of a mighty wind, of an earthquake, of a fire. All of these are found in the Scriptures as symbolic announcements of the appearance of God. But the actual appearance of the Lord, his presence to his prophet, is symbolized, not in those stirring phenomena of nature, but in "a tiny whispering sound."

Manifestly the whole scene is intended as a source of encouragement for Elijah. Still, perhaps the most remarkable aspect of the story is not the grandiloquent expression of God's announced appearance, but the faith of the prophet who could see the Lord in that "tiny whispering sound." Many an atheist has been shaken into a beginner's faith by the experience of the extraordinary. Only the person of deep faith can see that hand of God in the small and simple things of life.

The experience was a discovery by Elijah of the faith that he already had. And so, buoyed by the discovery he returned to his land to complete his mission. It is a powerful lesson for us who call ourselves Christians. Where do we find the source of our faith? Where do we look for it?

No one could miss the theme of faith in the Gospel story. In the early morning Jesus appears to the disciples walking on the waters.

Fearing a ghost, they are assured that it is the Master. Then Peter, impetuous as ever, asks to come to Jesus on the waters. But his faith fails him and, after a tentative beginning, he begins to sink. Jesus saves him but rebukes him for his feeble faith.

To appreciate Matthew's account fully, we must have some background information. To the best of our knowledge the evangelist was writing for a Christian community composed to a large extent of Jewish converts. At the time of his writing (about 80 A.D.) there was an increasing estrangement between the Jewish people and their former associates in the faith. Christian converts were being more often and more resolutely shunned by members of the synagogue.

Matthew's community was greatly affected by this. Some apparently, in the face of this pressure, renounced their Christian faith. Others were wavering. Matthew wrote his Gospel to bolster their faith. The many stories about Jesus reveal this intent.

Our present account is a good example. The fact that Matthew has borrowed the story from Mark (6:45-52) and then added the part about Peter indicates his faith concern. Even Peter, who is the "prince of apostles" in Matthew's Gospel (v.g., 16:13-20), wavers in his faith.

Unlike Elijah, who was content to find God in the "tiny whispering sound," Peter wanted to find him in the spectacular. This is human, and Jesus appreciated that. But he knew that it was not enough. Until the faith of the foxhole or the faith of a Lourdes becomes the faith of the daily office grind and of cooking the family dinner, it is not an adult Christian faith. We, like Peter, have to cry out to Jesus, "Lord, save us!"

Twentieth Sunday in Ordinary Time (A)
Isaiah 56:1, 6-7; Romans 11:13-15, 29-32; Matthew 15:21-28

The Gospel reading tells of an astonishing incident. It is about Jesus' encounter with a pagan woman. In the eyes of Jesus' contemporaries she had two marks against her: she was a pagan and a woman. Her meeting with Jesus was bound to capture the interest of Matthew's readers.

Note, first of all, that she addresses Jesus with the highest of messianic titles. She calls him "Lord" and "Son of David." The former title could be understood in an ordinary sense, such as "Master." But the context shows that the woman intended it in the religious sense it usually has in the New Testament. "Son of David" refers to the longed for descendant of David's throne who would restore the kingdom to God's people.

The woman would have heard of Jesus and would have known how he was looked upon by his followers. Did she really believe all this of Jesus, or was she "putting on an act" to gain his attention? In the light of the whole story we have to accept the first explanation. She really believed.

Jesus' initial response of utter silence is shocking to us. Throughout the Gospels he is presented as one concerned about those in need. But it is likely that the story was adapted a bit in later Christian circles to intensify the dramatic effect.

Still, Jesus would have shared the conviction that the Kingdom message had first to be proclaimed to the house of Israel. It was with them that God had originally sealed the covenant. As Paul says in the second reading, from the letter to the Romans, "God's gifts and his call (directed to Israel) are irrevocable."

The woman's faith and spirit are remarkable. When Jesus is initially silent, she "keeps shouting" after the disciples. When he mentions Israel's privileged position, she still pays him homage and asks for his help. When he speaks of not throwing the true children's food to the dogs (a strong statement), she begs for scraps from the table.

One important point of the story is that Jesus did come primarily for his own people. This is one of his few excursions outside the land of the Jews, and there is no indication that it was for the purpose of preaching to the Gentiles. The incident, in fact, is proof to the contrary.

This does not mean that Jesus did not foresee the conversion of the Gentiles. He knew about the story of Jonah's mission to the detested pagan Assyrians. He would have known about passages such as our first reading where "foreigners" (that is, Gentiles) are said to "join themselves to the Lord, ministering to him. . . ." But the mission to the Gentiles was to be the work of the missionary Church. Jesus was to bring the good news to his own.

Despite this restriction of Jesus' activity to the Jewish people, and despite the pagan woman's acceptance of this division between Jew and Gentile, her faith is strong enough to break through the temporary barrier. Jesus acknowledges that faith and grants her request. Her daughter is cured.

Throughout his Gospel Matthew is at pains to show what great things can be achieved through faith in Jesus Christ. He is writing for Christians who have already expressed that faith—and he is writing for us. For he knows that all Christians are in need of constant encouragement to grow in faith. Here he is telling us how effectively even this pagan woman believed. Could Jesus say to us what he said to her, ". . . you have great faith!"?

Twenty-first Sunday in Ordinary Time (A)
Isaiah 22:15, 19-23; Romans 11:33-36; Matthew 16:13-20

This Sunday the outstanding passage is that of Peter's confession and Jesus' reply in Matthew's Gospel. For Catholics this has always been a foundation text for our acceptance of papal authority.

Almost all scholars agree that Matthew used Mark in composing his Gospel. But in this section Matthew has added considerably to his source. Peter acknowledges Jesus not only as the Messiah, but also as "the son of the living God!" Jesus' response, which makes Peter the foundation stone of the Church, is wholly lacking in Mark.

Where did Matthew get this material? Some suggest it was part of a special resurrection appearance to Peter, others that it came from a later period in Jesus' ministry. In any case what is important for us is that it is part of Matthew's Gospel and so the Word of God.

As "Messiah" Jesus is the long-awaited son of David who ushers in the reign of God. As "son of the living God" he is the unique representative of God to all the people, possessing God's Spirit and enjoying an exclusive union with the Father. In our terms, he is divine. This is how Matthew understands Peter's confession.

In his reply Jesus acknowledges that such a confession can come only from revelation (not from reason) and that it is made in faith. Because of this Peter is made the foundation of the messianic community, the Church, which will never fail.

The "keys of the kingdom" given to Peter signify doctrinal and disciplinary authority in the Church. That is indicated by the reference to declaring what is bound and what is loosed. How extensively Jesus considered that authority to be exercised is not clear, but it is remarkable that the evangelist preserves this prophecy some twenty years after Peter's martyrdom.

In the past, Catholic theologians tended to read into this passage all that they saw being exercised in the papal office of their day. This fails to recognize development in ministry. But the passage is there and needs no apology. For Matthew it represents an important stage in his presentation of the message of the Kingdom.

The first reading, from Isaiah, was chosen because of its reference to the key of authority given to a royal official. Isaiah did not, of course, see this as pointing to the later conferring of the keys on Peter. The Church simply uses it to illustrate a common theme. The symbolism is similar.

Returning to Matthew, we note that he is much concerned about the Church. He is the only evangelist to use the term in his Gospel. For him the Church is where Christ is. "Where two or three are gathered in my name, there am I in their midst" (18:20).

The Church is closely associated with the Kingdom of God. Matthew realized that the Kingdom had not come in all its fullness. That was clear from the presence of sinners, even in the Church. Yet, Jesus had announced the Kingdom and had inaugurated it in his message and activity. For those who did not experience the earthly Jesus, the Church was the means of experiencing the Kingdom.

This doctrine of the Church should be a source of deep joy to all Christians. What Paul says in the second reading about the riches and wisdom and knowledge of God can be applied as well to the revelation about the Church. Part of God's mystery, it shares in the power of his Kingdom.

Twenty-second Sunday in Ordinary Time (A)
Jeremiah 20:7-9; Romans 12:1-2; Matthew 16:21-27

The reading from Jeremiah contains a stunning illustration of the
irresistible power of God's Word. The passage, however, must be
seen in its context. The prophet had just had a confrontation with the
priest Passhur. The latter had had Jeremiah scourged and imprisoned
overnight because of his prophecies of doom for Jerusalem and
Judah. Upon his release, Jeremiah proceeded to denounce Passhur
and to foretell the priest's own doom.

In the account of Jeremiah's call to the prophetic office we read
that God was sending him forth "To root up and to tear down . . ., to
build and to plant" (1:10). In our present passage, which is one of
Jeremiah's intimate "confessions" to the Lord, he cries that "violence
and outrage is my message." Because of that, God's Word has
brought him "derision and reproach all the day."

Jeremiah is wondering when he will receive words of building
and planting from the Lord. It has been only words of doom that he
has spoken. That is why he cries out that he has been "duped" by the
Lord. He has been deceived about the nature of his mission.

Still, despite this overwhelming feeling of deception, a feeling
that leads him to resolve not to speak of God's words any more, he
immediately confesses his complete impotence to remain silent.
Listen to the cry of this man grappling with a power greater than he is.
God's Word, he cries, "becomes like fire burning in my heart,
imprisoned by my bones; I grow weary holding it in, I cannot endure
it."

Jeremiah's need to bear witness to the Word was so great and so
compelling that he was willing to suffer the consequences of that
Word. He would like to say something good, a saving word—and in
time he would—but no matter what kind of word it was, it was God's.
It could not be suppressed.

This willingness to receive bad news, news that includes even
suffering for oneself, is, paradoxically, part of the "good news," the
gospel. Obviously the bad news is not in itself good news. Rather it is
simply a necessary part of the overall plan of God for salvation.
Jeremiah bears excellent testimony to this.

The Gospel reading, too, has the same message. Jesus tells his disciples of the "bad news" of his own coming passion and death. Peter, that man of faith who had just made his confession of Jesus as Messiah and Son of God, cannot accept this. He tells Jesus this cannot be. And the Master rebukes him and assures him that it is true.

Jesus goes on to say that not only must his disciples accept the bad news about himself, they must themselves follow in his footsteps. They, too, must take up the cross. They must give themselves in order that, in the long run, they might find themselves. That is the paradox of the Gospel, the "good news."

The dilemma in which Jeremiah and Peter were caught is one in which we are all caught. We believe in the Lord because of who he is. And by the instinct of faith we know he means good for us. Even the meaning of "Jesus" in the ancient language is "Yahweh is salvation." That is indeed "good news."

But so often we experience doom and destruction, suffering and sorrow. The "bad news" seems so often to prevail. All we have is the assurance that that "bad news" is somehow part of "God's standards," as Jesus reminded Peter and as Jeremiah discovered. In the end God's love, never really absent, will be recognized in victory. Our story really is "good news."

Twenty-third Sunday in Ordinary Time (A)
Ezekiel 33:7-9; Romans 13:8-10; Matthew 18:15-20

Election, covenant, community, loving kindness, pardon and forgiveness—these are the elements that constitute biblical religion. Our first reading and especially the Gospel have to do with fraternal correction and forgiveness. But these can be appreciated fully only in the larger context of these other elements.

By election we refer primarily to God's prior love whereby he chooses us to be his own. This love and this choice presuppose nothing in us. It is one of the most powerful aspects of biblical faith. God does not choose us because of something in ourselves, but because of something in himself, his free and saving love.

This electing love expresses itself in the form of a covenant, again in both Old and New Testaments. A covenant is a pact, a treaty, an agreement made between two parties. In this case God takes the initiative and establishes the relationship. He binds himself to us and we are bound to him.

The immediate effect of this covenant is the making of a community, since the covenant is not made with individuals but with a people. ". . . you are a people sacred to the Lord, your God" (Dt 7:6). ". . . now you are God's people" (1 P 2:10). It is this community, assembly, church through which God acts. Personal salvation has meaning only in the context of community or church. It is the meaning of covenant.

"Loving kindness" is an attempt to translate a Hebrew word that cannot be adequately expressed in English. It refers to the special relationship between the covenant partners, between God and people and between the members of the community. It is not the prior, electing love by which God freely chose us. Rather it is the love of loyalty, a love that recognizes its responsibility to the other because of a bond. It is covenant love.

All of this comes through to us as rich and wonderful. But there is an aspect of the human person that makes the last two elements in our opening sentence—pardon and forgiveness—necessary. That apsect is our weakness and sinfulness.

Because of our weakness and sinfulness we have to go before the Lord and call on his "loving kindness," that special love that exists between us and him, and ask for his pardon and forgiveness. The Lord sees this act of forgiveness as a special act of divine mercy on his people. He regards this as so important that he wants it mediated through his own human ministers (Jn 20:22-23).

But there is still another aspect of this covenant relationship, and that is the relationship between the human members. God made the covenant, not with individuals, but with a people. This binds the individual members together and makes them responsible to one another.

This is forcefully presented in the first reading where the prophet is told that if he does not remind his covenant partner of his sin, both the sinner and he will die. If he does warn him but with no effect, the sinner alone will die.

It is the same underlying covenant conviction that explains the

Gospel reading. We are, by reason of being church, community, God's people, committed to fraternal correction. Jesus adds that, as church, we can bind and loose, forgive and hold back.

Seen in this larger context, fraternal correction should lose any tinge of vindictiveness or sense of superiority. For all of us, from the very beginning, are what we are because of God's prior love. No one can ever boast of himself.

Twenty-fourth Sunday in Ordinary Time (A)
Sirach 27:30—28:7; Romans 14:7-9; Matthew 18:21-35

In the Scriptures forgiveness, like sin, is a constant theme. God forgives his people; his people forgive one another. This tells us much about biblical religion. In ordinary human society punishment for a crime is the expected reaction. If the State were to forgive every crime automatically, anarchy would result.

This necessary action on the part of the State, that is, of judging and punishing, tells us much about the human condition. The State cannot presume that forgiveness will unfailingly evoke reform. Experience tells a sadder story.

Still, despite this proclivity in human nature, God tells us to forgive. The reason for this attitude is that God's nature is a forgiving one, and anyone who belongs to God must imitate his attitude.

That is why we often find in the Scriptures a prayer to God for forgiveness without any motive adduced, such as the good intention of the sinner or the worthiness of the petitioner. God forgives because he is a forgiving God, not because the sinner deserves forgiveness. In fact, in Amos 7:2 God is asked to forgive Jacob precisely because "he is so small!"

It is true that we do find in the Bible references to God's anger and determination to punish. But in all these cases it is spoken of those who, in the end, reject God's forgiveness. Divine forgiveness flows from a creating and unmerited love and a new creation results. If that creating love is rejected, it is clear that the chaos of sin remains. Punishment is the necessary result. But as long as life remains, the forgiving hand, of God is outstretched to all.

In the first reading we immediately hear about the Lord's vengeance, a theme found elsewhere in the Bible. But this must be understood in the light of what has just been said. Vengeance is final only when the refusal of forgiving love is final.

I suspect that anyone would rejoice in hearing of this forgiving love on the part of God. Strangely enough, the difficulty arises in knowing whether we have actually accepted God's forgiveness. The word of forgiveness is a good word, and we can easily recognize it as good. But recognizing it as good and accepting it in our hearts are not the same.

And that is what our first and third readings are primarily about. How do we know that we have accepted God's forgiving love? Only when we can forgive others. "Should a man nourish anger against his fellows and expect healing from the Lord?"

Sirach proposes several motives for forgiving others. Thinking of our own death is one. What good will hatred of others do after we have died? God's commandment not to hate our neighbor is another. But the best of all is "the Most High's covenant," that is, the Lord's own loving forgiveness of us.

Jesus' parable in the Gospel illustrates this motive even more powerfully. The huge amount of money written off by the king is contrasted with the tiny amount that the official refuses to forgive. Jesus is saying that the official did not really understand and make his own the great forgiving act of the king. If he had, he would have readily forgiven his fellow servant. Because he did not, his own debt remains.

We are fortunate that we can experience in a concrete way the forgiving love of God in the Sacrament of Reconciliation. But it is not magic. We show that it is not magic when we find ourselves forgiving others.

Twenty-fifth Sunday in Ordinary Time (A)
Isaiah 55:6-9; Philippians 1:20-24.27; Matthew 20:1-16

If the Church were ever to become completely relevant to the modern world, she would have betrayed her role as the Body of Christ. If anything emerges from the readings for this Sunday, it is that. Unpalatable as it may be to think of, the Church, like her Founder, is destined always to be "a sign of contradiction."

To study all the implications of that statement would require a course in Christianity. Let's simply reflect on our readings, especially the first and third, and draw some conclusions.

The Isaian passage is addressed to the Jewish people, returned from exile in Babylon. Dispirited by their experience of a devastated homeland, they have become weary of their faith and their vaunted heritage. The prophet invited them to return to the source of all life and strength. God has not abandoned them; they have abandoned God.

They have abandoned him because they tried to cut him down to their size, but he didn't fit. They wanted to make their thoughts his thoughts, their ways his ways. But his thoughts and his ways are "as high as the heavens are above the earth."

They wanted to repay their enemies for the losses inflicted on them, but the Lord was for mercy. They wanted vengeance, but the Lord "is generous in forgiving." They wanted their own "closet God" who would take care of all their needs as they felt them, but he is Lord of heaven and earth.

And yet, this Lord is near to them. "Seek the Lord while he may be found, call him while he is near." Only recognize the Lord as God, the prophet urges them, and surrender your petty ambitions and selfish desires. Then will you experience how generous this God can be.

Does the Gospel parable say anything else? It is the story of the estate owner who went out at various hours of the day to hire laborers for his vineyard. At the end all are paid a full day's wage.

We must not try to find a meaning for each of the details. The estate owner is not God, nor are the earliest workers "cradle Christians," nor the latest workers deathbed converts. Jesus was telling a simple agricultural story whose meaning was not in the details but in the story itself. In the Father's Kingdom all are equally loved. Human standards are not to be used to measure God's generosity.

In these two readings the divine "irrelevance" to the world, which the Church must imitate, is expressed especially in terms of forgiveness, generosity, and love. God forgives and loves as the world does not know how to forgive and love. The Church must do likewise.

God's thoughts and his ways are high above the world's in other matters too. His ideals of justice, concern, and respect for the life and freedom of all, as these are expressed by the prophets and especially by Jesus in the sermon on the mount, have never been matched by any purely human program. To turn the other cheek, to go the extra mile, to hand over the coat as well, to become a eunuch for the sake of the Kingdom—all of this must seem ridiculous to the world.

But all these other "thoughts and ways" of God flow from his "ridiculous" standards of generosity and love, of which our readings speak. And that is why they are so gloriously fulfilling of the human spirit even while the world finds them absurd. But that, too, is why the Church, all devout Christians, must never strive to be relevant to the world. That's not aiming high enough.

Twenty-sixth Sunday in Ordinary Time (A)
Ezekiel 18:25-28; Philippians 2:1-11; Matthew 21:28-32

For me the magnificent hymn to Christ in Paul's letter to the Philippians (vv. 6-11) overshadows the first and third readings for this Sunday. It is called the kenotic hymn from the Greek word meaning "to empty out."

Scholars generally concede that Paul has taken over a hymn that already existed in the Christian community. This means it would have been composed within some twenty years after Christ's death and resurrection. This indicates how rapidly a strong and rich Christology (doctrine about Christ) developed within the Church.

Christ is presented as having existed before his earthly, historical life, and indeed as God. Still, all the external glory associated with that divinity ("the form of God") was not considered so priceless that it could not be temporarily abandoned for the sake of some higher good.

This Christ did. He "emptied himself" of that glory and became a slave, a servant in the form of man. His self-emptying or self-humiliation went so far as to accept obedient death, even (and Paul adds this) death on the cross. Thus in three short, concise verses is depicted the most compelling drama in human history. Nothing remotely similar ever happened before; nothing ever will again.

But that is not the end of the story. The Father did not say, at the time of the crucifixion, "How good of my Son to do that!" Rather, *because* he did it, the Father exalted him on high. Now we have the reversal of the downward movement, the fulfilling after the emptying out.

What the Father did was not just to reverse the movement, not just to fill up what had been emptied out. He did more. He gave Jesus a name indicating a role Jesus now exercises that he did not exercise before. The name is *LORD*.

Exalted on high with the Father, Jesus Christ now has a relationship to the world and especially to all human beings that he did not have even as Son of God. He is now their Savior, a function he has precisely because he is Lord. And, as the first half of the hymn shows, he knows what it is that is to be saved.

These words of explanation seem shallow in the brilliant light of the hymn itself. It says so crisply and so powerfully what we must belabor ourselves to say in many weak words. It is a confirmation of the special presence of the Spirit in the community that produced the hymn. It is one reason we speak of inspiration.

How might we apply this hymn to ourselves? In the prologue to it Paul had encouraged the Philippians to strive for unity, to humble themselves for the sake of others. He adds, "Your attitude must be that of Christ." Then follows the hymn.

But we can never imitate what Christ did; we are not divine. Paul, of course, knew that. What he is implying here is that *because* Christ did what he did and the Father did what he did in response, we also are able to "empty ourselves" out for others within our human bounds. Christ's kenotic action led to lordship. Because of that we can be "united in spirit and ideals" with Christ.

It does not require a great leap of the imagination to understand the Gospel in the light of this hymn. It is not what we were or thought at first that counts anymore. As reluctant servants, sinners, prostitutes, unjust dealers, we must "empty ourselves," and believe in Jesus the Lord. We can do it, because he has made it possible.

Twenty-seventh Sunday in Ordinary Time (A)
Isaiah 5:1-7; Philippians 4:6-9; Matthew 21:33-43

An insidious form of Christianity exists in America today. It claims that all one must do is confess Jesus as Lord and Savior and place one's trust in him. Whatever a person does after that is of no significance for salvation. Even sin cannot affect the reality of God's love in Jesus Christ.

This form is insidious because so much biblical truth is in it. Above all, the nature of God is presented as love. "God is love, and he who abides in love abides in God, and God in him" (1 Jn 4:16). If God *is* love, then he *must* love, and we cannot change him.

Then, too, there is the conviction expressed in the Bible of God's prior love for us. Before we were even able to know him, God loved us. He loved us, not because of some good that he found in us, but completely out of his own free choice.

Moses told Israel, "It was not because you are the largest of all nations that the Lord has set his heart on you and chose you, for you are really the smallest of all nations. It was because the Lord loved you. . . ." (Dt 7:7-8). And John again tells us the same, "Love, then, consists in this: not that we have loved God but that he has (first) loved us. . ." (1 Jn 4:10).

Also, St. Paul's teaching on justification by faith, and not by works, seems to argue the same way. ". . . we too have believed in him in order to be justified by faith in Christ, not by observance of the law. . ." (Gal 2:16). We cannot "earn" salvation; it is a free gift of a loving God.

All of these biblical passages we accept as true. God *is* love, and he has first shown his love for us. It is by our acceptance of Jesus Christ as Lord and Savior in true faith that we are justified in God's sight. To hold anything other than these truths would be false to the Word of God.

What is wrong with this form of Christianity is not what is said but what is *not* said. While God loves us with an unfathomable love that will never be withdrawn, still that love must be accepted and responded to by us. If there is no response manifested in our lives, then we have made a mockery of God's love for us.

The same John who said that God is love also said, "Beloved, if God has loved us so, we must have the same love for one another" (1 Jn 4:11). In other words, we must make God's love work in our lives. The same Paul who said we are justified by faith in Jesus Christ also said that God "will repay every man for what he has done" (Rm 2:6). In the same letter he said that "it is those who keep it (the law) who will be declared just" (2:13).

All that we have said is the necessary background for understanding this Sunday's readings. Isaiah's canticle of the rejected lover is surely to the point. All that the owner did for his vineyard is depicted in aching words to emphasize the tremendous love of God for his people. And yet the vineyard (Israel) brought forth only wild grapes. There was nothing for God to do but punish her.

In his Philippian letter Paul makes a similar point. "Live according to what you have learned and accepted, what you have heard me say and seen me do. Then will the God of peace be with you." In the Gospel parable we have a Christian version of the song of Isaiah. "He will bring that wicked crowd to a bad end and lease his vineyard out to others who will see to it that he has grapes at vintage time."

We must, by all means, believe firmly in God's prior love for us. We must confess Jesus Christ as our Lord and Savior. And we must also remember that our Lord has said to us, "It was not you who chose me, it was I who chose you *to go forth and bear fruit*" (Jn 15:16).

Twenty-eighth Sunday in Ordinary Time (A)
Isaiah 25:6-10; Philippians 4:12-14, 19-20; Matthew 22:1-14

One of the most pleasant of human activities is the family or community meal. In its ideal form it is a time when those who love one another not only share the food they eat but also share with one another their hopes and fears, their experiences and future plans. The love that already binds them is made even stronger.

The Scriptures attest to the fact that a meal is expressive of a wide range of human attitudes and emotions. It can be a powerful testimonial to a friendship that many would doubt could exist, as when Jesus accepted the invitation to dine with a despised tax collector (Mk 2:13-17).

When the forgiving father welcomed home the prodigal son, the most impressive way in which he could make that welcome ring true, as the older brother was quick to realize, was by having an elaborate meal prepared for him. The "fatted calf," shared by the reunited family, was a symbol of the richness of the joy of father and son (Lk 15:11-32).

Abraham provides us with still another example of the symbolic value of a meal. When he beheld the three men coming down the dusty road, wearied from their journey, he quickly told Sarah to prepare a meal that disclosed the gracious act of hospitality being offered by the patriarch (Gn 18:1-8). Similarly, Raguel slaughtered a lamb to welcome his relative, Tobiah (Tb 7:9).

All mankind seems to be aware of the fact that a shared meal either creates or strengthens a community of life among the participants. That is why this most human of activities would also be used to symbolize a community of life between human and divine participants. Somehow, God, or the gods, were thought to share a meal with their worshippers.

In the pagan religions this sacred meal was often associated with orgiastic rites that debased those who took part in them. Though many Israelites succumbed to the lure of these celebrations, the inspired authors were always careful to avoid any semblance of degradation when speaking of the sacred meals shared by Yahweh.

This explains the rather mysterious reference to Moses and the elders on Mount Sinai: "After gazing on God, they could still eat and drink" (Ex 24:11). Despite the majestic presence of the Lord, they were still able to share the meal with him. In doing so they confirmed the bond of covenant love that God had just established.

This sharing of a common life and love is behind the Lord's choice of the Eucharistic meal that he offers his followers. Made much more real (as Paul points out in 1 Cor 10:16-17 and 11:23-29) by the change of the bread and wine into the Body and Blood of Christ, the Eucharist becomes the supreme expression of the covenant bond between the participants.

We have given this background to heighten appreciation of our first and third readings. The Isaiah reading describes in rich imagery what is commonly referred to as the eschatological or end-time meal.

In his description of this meal the author is trying to bring home to the people the exquisite joy of that final day when they would be united with the Lord forever. A common life and common love are symbolized. "This is the Lord for whom we looked; let us rejoice and be glad that he has saved us!"

The banquet of which Jesus speaks in the Gospel is the same, an eschatological meal. But here we are told more about the participants. They will not be simply those you might expect on a royal wedding list. They will be all those who want to come, those who sincerely look for the Lord. This is understandable, since they alone would know how to share the life and love of the Lord.

Twenty-ninth Sunday in Ordinary Time (A)
Isaiah 45:1.4-6; 1 Thessalonians 1:1-5; Matthew 22:15-21

The Gospel reading for this Sunday is especially familiar because of the apparently clever way in which Jesus answers his opponents' question without falling into the trap they set for him. It is probably better known to scholars because of the differing interpretations given to Jesus' reply. The interpretation proposed here is based, in part, on the import of the first reading that the Church gives us as a companion piece.

In the Gospel story some Pharisees send their disciple, together with "Herodian sympathizers," to Jesus to ask him whether it is right to pay tax to the Roman emperor. This is a trap because if he says yes, he would alienate a large number of people, including the Pharisees, who resented Rome's sovereignty. But if he says no, he would alienate groups like the Herodians, who were fiercely loyal to Rome. Also in this case he could be subject to arrest by Roman soldiers for fomenting rebellion.

Jesus' famous reply, based on Caesar's image and inscription on the coin they showed him, was, "Then give to Caesar what is Caesar's, but give to God what is God's." He apparently answers yes to the question but obviously in a way that confounds his questioners. They were "taken aback by this reply. . . ."

In one sense Jesus evades the question. They wanted to know whether it is right or legal to pay taxes. All he says, in effect, is, "Look, this coin has Caesar's name on it. So give it to him. If you always give people, even God, their due, you'll do the right thing." Thus, they still have to make up their own minds whether taxes are due to Rome.

Some have falsely interpreted the reply as meaning that we shouldn't mix politics and religion. Some parts of creation belong to mankind; other parts belong to God. Politics is for politicians just as praying is for believers. Or, Sunday is for God; the rest of the week is for us.

This kind of mentality is foreign to Jesus. He would never think of dividing creation into two spheres, God's and our's. One of the reasons he would not is because he knew his Scriptures, the Old Testament, in which a different picture was painted.

A striking example of that different picture is our first reading. The oracle is addressed to Cyrus, the Persian king who conquered Babylon and who, at a later period than this prophecy, released the Jewish people from cpativity.

What is so remarkable is that God calls this pagan emperor "his anointed." The Hebrew word is *mashiach*, from which our English "Messiah" comes. God calls Cyrus his messiah, a title given otherwise only to someone in Israel, usually the king, or in later Judaism to the end-time figure who would usher in the "messianic" age.

Moreover, God directs all Cyrus' operations. He even arms him, "though you know me not." And the reason for this is "simply" that "I am the Lord and there is no other, there is no God besides me." *Whatever* happens, at *any* time, at *any* place, happens under God's control. *All* is his.

Jesus knew this. He knew that, while Israel was the chosen people, the others did not act independently of God. Everyone and everything comes from that God; everyone and everything belongs in its own way to that God. There is nothing that is not his.

So Jesus is really saying to his opponents, "You can give that coin to Caesar and still be giving it to God." Each one "owns" it in his own way. God's ownership is absolute and eternal. Ours is relative and temporary. And that, if we think about it long enough, is a consoling thought.

Thirtieth Sunday in Ordinary Time (A)
Exodus 22:20-26; 1 Thessalonians 1:5-10; Matthew 22:34-40

Secularism as a movement for the interpretation of life was given that name about the middle of the last century. Its purpose was to do away with what was considered the magic of religion by seeing the world (*saeculum* in Latin) as having its own meaning independent of any transcendent or divine reality. A form of atheism, its stress was on the meaningfulness of the world of and by itself.

Secular humanism is another expression of this movement. Its emphasis is on the proper attitudes that we should have for the whole of human society. Social progress, therefore, and the elimination of all injustice are its exclusive aims. Like secularism, it dismissed the need for any divine reality to carry out its program.

Our first and third readings for this Sunday champion a biblical humanism. This movement, a few thousand years older than the other two, proclaims the necessity of an acting, saving God and a human response in the form of love both for God and for all his creatures. Another name for this is Judaeo-Christianity.

The claim of this movement to a more intense humanism than the other two is based on the conviction that it is God's saving love that has made us what we are. Within us, therefore, is a divine spark or transcendent principle, a "grace," that makes us capable of a love for others that exceeds normal human dimensions.

Many studies have been made comparing Israel's law code with those of other ancient peoples. Its humanism has been shown to excel that of the others in many ways. Some examples are found in our first reading from Exodus.

The "alien" or non-Israelite was not to be mistreated. The motive for this, Israel's own experience as aliens in Egypt, is unique among the nations. Widows and orphans were the special object of concern in most societies. But there God himself is the divine "kinsman" who will come to their aid.

In the Babylonian Code of Hammurabi interest was permitted on any loan. In Israel it was not to be demanded of the poor. The neighbor's concern, which included consideration of the social condition, was every Israelite's concern.

It is true that these humanitarian laws say nothing about an attitude toward God. But the framework in which they are placed, the context of which they are a part, is that of a covenant between God and his people. That covenant says, in effect, "God has saved you in his everlasting love. Therefore, you must hold him above every other object and show love and concern for his people."

In the Gospel reading this twofold attitude, toward God and toward others, is given its most concise expression. Asked to sum up the 613 precepts of the Jewish Law, Jesus does so by saying that we must love God with all our being and we must love our neighbor as ourselves.

Note that the love of God is placed first, not just because he is worthy of a special love, but also because our love of others is most intense when it flows from our love of God. That love of God is possible only because his love has first placed that spark, that "grace," within us.

If secular humanism is attractive to the human spirit, biblical humanism should be all the more so. But it will win out only when we who proclaim it will live it.

Thirty-first Sunday in Ordinary Time (A)
Malachi 1:14—2:2, 8-10; 1 Thessalonians 2:7-9, 13;
Matthew 23:1-12

According to the Bible, it started in a garden. There the serpent presented himself as something he was not, the ultimate judge of human conduct. And Eve strove to be what she could not be, like God himself. From the beginning the lure of deception has plagued the human condition.

What God wants us to be is stated symbolically but forcefully in the verse preceding that first fall from grace: "The man and his wife were both naked, yet they felt no shame" (Gn 2:25). There were no barriers between them, nothing to interfere with honest communication and dialogue.

Modern writers describe this as transparency. We are transparent to others when they can "see through us" with ease, when we present not obstacles to their understanding who we really are, when our actions describe truly all that we feel. Jesus was thinking of the original Israelite, Jacob, who practiced deception in order to obtain the birthright, when he described Nathanael as "a *true* Israelite," one "without guile" (Jn 1:47). He was transparent to others.

This theme of deception versus transparency is in our readings this Sunday. The first verse of the reading from Malachi supports this: "Cursed is the deceiver. . . ." A few words about the background of the reading will help in understanding it better.

The pseudonymous author (the name Malachi means "my messenger"; cf. 3:1) was writing in the period after the exile and at a time of serious religious abuses. The priests had become the dominant party since the fall of the monarchy and used their power in many deceptive practices.

One of these is described in the opening verse as substituting a gelding for a male animal at the sacrifice. In the preceding verse the priests were accused of offering the lame and sick animals instead of whole ones. They felt perhaps that they were deceiving the people who were not able to "see through" their actions.

The ultimate reason for Malachi's rage is, of course, the holy God. They are trying to deceive him who can see into their hearts. And because he does see, the prophet foretells the time in the future when the true worship of God will be offered by the Gentiles. ". . . my name will be feared among the nations."

The Gospel reading is the epitome of condemnation of deception. Because of the strong denunciation of Pharisees here, the evil of hypocrisy has been unfortunately attributed to all Pharisees of all ages. That Jesus did condemn some Pharisees of his day there is no reason to doubt. But the present reading's intensity is probably due more to the historical situation in Matthew's day in the latter part of the first century.

In any case the only way in which this can be properly interpreted for us is to ask whether we are guilty of this kind of deception. In all of us is the temptation to be thought of as better than we really are, to have our clothes or other ornaments say something about us that we are not.

Jesus doesn't condemn phylacteries and tassels; we read that he wore the latter himself (Mt 14:36). He condemned the way they were worn, to suggest a holiness that was not there. He denounced the lack of transparency.

Openness to God and to one another should be the goal of all God's children. No doubt we can impress others at times and be honored for what we are not. But God sees us as we are; to him we are transparent.

Thirty-second Sunday in Ordinary Time (A)
Wisdom 6:12-16; I Thessalonians 4:13-18; Matthew 25:1-13

Throughout the history of the Church the *parousia*, or second coming of Jesus Christ in glory at the end of time, has been taken most seriously. There is no Christian doubt about it. History will come to an end, and the end will be marked by some kind of manifestation of the risen Lord.

At times the seriousness with which the *parousia* is taken is marked with excessive zeal. People become convinced that they know the precise day and hour of the end and prepare for it in bizarre ways. They climb a high hill and wait in eager anticipation. Or their "prophets" go about with signs proclaiming, "The end is near."

This is not what Jesus meant when he told his disciples to "keep your eyes open," or to "be ready for the coming." While a really thorough understanding of what he did mean would require a study of numerous texts, our readings for this Sunday can help put us on the right track.

Let's begin with Paul's advice to the Thessalonians. He writes to them, not to convince them of the *parousia*, since they already had a marked conviction about it. Rather, he wants to assure them that their deceased families and friends would also share in that glorious day. Apparently they thought that only the living would take part in it.

The reading should be familiar to many since it is used so often in the Eucharistic liturgy for the dead. It is a consoling passage. Some of the language is technical (more precisely, *apocalyptic*) and difficult to understand. At any rate, we need not interpret literally such items as the archangel's voice, the trumpet of God, or the catching of people up into the clouds. These phrases have their own special meaning.

What is really the heart of Paul's message is found at the end where he says, "Thereafter we shall be with the Lord unceasingly." Here is the heart of *parousia*, full enjoyment of the Kingdom with the Lord and with one another.

The parable in Matthew's Gospel gives a further insight. The groom represents the Christ awaited in his *parousia*. The midnight hour does not mean a designated time. Rather it conveys the uncertainty (they are in the dark) concerning the time of his coming. The two groups of bridesmaids represent those who will and those who will not share in the event. Preparedness is the ultimate criterion.

The theme of preparedness is certainly one of the reasons why the Church reminds us of the *parousia* at several places in the Eucharistic prayer. If our eyes are on that glorious goal, we are more likely to keep our spiritual lamps lit and ready for the reception.

But we can find another insight here. Just as the groom did not appear out of nowhere, but had to approach the trysting place, so the Lord is already on his way. In fact, his approach began at the time of his death and exaltation. Those were the sources of his saving power, the paschal mystery that contained within it the final saving coming.

So, just as the Church continually rises to her source in the paschal mystery, she continually rises to meet the coming Lord. The *parousia*, in this sense, is now. When we rise to meet him now in the Eucharist, we are also rising to meet him at the end.

Like personified wisdom in the first reading, Christ is searching for us. When we look forward to meeting him, he "graciously appears to us in the way and meets us with all solicitude." Then we experience *parousia*.

Thirty-third Sunday in Ordinary Time (A)
*Proverbs 31:10-13, 19-20, 30-31; 1 Thessalonians 5:1-6;
Matthew 25:14-30*

"Man is not saved by works, but he is not saved either without works. . . ." (F.J. Leenhardt). This is the way one modern author tries to express the Pauline teaching on salvation. By reflecting on what he means we can appreciate better all three of this Sunday's readings.

Over and over Paul insists in his letters to the Galatians and to the Romans that we are not justified (that is, brought into a right relationship with God) by works but by faith. By "works" he meant, first, all those things commanded by the Law of Moses. By extension, he also included any good deeds we do. By "faith" he meant a total surrender to God, an openness to his love which allows that love to pour into our hearts and act on our personalities.

We can see, then, what our modern author meant by his first statement. No one approaches God on his own. No one can earn his love. Only through the gift of faith are we brought into his presence and, when we are, the life we live is not ours, but is that of Christ, who is living in us (Gal 2:20).

We, however, must continually accept the divine life, we must continually respond to it. When we do, then there are "good deeds," the fruits of our new life. Since these good deeds are the result of a divine gift, we cannot say that we "earn" final salvation, even though those deeds are necessary for that salvation. This is what the author meant by the second part of his statement.

All three of our readings, each in its own way, stress the second part of the statement. We cannot be saved without good works, since these are the acknowledgment of our new life with God. To put it in Paul's words, ". . .it is those who keep it (the interior law of love) who will be declared just" (Romans 2:13).

The reading from Proverbs depicts the ideal wife of ancient Israelite society, an industrious, charitable, prayerful woman whose "works praise her at the city gate." It would be grossly unfair to condemn the poet for extolling certain qualities that the modern American woman may not particularly prize. He was a product of his culture and expressed its values, not ours.

The heart of our reading is that this woman, who had been caught up in a covenant relationship with her people's God, had generously responded to his love by giving herself in the best way she knew how. Her works said something about her inner life.

The same truth is the essence of the passage from Paul's letter to the Thessalonians. While we await the glorious coming of the Lord, we must live the Christ-life, the life of light, not of darkness. This means doing the deeds of light.

And who can miss the meaning of the Gospel parable? By indulging in a bit of allegorizing, as Matthew did, we can see the money given to the three servants as the gift of new life that God gives us through faith. We must not hide that life under a basket. We must live it and let it grow. Only in this way can we attain the ultimate gift of salvation.

The application of all this should be clear. Each time we sin we reject a gift, we say "no" to God. Each time we lend a helping hand or cheer a grieving heart we affirm a gift within us. Then we can and must thank the Lord for allowing us to "share the master's joy."

Christ the King (A)
Ezekiel 34:11-12, 15-17; 1 Corinthians 15:20-26, 28;
Matthew 25:31-46

A different kind of king. That is the only and necessary way of speaking of this Sunday's solemnity. Some, however, favor doing away with this title for Jesus Christ. They maintain it smacks of authoritarianism and luxurious living. But let's retain the title—and always keep in mind that Jesus is a different kind of king.

First, he is a king who *serves* his people. Like earthly kings, he does this through his representatives, those who are called by him in the vocations of priesthood, religious life, diaconate, and lay ministry. He takes a risk in serving them in this manner, for often his service will be judged by the all-too-human and imperfect service of those he has called. But he has willed it, for he has called them.

Second, he is a different kind of king in that he also serves his people *personally and directly*. This is what he means when he said that he would be with us always, even to the end of time. He is the Emmanuel (God-with-us) king, predicted by Isaiah as coming from the royal line of David (7:14), a prophecy fulfilled at Jesus' birth (Mt 1:23). He is with us to serve us.

This is what the Church means to teach us in giving us the first reading, from Ezekiel. In the larger context the prophet condemns the earthly kings of Israel because they "did not look after my sheep"

(34:8). We should not be surprised to find the king described as shepherd. It was a common identification in the ancient world and meant to suggest the very kind of service that these kings were neglecting.

The prophet goes on to say that the Lord God will personally take over this service. "I myself will look after and tend my sheep. . . .The lost I will seek out, the strayed I will bring back, the injured I will bind up, the sick I will heal. . . ." The Church sees these as the words of Jesus, the shepherd-king.

But Jesus Christ is also a king who *reigns* over his people. Again, his is a different kind of reign from that of earthly kings. There is, it is true, an exercise of power and authority, and that is why we must retain the title of king for this Master of ours. But he exercises them not for their own sake, but *in favor of his people*. It might be better, then, to say that he reigns *among* his people rather than *over* them.

This is the import of the beautiful parable in the Gospel reading. All those people who had served the hungry and the thirsty and anyone in need were doing it for him. This must mean that his love for them was empowering them to serve the King they did not consciously acknowledge. Only at the end would his identity as the King they served be revealed when "he will sit upon his royal throne."

Paul, too, speaks of this different kind of king in his letter to the Corinthians. His subject is the resurrection of Jesus Christ. After speaking of the reality of it, he addresses its consequences. One of these is, of course, our own resurrection to new life.

But Paul speaks of a cosmic authority of this King Jesus as a result of his resurrection. "Christ must reign until God has put all enemies under his feet, and the last enemy to be destroyed is death." This may sound too overpowering for our Emmanuel-king. But it should not, for it is all done in favor of "all those who belong to him."

In the end what matters is this: we must be among those "who belong to him," who accept him as king in their lives. It isn't hard, for he is a different kind of king, one whose crown was made of thorns.

THE WORD ALIVE

Cycle B

First Sunday of Advent (B)
Isaiah 63:16-17, 19; 64:2-7; 1 Corinthians 1:3-9; Mark 13:33-37

One of the distinctive characteristics of biblical religion is its insistence on hope in the future. Hope pervades both the Old and New Testaments. It is why we celebrate a season of Advent in our liturgical year, for Advent is essentially hope in the future coming of the saving God. In him is our hope, as the New Testament Scriptures make abundantly clear.

What is the source of this hope? How, in the face of crises, frustrations, and disappointments, can it have such power? The reason is an equally strong faith in the past, a belief in what God has already done to prove his love. The reasoning is that, if he has done so much for us already, how much more must he have in store for us! Thus, in Advent hope and faith are expressed equally; we can hope because we believe.

The first reading from the book of Isaiah seems at first glance to be a cry of anguish more than of hope. It was written at a time when Jerusalem lay in ruins, and the people's only hope was in God. God, however, seemed so remote, his wonderful redemptive deeds buried in a distant past. Isaiah, nevertheless, unites himself with the sinful people and pleads their cause before God.

The point is that he *does* plead that cause. Even if salvation did *seem* buried in the past, his stubborn hope gives rise to prayer. Thus what on the surface appears a cry of anguish is, more profoundly, a cry that is suffused by hope. If he did not hope, he could never have prayed.

We see here the role of suffering in hope-filled history. It tests that hope, forcing it to assert itself. "Yet, O Lord, you are our father." Such a prayer could never have been uttered in abject despair.

The second reading, from Paul, was chosen because of its reference to the expectation of the Lord Jesus Christ's revelation at the end of time. "He will strengthen you to the end, so that you will be blameless on the day of our Lord Jesus."

The church at Corinth, too, was experiencing its crisis. The community was racked by factions and by disorders of every kind. Paul would deal with these at length in the rest of the letter. But here, at the beginning, he expresses his confidence in the final outcome. It is a confidence sparked by hope.

Note that Paul can have that confidence because of his belief in what Christ has already done for the Corinthian church. "I continually thank my God for you because of the favor he has bestowed on you in Christ Jesus, in whom you have been richly endowed with every gift of speech and knowledge."

For the Christian, of course, that hope centers on the second coming of Jesus Christ in glory. Paul alludes to it in passing, as we have seen. But in the Gospel reading from Mark it is the sole concern of Jesus' words. A new note, however, is struck here. Hope in the coming of Christ must be marked by a spirit of preparation and a state of readiness.

Mark, even more than Paul, was writing at a time of crisis. The church in Rome was beginning to experience persecution. The threat now was from without. It was not a case primarily of renewing the church from within, but of standing firm in the faith they had received and in the hope of future glory.

That is why Mark stresses Jesus' words of need for watchfulness. "Be constantly on the watch! Stay awake! You do not know when the appointed time will come." These words of exhortation have perennial value. If we really do believe what God has done in Jesus Christ, and if we really hope in his coming, we must strive to be prepared. Then Advent will be a season of joyful expectation—and that is what it is meant to be.

Second Sunday of Advent (B)
Isaiah 40:1-5, 9-11; 2 Peter 3:8-14; Mark 1:1-8

"A herald's voice in the desert. . ." is more than a description of John the Baptizer in this Sunday's Gospel. The phrase expresses a stance that is at the heart of biblical religion.

In the Scriptures "herald" is a word rich with meaning. Basically he is one who proclaims, an announcer charged with enthusiasm. What he proclaims is good news, "gospel," a saving word. The good news is victory, the conquest of evil. The victory is that of the king, the leader of the people who are or will be saved. And the herald must "go forth" among the people.

In the reading from Isaiah we find all these elements expressed in an exuberance of language that betrays the overflowing joy of the prophet. ". . .the glory of the Lord shall be revealed, and all mankind shall see it together." "Cry out at the top of your voice, Jerusalem, herald of good news!. . .Here comes with power the Lord God, who rules by his strong arm."

Those words, written from the place of exile, Babylon, describe the long-awaited release from captivity. As he wrote, the prophet knew that the enemy was already on his knees and that the victorious army of liberation would soon sweep away all resistance. For the prophet the victory was that of the Lord his God and King.

The conviction of this presence of the Lord explains the rich profusion of the prophet's language. And his words can be applied to any of the saving events of salvation history. They can be most aptly applied to the victory of Jesus Christ. Mark knew that when he identified John the Baptizer as the herald who "makes ready the way of the Lord, clears him a straight path."

The Baptizer may seem, for some, a strange candidate for a king's herald. His appearance "in the desert," his clothing of camel's hair and leather belt, his food of grasshoppers and wild honey—these are hardly the marks of the trumpeting heralds of earthly kings. But Israel recognized its own and "went out to him in great numbers."

Like any faithful herald, John realized that he was but the one who comes before. He was not the victor, but the victor's proclaimer.

"One more powerful than I is to come after me. . . . I have baptized you in water; he will baptize you in the Holy Spirit."

The One whom the Baptizer heralded, as we confess, has already come. He has defeated the ancient serpent. He has gained the victory through his death and resurrection. The good news, the gospel, is that of salvation won. But we also know that he must yet come into the lives of many who do not know him. And he must come again at time's ending, as Advent reminds us.

In the meantime, as we live this Advent of a pilgrim Church, we who have been baptized by the "Stronger One" must be his heralds to the world. We must, each in his or her own way, bear witness to the Word, to the good news, to the gospel of victory and salvation.

One obvious way to do it is by proclaiming the Word as the Baptizer did, a ministry given by the Church to those whom she calls. But one can be a herald, a witness in many other ways. One who teaches with the conviction of faith is bearing witness. One who lives a life of love for others is testifying to the presence of the God of love.

Finally, all those who suffer in union with Christ are witnesses in a special way. It is no coincidence that, in the early Church, those who suffered and died for their faith were called martyrs, for the word, "martyr," in Greek, means "witness." They are among the heralds of the gospel of Jesus Christ.

Third Sunday of Advent (B)
Isaiah 61:1-2, 10-11; 1 Thessalonians 5:16-24; John 1:6-8, 19-28

In Matthew's Gospel John the Baptizer sends his disciples to ask Jesus if he is "He-who-is-to-come" (11:3). By the time of Jesus this expression, which is one word in the Greek, was a technical term for a special figure expected by the Jews. Matthew himself would have understood it as another title for the Messiah, the "Coming One."

The prophet Malachi speaks of God's messenger, the messenger of the covenant whom the Jews desire. And Malachi adds, "Yes, he is coming, says the Lord of hosts" (3:1). When John's disciplesthen spoke of the "Coming One," they knew clearly what they were referring to.

This Sunday's Gospel reading centers on John the Baptizer. But it is evident that the whole point of the passage is to contrast him with Jesus Christ. The first part shows that John came "only to testify to the light, for he himself was not the light." The passage continues with, "The real light . . . was coming into the world." Here the "Coming One" is identified as the "coming light of the world."

In the second part of the reading John's encounter with the Jewish representatives emphasizes again the secondary or preparatory role that the Baptizer plays in contrast to Jesus. In one place John refers to Jesus as "the one who is to come after me." This must mean the one who will come and fulfill all your expectations.

It seems that the early Church had to stress the absolute distinctiveness of Jesus in the face of a strong Baptist movement that looked on John as a possible candidate as Messiah. But Jesus, as a transcendent figure (and the evangelist John in his prologue designates him as God made flesh), simply cannot share the messianic role with anyone. He is unique.

Our contemporary world tends to deny absoluteness in any form. Everything is relative, which is "nice" because it allows for pluralism of thought and expression. There is no danger of "cutting off the dialog." It is a world that gladly permits many John the Baptizers but no Messiah.

So much is true in this position. In the secular order of reality we must beware of simplistic absolutes that can lead to a deadly fanaticism. These absolutes may be in the social, political, economic, or moral order. When pursued relentlessly they bring on tensions and diversions that are healed only with difficulty.

At the same time it is certain that biblical religion is based on the conviction that the Absolute has entered history. That Absolute is the one God who has revealed himself to us and made it possible for us to crave eternal life. As Qoheleth put it so beautifully, he "has put the timeless" into our hearts (Ecclesiastes 3:11).

That is why the prophet in our first reading could write so movingly of Jerusalem's future. That future was determined by the Absolute's association with it. The "new name" she will receive will mark her as unique because her Lord is unique.

That is why John the Baptizer could speak of a "Coming One."

That "One" is unique, the Absolute, God's Son in whom the hope of the world is realized. That is why it is possible to have an Advent. For Advent means, literally, the season of the "Coming One." The depth of our faith in him will determine the intensity of our celebration.

Fourth Sunday of Advent (B)
2 Samuel 7:1-5, 8-11, 16; Romans 16:25-27; Luke 1:26-38

Celebrating Advent is like walking through a long tunnel. Even at the start we can see the patch of light at the end, but it seems so distant. As we approach the end, however, the light becomes brighter until we step out into the open and see the new world around us.

In the first Sunday of Advent we were told just to stay awake, to be on guard. Or, to use our tunnel figure, we were to keep walking with the assurance that there would be a bursting out into glory. In the second Sunday we heard of John the Baptizer clearing a straight path. And last Sunday he spoke openly of the Coming One.

On this fourth Sunday we are so close to the end that we even glimpse the Coming One. At least we are told of his conception in his Mother's womb and hear remarkable things about him: "He will rule over the house of Jacob forever and his reign will be without end." The light that is almost upon us will, when it appears, shine forever.

Tracing the development of biblical revelation from the beginning is like traversing a tunnel too. In fact, the liturgical season of Advent is an abbreviated Bible. Its readings are intended to catechize us in the way that God prepared his people for the coming of his Son.

Sometimes that preparation seemed to be for nothing. The light at the end wasn't even visible. During the wilderness experience Moses was ready at times to call the whole thing off. Israel forgot about the tunnel's end and only wanted to go back to the flesh pots of Egypt, as if there were no reason for the journey.

But at other times the light at the end appeared so brilliant that the sojourners might have thought they had reached the end. One of those times is recorded for us in the first reading for this Sunday. The biblical author notes that the Lord had given David "rest from his enemies on every side." That is almost an end-time figure of speech for our author. It is the final resting place that Israel longed for in the desert (Deuteronomy 12:9). David is now enjoying it.

Even more, David is made the object of a blessing by God which might suggest that God's story had come to its dramatic and hoped for conclusion. God is going to make him "famous like the great ones of the earth." And above all, "Your house and your kingdom shall endure forever before me; your throne shall stand firm forever."

But we know that it was a promise *to be* fulfilled. In the stories that follow in 2 Samuel we hear some less than glorious things about David, about his adultery, his murder of Uriah, his problems with his own family. But the promise still stands. God remains faithful to his Word. In all that terrible darkness there is still that light at the end.

The Gospel reading assures us that the promise made a thousand years earlier is being fulfilled. This Jesus, who is "Son of the Most High," will take over "the throne of David his father. . .and his reign will be without end." Mary's *fiat* is the human touch that makes it possible now.

Still celebrating the season of Advent, we remind ourselves of the need to keep walking. The light of the world is almost in our grasp. Tomorrow he will be among us. And when we come upon him, then, like St. Paul, we must bear witness to him in our lives. For he is the gospel, the good news, "which reveals the mystery hidden for many ages."

Vigil of Christmas (ABC)
See page 9

Christmas: Midnight Mass (ABC)
See page 11

Christmas: Mass at Dawn (ABC)
See page 13

Christmas: Mass during the Day (ABC)
See page 14

Holy Family (B)
Sirach 3:2-6, 12-14; Colossians 3:12-21; Luke 2:22-40

In his book *The Secular City* Harvey Cox pinpointed some of the factors that contributed to and characterized the phenomenon we know today as secularization. For example, mobility, or the ease of getting from place to place, or "having wheels," makes it possible to escape unwanted influences and to "do one's thing" as one wishes. Closely associated with this is the factor of anonymity, the ability to conceal one's identity and so also reduce one's responsibility.

In a secular society, where these factors are at work without control, the human family is exposed to gradual disintegration. Without the sense of responsibility to others that the family fosters in a basic way, every form of responsibility, even to a transcendent Lord, will slowly erode.

It is probably no coincidence that devotion to the Holy Family arose at a time when the disintegration of the human family began. Such a special devotion did not exist in the first 1600 years of the Church when family ties were strong. And it was only in 1921 that our special feast of the Holy Family was instituted. We can see it as providential. In our readings for this feast we will note the call to responsibility to others and to the Lord.

In the reading from Sirach the total emphasis is on the children's responsibility to their parents. It was presumed that the parents would do what was needful for their children since they had already shown their responsibility by having children.

The biblical author is really expounding on Exodus 20:12 where the fourth commandment enjoins the honoring of one's parents as a necessary part of their covenant relationship with God. In other words, this is all seen in a religious context. It's not just the "nice" thing to do. That is why Sirach can say that one "who despises his father" is a blasphemer.

This is an important observation. Responsibility of family members one to another does not flow only from their natural relationships. It flows also and more profoundly from the special relationship they have to the Lord. When they respond to one another's needs, they are responding to God's covenant call of love.

Paul, too, makes this relationship to the Lord the basis of his injunctions concerning Christians' relationships to one another. The reading from Colossians begins, "Because you are God's chosen ones . . . ," and then proceeds to enumerate the attitudes of responsibility we should have for one another.

Only in the latter part does Paul concentrate on the Christian family. Again mutual responsibility is the guiding principle. But also, this must be done "in the Lord." Love, honor, and respect between parents and children come "naturally" to those who reverence the Lord.

The Gospel reading was chosen presumably because it illustrates the concern of Mary and Joseph to fulfill their religious obligations. Luke recounts that when the prescriptions of the law had been fulfilled "they returned to Galilee and their own town of Nazareth."

And it was precisely within the context of the life of the "Holy Family" that Jesus grew "in size and strength, filled with wisdom, and the grace of God was upon him."

The lesson is clear. Every Christian family must be holy. Members will look on their fulfillment of mutual responsibilities as a response to God's prior call.

Mary, Mother of God (ABC)
See page 18

Epiphany (ABC)
See page 20

Baptism of the Lord (B)
Isaiah 42:1-4, 6-7; Acts 10:34-38; Mark 1:7-11

The baptism of Jesus by John the Baptizer, the feast we celebrate on this Sunday, has always enjoyed particular favor in the history of Christianity. This is true despite the misinterpretation that could be given to it. We shall see the source of this possible misinterpretation and then consider the significance of the event for us.

Jesus being baptized by John could be understood as indicating the superiority of the latter. Normally the baptizer would be thought to have a power not had by the baptized. One could even think that the baptized would thereby be considerd a disciple of the baptizer.

Already Mark, the earliest evangelist, recognized this possible source of misinterpretation and took steps to avoid it. He records John's statement that "One more powerful than I is to come after me. . . .I have baptized you in water; he will baptize you in the Holy Spirit." John is obviously referring here to Jesus.

If one were to examine the parallel scenes in the other Gospels, it would be clear that these evangelists are even more concerned to avoid any misinterpretation. This suggests that, by the time they were writing, in the latter half of the first century, some people were extolling John over Jesus. All the Gospels make it clear that this was a mistake.

Why, then, did Jesus permit himself to be baptized by John? One reason is that he recognized the validity of John's mission and wished to encourage it. John was bringing many people closer to God and so preparing for the messianic mission of Jesus. The Baptizer was the climactic figure of the Old Testament period and, as such, a fitting forerunner of the Christ.

A second, more profound reason was that Jesus, even though without sin, wished to identify himself with sinful humanity. His mission was precisely to be one of calling sinners into the Kingdom. Thus the initial event in his ministry is an implicit invitation to sinners to come to him. It can still have that meaning for us today.

Some of the early Fathers of the Church saw in this event the symbolic institution of the Christian sacrament of baptism. The basis for this is the appearance of the three persons of the Trinity in the baptismal scene. The voice of the Father and the descent of the Spirit on the Son would symbolize the baptism "in the name of the Father, and of the Son, and of the Holy Spirit." The actual commission to the apostles to baptize "all nations" in this way is recorded in Matthew's Gospel (28:19).

The second reading from the Acts of the Apostles indicates again the importance accorded Jesus' baptism by John in the early Church. Peter sums up the whole ministry of Jesus in three "events." These are the baptism, the actual ministry of doing good and healing the sick, and the death and resurrection. It is remarkable that the baptismal event features so largely in the summary.

It was considered so important because it represented the inauguration of his mission in the power of the Holy Spirit. For Luke, the author of Acts, the entire public ministry of Jesus was exercised in the power of the Spirit. That is why he emphasizes Peter's reference to the baptismal scene.

Finally, the first reading, from the book of Isaiah, is chosen by the Church to indicate the messianic preparation for the ministry of Jesus. The mysterious "servant of the Lord," mentioned in Isaiah, is now seen to be identified with Jesus Christ. On him God has placed his Spirit and sent him out to "establish justice on the earth." Thus does the baptism of Jesus tell us so much about him and about his mission to all of us.

First Sunday of Lent (B)
Genesis 9:8-15; 1 Peter 3:18-22; Mark 1:12-15

A new beginning! That is what our readings for this Sunday speak about to us. And, while we generally associate Lent more readily with penance, the notion of beginning anew is more positive and is a helpful approach to this important time of the Church's year.

The passage in Genesis speaks of a covenant God made with Noah and his sons after the disastrous flood. The priestly author of this narrative was also responsible for the first creation story in chapter one, and scholars suggest that he understood God's words there to the first man and woman to be the expression of a covenant also (1:28-30).

That first covenant had been shattered by human sinfulness. Reflecting on the enormity of sin, God "regretted that he had made man on the earth, and his heart was grieved" (6:6). The flood was seen as the divine reaction to the human rejection of God. But there was a note of hope, for "Noah found favor with the Lord" (6:8).

Now the past is done with. Noah and his family stand waiting for the Lord. And he takes the initiative. He forms a new covenant with these people. It is as though God were saying, "Let us forget the past. We'll begin anew with peace between myself and humankind and, indeed, between myself and all creation. The rainbow will be its sign."

One of the significant aspects of this covenant is that "every living creature" is associated with it. It might seem strange to think of God making a covenant with dogs and birds and fish. But it is a constant biblical theme that God made all things good and that, in the end, all creation will be transformed (cf. Romans 8:18-22). A recognition of this bond between ourselves and all of nature is a mark of this new beginning.

The Gospel reading tells us of Jesus' forty-day stay in the desert, the origin of the Lenten season. But it includes also his appearance in Galilee and the initiation of his preaching mission. This, too, is a new beginning.

That Jesus' appearance marked a radical new beginning is accepted by all who recognize him as Son of God. Mark had indicated that in the scene just before our present reading, the scene of Jesus' baptism. The Father had declared him to be his beloved Son. This God-man was now visiting his people in the flesh.

Also in that scene Mark noted that the Spirit descended on Jesus "like a dove." No complete agreement exists among scholars on the meaning of that phrase. But it is possible that Mark was thinking of God's spirit hovering over the primordial chaos in the first creation story. If that is the case, then the theme of a new beginning, a new creation, is all the more vigorous.

In writing of Jesus' stay in the desert Mark says that "He was with the wild beasts. . . .'' This is commonly seen as an allusion to the messianic period when "the wolf shall be a guest of the lamb, and the leopard shall lie down with the kid" (Isaiah 11:6). Once again, as with Noah, all of nature is seen to share in this new beginning.

What is important for us is not so much what we actually do during this Lenten season, whether it be attending daily Mass, visiting the sick and the elderly more often, or foregoing some special pleasure. All these are fine. But what is essential to Lent is our resolve to begin anew. One thing is certain: God's covenant love is here to strengthen and comfort us.

Second Sunday of Lent (B)
Genesis 22:1-2, 9-13, 15-18; Romans 8:31-34; Mark 9:2-10

This Sunday's readings present us with the challenge of faith. Can we honestly believe in the enormity of God's love for us—and accept that love?

The reading from Genesis is familiar. That may pose a problem. Like Chesterton's man who was so tall he couldn't be seen, this story may be so familiar its power is not recognized. We have to remove from our eyes the scales of familiarity and take a fresh look.

The story is about Abraham and his son Isaac. "His son" are the operative words here. For any parent the two words will have a strongly emotive effect. And anyone whose humanity has not been exhausted must appreciate the deep and poignant pull of "father and son."

If I seem to make so much of the relationship, it is because the author of our story does so. In God's command to Abraham to offer his son Isaac in sacrifice in the land of Moriah, we hear these words (as the Hebrew text suggests): "Take your son . . . Isaac . . . your only son . . . the son whom you love . . . and go to the land of Moriah." It is as though God were pronouncing each word slowly and deliberately in order that the full significance of each repeated word might penetrate Abraham's heart.

Abraham's response at first seems insensitive, even indifferent. "Early the next morning Abraham saddled his donkey, took with him his son Isaac . . ." and proceeded to the land of Moriah. There is no word of protest, not even a plea for an explanation.

The author was certainly aware of what might be naturally expected. But he wants to bring out as effectively as he can the apparent absurdity of the whole thing. God, the mighty God, the God who had brought Abraham to this land in the first place, now imposes this enormous and inhuman obligation.

What is all the more absurd is that this God had made a promise to this Abraham that a nation would spring from his loins. And this child, Isaac, was the only medium for the fulfillment of the promise. Abraham had believed in God, and Isaac was the apparent confirmation of his faith. With him, it seems, would go the father's faith.

We know how the story ends. The child is saved at the last moment by God's command. And we ask, Why? Why this strange ritual only to have things end up, happily, as they were before? The answer can only be to show the enormity of the act of faith.

Faith's object is not, primarily, a promise, but God himself. When one gives oneself completely to the transcendent Lord in faith, then one knows with an absoluteness that may appear to be indifference that he will be faithful. "If we are unfaithful he will still remain faithful, for he cannot deny himself" (2 Tm 2:13).

The burden of faith is exposed even more in the Gospel reading. In this case, however, the burden is not that of giving up something. Rather it is in being asked to accept something. We are asked to accept this Jesus as God's Son, as his beloved Son. We are asked to accept him as a Son who will be offered up—for us!

The words of the Father in the transfiguration scene are a clear allusion to the words of command to Abraham. Another "Father and Son" are involved in a sacrifice motivated solely by love. This one will be consummated. Can we believe that love—and accept it?

Third Sunday of Lent (B)
Exodus 20:1-17; 1 Corinthians 1:22-25; John 2:13-25

The heart of Jesus' message was the presence of the Father's kingdom. Telling about Jesus' first public appearance in Galilee, Mark summarized the message in these words: "This is the time of fulfillment. The reign of God is at hand! Reform your lives and believe in the Gospel!" (1:15).

The awesome reality of God's reign or kingdom underlies every page of the New Testament. It is the motivating force behind every word and deed of Jesus, behind every paradoxical statement and every startling action of the early Christians. God's reign, initiated in the coming of Jesus, made all things different.

The reign of God means the prior action of God in making the world whole again, in reconciling all things in his Son, in establishing the fullness of relationships between himself and his people and between the various members of his people. But, because this involves a world shattered by sin, God's reign will be marked by the unexpected until it is fully established.

These thoughts come to mind as we reflect on the Gospel reading. In a wholly surprising move Jesus takes a whip of cords and drives sheep and oxen out of the temple area and knocks over the tables of the money changers and spills their coins all over the pavement. The Church would have been too embarrassed to have made up this story. She told it because she knew it happened.

All kinds of revolutionary movements have used this story to justify their own brand of violence. But if they are to use it, they must recognize that it is to be on Jesus' terms. Only if their zeal is for "the Father's house," for the reign of God, can they presume to affect radically the lives of others. And if their zeal is such, then their violence will be as restricted as was that of Jesus, who wanted to win peoples' lives, not destroy them.

The recognition of the divine initiative and of the primary goal of restoring relationship with the Lord must characterize any Christian revolution, any Christian movement for liberation. The first reading, from the book of Exodus, provides us with an excellent preparation for Christian action.

In that reading God establishes a covenant with his people Israel. That it is God's movement, his initiative, is clear from the beginning: "I, the Lord, am your God, who brought you out of the land of Egypt, that place of slavery." That its primary goal concerns proper relationship with the Lord is evident in the first of the covenant's stipulations: "You shall not have other gods besides me."

When Israel failed to be guided by those principles, then the violence fell upon her. Then *she* had to be stripped naked, made like the desert, reduced to an arid land, and slain with thirst (Ho 2:5). But the purpose of such violence was that she might once again respond to the Lord as in the days of her youth and call him, anew, her husband (2:17).

It is not easy to recognize the presence of the kingdom, to know what it is demanding of us here and now. It deals with the transcendent. As Paul tells us, the cross of Christ can be a stumbling block and an absurdity, or it can be the power and wisdom of God. For his folly is wiser than we are, his weakness stronger than we.

This much is certain. Just as peace must be an attitude of mind and heart before it can be a program of action, so, too, Christian revolution must begin in our own hearts and in our own lives. That is what this season of Lent asks of us. Then we will recognize the kingdom and know what to do.

Fourth Sunday of Lent (B)
2 Chronicles 36:14-17, 19-23; Ephesians 2:4-10; John 3:14-21

"Just as Moses lifted up the serpent in the desert, so must the Son of Man be lifted up. . . ." That is hardly an auspicious way to begin a reading that is supposed to move people to enthusiastic service of the Lord. But this simply proves that the Bible is an adult book and needs an adult interpretation. That is what the homily is all about; it is called "breaking the Word."

Actually the passage from John's Gospel is rich with meaning. Together with what follows, it can provide enough material for a whole Lenten week's reflection. Perhaps we can help by "breaking" a few of the words here.

The serpent story is in Numbers 21:1-9. The grumbling Israelites were punished by the Lord with poisonous serpents. When they acknowledged their sins and cried for help, Moses, at the Lord's command, made a bronze serpent and mounted it on a pole. All who looked up at it recovered.

There is not space here to explain the meaning of that story as understood by its original author. For John it serves simply as a powerful illustration. Like the serpent, Jesus is "lifted up" on the pole of the cross. All who look up at him in faith will have eternal life.

Jesus is called "Son of Man." That title was applied in the Old Testament to a glorious figure to whom the Father would give dominion and kingship and whom nations and peoples would serve (cf. Dn 7:13-14). Obviously John is here anticipating the glory of the risen Jesus. During his earthly life Jesus begins to manifest the saving effects of his crucifixion and resurrection.

The mention of being "lifted up" does, as we have noted, refer to Jesus' crucifixion. But in John's Gospel it also refers to his resurrection and ascension (cf. also 8:28 and 12:32). There is one sweeping movement from earth to cross to heaven; this is his "being lifted up." All of it constitutes Jesus' paschal entrance to glory.

To believe this is to surrender one's self to the power of the exalted Lord. It is to enter into a new kind of life. John calls it "eternal life." This doesn't mean, primarily, life that doesn't end. Rather, it means a life lived in union with God, a sharing of his life. Because it is that, it will never end.

What follows in the Gospel passage elaborates on that basic insight of faith. What happens to Jesus is the climactic demonstration of God's love for the world. Could anyone believe in that Jesus and doubt God's love?

Still, some do not believe. God does not condemn them; he is too busy showing his love. Rather, they who do not believe condemn themselves. Their rejection of God sets them in that irreversible movement that leads to total estrangement from the Good. Such a person "is already condemned. . . ." Only a radical conversion can signal a change.

Are we part of that upward sweep with Jesus to eternal life? Or are we part of that downward movement to condemnation? The Gospel poses that question and tells us how we can know. "You will know them by their deeds" (Mt 7:16). Or, as our Gospel for today tells us, "Everyone who practices evil hates the light. . . . But he who acts in truth comes into the light, to make clear that his deeds are done in God."

God loves. Jesus saves. We believe and live his life. That is the sum of it.

Fifth Sunday of Lent (B)
Jeremiah 31:31-34; Hebrews 5:7-9; John 12:20-33

Taking care of "Number One" is a popular attitude now. There is no mistaking who is meant by "Number One"; it is one's own self. Selfishness has been made into a virtue, and sacrifice for others is seen as the act of a fool. This is the era of The Me Generation.

I doubt that anyone would seriously question the prevalence of this attitude. A rash of books has appeared in recent years with detailed information on how to look out for "Number One." Ayn Rand, the novelist, has openly championed selfishness in her writings. Christopher Lasch has described "The Culture of Narcissism." And advertisers, always among the first to latch on to current trends, are encouraging us to indulge in the luxuries they offer because "You can't do enough for yourself."

This is not just a matter of relaxing after a hard day's work, nor is it the case of an enjoyable vacation. It concerns a basic human attitude whereby the self must be served even at the expense of another. Even religion can be "used" for such a selfish purpose. It's easy to "find" God's love and use it as an escape from concern for others.

The philosophy of Number One is contradicted by today's Gospel reading. This passage from John is not, of course, the only one that places selflessness at the heart of biblical religion, but it is one of the most powerful.

The context of Jesus' words is the desire of "some Greeks" to see him. Apparently they are Greek-speaking Jews or Greek converts to Judaism. Their request is relayed to Jesus.

Jesus probably reads the request correctly as a desire to see some display of power. The recent raising of Lazarus had caused a furor. The Pharisees were plainly concerned that "the whole world has run after him" (12:19). Everyone wants to share the limelight. What better occasion for Jesus to say what he expects of his followers!

His words are totally unambiguous. No one can mistake their meaning. " . . . unless the grain of wheat falls to the earth and dies, it remains just a grain of wheat. But if it dies, it produces much fruit. The man who loves his life loses it, while the man who hates his life in this world preserves it to life eternal."

Some typical Semitic exaggeration here should be explained. "Hate" is often used in the Scriptures in the sense of loving less, of preferring something else, in fact, of making someone else "Number One." That is the meaning here. The use of our abilities, our talents, our lives for the service of others is the only way in which we will be truly fulfilled. We must "die" if we are to grow.

Jesus tells us this, and we want to do his will. We want to be the kind of follower that he wants us to be. And we know how difficult it is at times. Old "Number One" keeps demanding attention.

But we have a solid basis for hope in Jesus himself. He empowers our weakness with his strength. He had come, as we learn in this Gospel, to his "hour," the hour of crucifixion and glory. He was ready to be raised up on the cross and in resurrection, to lose his life and save it for all of us. " . . . and I—once I am lifted up from the earth—will draw all men to myself.

The choice is ours. We can determine to make ourselves "Number One" and end up an empty shell. Or, with Jesus, we can make the neighbor "Number One" and end up with more fulfillment than we ever dreamed of.

Passion Sunday (B)
Isaiah 50:4-7; Philippians 2:6-11; Mark 14:1—15:47

What is the Church trying to tell us in the readings for this Passion (Palm) Sunday? One writer says we are "to follow his (Christ's) example of humility, to die to self with him, that we may enter into eternal life with him." We must imitate Christ in his sacrificial death and then we will imitate him in exaltation to glory.

Excellent support exists for this interpretation. As an introduction to the hymn that he quotes for the Philippians, Paul tells them they should be humble and have Christ's attitude. Then the humility of Christ is starkly portrayed in his self-emptying to become "of human estate" and obedient to death on a cross.

The account of Jesus' passion and death is the Gospel reading. That Mark intends this as a reminder to Christians of what they, too, must be willing to imitate is made clear by him at the beginning of the second part of his book. There, after Peter's confession of Jesus' messiahship, Jesus explains his doctrine of the cross (8:34-38).

That doctrine can be summed up in Jesus' own words, "If a man wishes to come after me, he must deny his very self, take up his cross, and follow in my steps" (8:34). No doubt Mark had in mind, as he recorded this saying, that the reader of the Passion account would reflect on the possibility of imitating Jesus even literally in this kind of suffering. Some Christians have. But he would also, and more generally have in mind the acceptance of any kind of suffering for Jesus' sake "and the gospel's."

Both Paul and Mark emphasize the need to accept suffering in order to fulfill the Christian life. But they do this with the full realization that this is not a lonely, unassisted struggle. Both of them know that it is done "in Christ." And that means it is done in his strength, in the power of his suffering love for us. Jesus, for Mark and Paul, is more than a guru whom we follow; he is the very source, the ground of our ability to follow.

When we examine more closely the hymn to Christ, this becomes quite evident. It tells of him being "in the form of God," and *then* emptying himself to take "the form of a slave." Later it speaks of his exaltation on high and of his being given the name of "Lord."

As one scholar puts it, "Who could possibly imitate such an act or follow such a cosmic path?" This is not just a model for Christian living; this is divine redemption. Christ's ethical decision to empty himself of the external trappings of Godhead was not made to provide an incentive, but to provide salvation. *Because* the Christ did what he did, we can do what he asks us to do.

Throughout Mark's Passion account we can find a number of redemption themes that tell us exactly what the hymn tells us. When Mark notes that Jesus makes preparation for the feast "when it was customary to sacrifice the paschal lamb," could anyone doubt that he was also speaking of the *real* sacrificial lamb?

The redemption theme breaks powerfully into the open in the Eucharist account. Jesus says, "This is my blood, the blood of the covenant, *to be poured out on behalf of many*." Again, when he notes that, on Jesus' death, the temple veil was torn in two, what else did Mark have in mind except that a new era had just been inaugurated? Jesus' suffering and death now made direct access to the Father a possibility for all, not just for the high priest.

We are asked to see in Jesus a model for obedient suffering. This is what Passion Sunday tells us. But more profoundly it tells us that in Jesus we have the strength to suffer. In accepting him we accept the power to do as he did—all the way.

Easter Sunday (B)
Acts 10:34, 37-43; 1 Corinthians 5:6-8; John 20:1-9

Alleluia! That word belongs to Easter. We can understand why when we examine its meaning. It is a composite of two Hebrew words. The first, "allelu," is the second person, plural, imperative form of the verb *hallal*, meaning "to praise." The second word, "ia," is a shortened form of the personal name of God, Yahweh. Together, then, "alleluia" really means "praise the Lord!"

"Alleluia" was the outburst of the ancient Christian Church upon hearing of the resurrection of the Lord Jesus. It is presented in the book of Revelation as the victory song of the great assembly in heaven before the throne of the exalted Lord (19:1.3.4.6). For almost two thousand years now it has been the Christian response to the Easter event.

If Easter is true, then response there must be. "Alleluia"is an expected exclamation that acknowledges with wonder the author of the event. Our readings for this Sunday tell us of other responses to the Easter event.

One response is the proclamation of the story by designated witnesses. This is what we find in the first reading. The resurrection was witnessed by many people, as Paul tells us in 1 Corinthians 15:3-8. But that experience had to be interpreted and officially proclaimed. Peter did so that day in Caesarea.

Easter's meaning, Peter tells us, is that God has set this Jesus apart "as judge of the living and the dead." Exalted on high, he is now able to exercise that lordship that was only hinted at during his earthly existence. Then he had gone about doing good, healing, attesting to God's presence. Now he is truly Lord of all.

So much is this so, Peter adds, that "everyone who believes in him has forgiveness of sins through his name." Jesus' lordship, which results from his resurrection, is not some kind of cosmic composure that we admire from afar. It is real *for us*. If we truly believe in him, which means giving ourselves to this risen Lord, our sins are forgiven.

The second reading provides another response to the resurrection. It is closely tied to the first. If we truly believe in him and experience the forgiveness of sins, then our lives will be changed. We'll be singing our "Alleluias" in a renewed spirit and with clean hearts.

Paul gets this across to the Corinthian Christians by a play on the words used to describe the Jewish feast that Christians now celebrate as Easter. On the feast of Passover a lamb was sacrificed to celebrate Israel's liberation from slavery. And for one entire week unleavened bread was eaten to symbolize the newness of life; no yeast from the old life of slavery was used.

Paul sees Christ as the Passover lamb sacrificed for our freedom. And the unleavened bread represents our new life purged of any taint of the old life of sin. "Get rid of the old yeast to make of yourselves fresh dough, unleavened loaves. . . ." The newness of Easter Sunday must mean a newness in our lives.

And the third reading? It is the account of the discovery of the empty tomb. It tries to make those apostles' experience our experience. The response simply, yet profoundly, is, "He saw and believed." We get back again to the first movement of the human spirit responding to the resurrection—faith. Only in faith can we sing "Alleluia," "Praise the Lord!" For faith alone can tell us why we praise him.

Second Sunday of Easter (B)
Acts 4:32-35; 1 John 5:1-6; John 20:19-31

"Peace be with you." ". . . forgive men's sins." These two statements from the Gospel reading, one a prayer, the other a commission, can be seen as providing our theme for this second Sunday of Easter. The two are indissolubly related. Peace can only be had when one is united in faith and love to the Lord. When Jesus wished the disciples peace, forgiveness of sins was a necessarily accompanying charge.

In the biblical world peace is a dynamic reality best expressed as the fullness of God's blessings and, consequently, as the fullest relationship between ourselves and God, and ourselves and one another. We can readily see why peace in the biblical sense is incompatible with sin.

We can also understand why the whole of the Bible story could be titled "The Quest for Peace." The Bible story opens with the shattering of relationships between man and woman and God, between brother and brother, between nature and mankind, between all members of the human society (Gn 3-11). The Bible story closes with the prayer for the Lord's coming and for his grace uniting all (Rv 22:20-21).

The account of Easter Sunday's appearance of the risen Lord is an anticipated fulfillment of Revelation's prayer. Jesus grants them peace (his wish is already a grant!), breathes on them the Spirit, and empowers them to forgive sins. The fullness of the relationship now between the disciples and their Lord is vividly illustrated in Thomas' unreserved acceptance of his Lord and God. He needs no "proof"; Jesus himself is his assurance.

The first reading hardly needs a commentary. At least in the context of our theme there could be no clearer illustration of the kind of peace we have described above. The Christians "were of one heart and one mind." Each was concerned about the needs of the others so that the Christian community was marked by a true spirit of harmony and love.

Scholars are generally agreed that Luke has composed here an idealized summary of Christian history. There are two other such summaries in this part of Acts (2:42-47 and 5:11-16). They are idyllic pictures of the springtime of the Church. In Luke's mind, they are the emergent of the work of the Spirit, who came as the fruit of the resurrection. They are, therefore, "Easter pictures" painted by Luke.

The summaries are firmly rooted in history. While Luke has generalized and idealized that history, holding up to all Christian communities of all ages a mirror of what they should be, some Christians did live this kind of Easter peace. In Christianity the ideal and the real unite in those wondrous "surprises of grace."

In John's letter, the second reading, peace and forgiveness of sins are not mentioned. But he does emphasize the union of love between Christians and the Father that is the expression of peace. All of this he sees as the work of faith in Jesus the Christ, the Son of God.

Indeed, John uses the bold imagery of world conquest when he speaks of this faith. The world here is the world of sin, of Satan's domain. When this world lies defeated at the feet of the believer, then peace reigns in the believing heart. The union of love is achieved. Easter's work has been accomplished. Sins are forgiven and peace lives.

Third Sunday of Easter (B)
Acts 3:13-15, 17-19; 1 John 2:1-5; Luke 24:35-48

We hold the Bible to be inspired. By that we do not mean that the biblical authors were "inspired" as the poet or painter is said to be. Rather, we mean that God was actively at work in them, in no way restricting their own freedom of expression, but joining with them to produce these books. Because of inspiration we call the Bible the Word of God.

This has many important consequences, such as the power of the Word and its saving truth. But one consequence not sufficiently reflected on by many is the unity of the Bible's story. We should expect unity, since the one God is at work throughout. But what makes that unity remarkable is the vast diversity of human authors, of times and modes of composition, of historical situations and circumstances. Despite all this, it is one story.

Our first and third readings for this Sunday of Easter bring out one aspect of this magnificent unity. Peter's address, in the reading from Acts, begins with a mention of "the God of Abraham, of Isaac, and of Jacob. . . ." We might well wonder what these patriarchs are doing in the context of the cure of a crippled man. Perhaps these long dead fathers of the Jewish people were specially invoked by crippled persons in Jesus' time.

Actually, the reason for their mention is much more profound than that. Peter, like all the Jewish people of his day, had a strong sense of the unity of all history and of the unity of God's revelation in that history. God's curing of the crippled man in Jesus' name was one more act of saving grace that had begun with his call of the patriarchs.

In a sense, every time there is an act of saving grace, as here, a new and climactic bursting forth of God's love takes place. But, while this is wonderful to behold, it is really the continuation of an event begun with the patriarchs. One can say that, when God acted in their favor, history became pregnant with the cripple man's cure. Peter may not have put it in those words, but that is in effect what he is saying when he mentions those names.

That is the kind of unity the Scriptures unfold, the unity of a story that can be shared by all. And how do we know we are part of that story? By faith. As Peter says, it is faith that "strengthened the limbs of this man . . . , " faith in Jesus' name that brought him into the healing stream of God's saving history.

Note that the Gospel reading begins with a story. The disciples "recounted what had happened on the road. . . ." Granted, this is only a brief story, telling about what had happened that day. But St. Luke makes clear it is part of a much longer story, going all the way back to Moses. For the disciples the story of Jesus is everything, but Jesus reminds them that he can be understood only in terms of something that went before.

In a sense, Jesus is the story fully told. But even he does not stand in isolated splendor. The "law of Moses and the prophets and psalms" had spoken of him and prepared for him. Without them he cannot be fully known, for he is the final and climactic chapter of a story peopled by many others before him.

It is this unity of the Scriptures, the unity of a story to which we as Christians belong, that we need so badly today for our reflection. We of Western culture have become a mass of fragmented, disoriented, value-less individuals, without a story that we can take pride in and without a destiny in which we can hope. We seek the "instant" brands of salvation that soothe the psyche but don't cure the disease.

We must become believers again, believers in our roots, in our story as Christians, a story that the Church has been telling for some two thousand years. It's never too late to believe, because the story never dies.

Fourth Sunday of Easter (B)
Acts 4:8-12; 1 John 3:1-2; John 10:11-18

For John God's love is prior to and essential for any human value. "Love, then, consists in this: not that we have loved God but that he has (first) loved us . . ." (1 Jn 4:10). So long had John reflected on this conviction that he came to the conclusion, "God is love" (4:16).

John is not saying something radically new. The Scriptures had spoken of God's love from the beginning. One is always stirred when reading Hosea's description of the divine love being so overwhelming that it cannot destroy, "for I am God and not man . . ." (11:3-4.9). John's "God is love" is a fitting climax to a powerful biblical theme.

I mention this, not only because it is a theme always worthy of reflection, but also because it is a theme that ties our readings together. The Gospel reading offers several bits of evidence. The image of a shepherd, as Jesus pictures himself, speaks loudly of love and concern. In fact, Jesus would surely not have used the image (people might tend to overemphasize their own identity as the mindless sheep—hardly complimentary) had it not been for the picture of unceasing care that "shepherd" conveys.

As the good shepherd, Jesus is contrasted with the "hired hand" precisely in that the latter "has no concern for the sheep." He goes on to say that he "knows" the sheep. In the biblical world, to "know" a person is to embrace fully, not just with the mind but also with the heart. It is a special way of saying "love."

Finally, the word "love" is actually used when Jesus says, "The Father loves me for this. . . ." That could be misleading. It could suggest that the Father begins to show his love for the Son when the latter lays down his life for the sheep. That would be contrary to John's definition of God. Rather, it means that in the Son's laying down of his life for us the Father's love is fully manifested. Or, Jesus' love of us is really a sharing in the Father's love of Jesus.

The second reading is from the first of John's letters. From the very first line we are assured that love is the topic. Note that the love is seen as expressed in our relation to God. We read that God's love is found "in letting us be called children of God! Yet that is what we are." Again, as in the shepherd image, it is a relationship that expresses the theme. And the relationship between father and child is presumed to be one of love.

Certainly that is John's presumption when he says that being God's children shows "what love the Father has bestowed on us. . . ." By saying that, he is saying equivalently that being God's children means being filled with this love poured out. God's love both makes us his children and conditions our nature as his children. Thus, when John addresses his readers as "dearly beloved," as he does here, he is in a real sense defining what they are, people filled with God's love.

Admittedly, the theme of love is not explicit in the first reading, from Acts. It tells of Peter's explanation of the cure of a crippled man. He was cured "in the name of Jesus Christ. . . ." Peter concludes that "there is no other name in the whole world . . . by which we are to be saved."

The theme here, then, is salvation through Jesus Christ. But are we not justified in seeing this in the much larger context of why God sent his Son in the first place? Was it not to show his love? Peter knew that. Luke knew it, too. All we must do is live in the same conviction.

Fifth Sunday of Easter (B)
Acts 9:26-31; 1 John 3:18-24; John 15:1-8

When people get together, things happen. That's a sound sociological principle. In the arena of spirituality it is a necessary principle. Only in unity with others can growth take place.

Unity in community is a demand of biblical religion. Even in the direst period of Israel's history, when the people seemed scattered over the face of the earth, there was, as there had to be for survival, that "remnant" community. It was the seedbed required for a future.

Nowhere is this need for a united community illustrated in the New Testament so positively as in Luke's Acts of the Apostles. Several times in the early part of the book he offers summary statements on the growth of the young church. The explicit theme of these passages is that the believers "were of one heart and of one mind" (v.g., 4:32). Often there is mention of the extraordinary growth in members (v.g., 2:47). When people get together for good, good things happen.

That theme of unity and consequent growth is explicitly stated in our first reading in the final verse. But note how it is cleverly suggested by Luke in the preceding account about Paul. He arrives in Jerusalem for the first time after his conviction. Before that, as we know, all Jerusalem, Jewish and Christian, knew him as a zealous persecutor of the Christian Church. How would they see him now?

Luke tells us that the Christians "were all afraid of him. They even refused to believe that he was a disciple." That is understandable enough. But can we imagine how the young church would have fared if this greatest of all converts had been rejected? Only as part of the community would he be able to do what God had in mind for him to do. Luke knew that, which is why he dramatizes the account.

We learn that Barnabas, a highly respected disciple, took matters in hand and overcame their fears with his account of what happened to this "Saul" on the road to Damascus. Then Paul could walk about freely and speak openly about the Lord. That, in part, is why Luke can conclude with his mention of peace and growth. When Christians get together, Christian things happen.

In the Gospel reading the deepest roots of this "togetherness" are traced for us in the allegory of the vine and the branches. In order to be one with one another, Jesus tells us, we must be one with him and in him. If we do not live in him, we become "a withered, rejected branch. . . ." Withered and rejected, we can do nothing. Our deepest source of unity is absent.

In him we are "automatically" with others. Jesus hardly had in mind a vine with a single branch. And with them in him we "will produce abundantly. . . ." When Christians are together in Christ, they necessarily bear fruit.

What happens when Christians get together in Christ is spelled out in the second reading. Love, truth, and peace happen. For John love is primarily how God relates to us, but that love finds its necessary extension in our relation to others. When Christians get together in Christ, an explosion of love takes place.

For John truth is God's revealing Word, which becomes a principle working within us. It is there when we "believe in the name of his Son. . . ." It is loyalty to that belief and to the faith community. Truth is the expression of our unity in Christ.

For John peace is the fruit of Jesus' victory over the world. It is the bridging of the gulf between ourselves and the Father, the absence of discord and factions in the community. More positively, it is the wholeness of our own being and of the community in Christ. When Christians get together in Christ, wonderful things happen. Let them!

Sixth Sunday of Easter (B)
Acts 10:25-26, 34-35, 44-48; 1 John 4:7-10;
John 15:9-17

What comes down from heaven must be spread throughout the world. This is the pressing truth urged on us in the second and third readings this Sunday. God's love comes down to us in his Son. The Son extends that love to us. We must bring it to others. "As the Father has loved me, so I have loved you. Live on in my love." That is the way John's Gospel reading has it.

Of all the New Testament writers, John probed the mystery of Christianity most deeply. We find this both in the Gospel and in the Letters. That is why they make excellent companion readings. They almost always have a common theme.

This is not intended to belittle at all the power of Paul's insights or the beauty of the Synoptic Gospels' description of the Christ-event. They have explored for us the full extent of the Paschal Mystery. Jesus Christ and his lordship come fully alive in those pages.

What John has done in a unique way is to trace this Mystery more surely back to its ultimate source, the Father. The following statistics alone say something startling: Matthew refers to the heavenly Father 44 times, Mark 5 times, Luke 17 times, and John 122 times. In his first letter alone John mentions the Father 12 times, more than any other New Testament epistle, though most of them are much longer.

By this means has John brought an all-embracing unity to the whole of biblical revelation. He sees that what happened in Jesus of Nazareth was the culmination of what happened "in the beginning" (cf. Gn 1:1 and Jn 1:1). Jesus completes the Father's work. "I have given you glory on earth by finishing the work you gave me to do" (17:4).

By this means John has not only shown the marvelous unity of saving history. He has also brought out the unity of each particular action of God. What we mean by this is exemplified in our two readings from John. The Father's love, the Son's love, our love are not all different loves. They are all one, the Father's. This is the meaning of the "as" and the "so" in the first verse: "*As* the Father has loved me, *so* I have loved you." The Son loves us with the same love the Father expressed to him.

This we can perhaps understand and accept. But is our love of others the same as God's love? Isn't that verging on the sacrilegious?

There are several statements in our readings that provide an answer. Jesus tells us, "Live on in *my* love." His love, which is the Father's, continues on in us. Moreover, he says, "Love one another *as* I have loved you." There is that "as" again, which above equated the Son's love with the Father's. It now equates our love with the Son's.

Or, most dramatically of all, in John's Letter we read, "Beloved, if God has loved us so, we must have the *same* love for one another." There can be no doubt what is meant: it is one love, the Father's, that we share. We can even be bold enough to say that when we love one another, we are *perfecting* God's love of us (1 Jn 4:12). That is John's idea, not mine!

There is, of course, a difference. What God is by nature, we share by grace. "God is love," as John tells us; his nature is love. But his love in us is gift—and a gift must be accepted. It must be opened, admired, and gratefully acknowledged. Above all, it must be put to use.

God's love has come to us in Jesus Christ. We must make it contagious so that what has come down from heaven will spread throughout the world.

Ascension (B)
Acts 1:1-11; Ephesians 1:17-23; Mark 16:15-20

The biblical reflection for this Ascension Day centers on the authority of the glorified Christ. The word "authority" is in the Greek text of both the first and second readings; it is implied in the third reading.

The Gospel passage (Mk 16:15-20) is found in what is known as the "longer ending." The main body of the Gospel comes to a close in 16:8. What follows in vv.9-20 is attributed to a later inspired author at the end of the first century. The Church accepts this passage as canonical. A number of the statements found in vv. 9-20 have parallels in Matthew, Luke, and John.

From a theological perspective vv. 17-18 present the most difficulty. Specific signs are to identify those who "profess their faith": expelling demons through invoking the name of Jesus, speaking new languages, handling serpents, and laying hands upon the sick so that they might recover. These signs are named elsewhere in the New Testament as well. There is one exception: the power to drink "deadly poison without harm." This latter sign is mentioned in some second century non-canonical writings, e.g. *Acts of John*. To defend their religion, Christian writers of the second century appealed to these signs as authenticating it against the onslaught of the detractors of Christianity.

The Gospel points out that Jesus transferred his authority to the disciples; the signs he worked, they were to work. He commissions the eleven to go out and preach "the good news to all creation." Even in the longer ending the author has remained consistent with Mark 1:14 where Jesus appears proclaiming the good news of God. In fact the first words Jesus utters in Mark's account occur in 1:15, "This is the time of fulfillment. The reign of God is at hand! Reform your lives and believe in the gospel." This is the same command of Jesus at his Ascension; the disciples will wait for the Holy Spirit at Pentecost in order to have the strength to fulfill that command.

Ephesians, the second reading, emphasizes that the ascended Christ is far above every spiritual being, "principality, power, virtue, and domination." His name *Lord* is above all names; it is far better than even the names of the angels (Heb 1:4). In the parallel passage to Ephesians found in Colossians 1:16 Paul attacks the syncretistic religious systems of his day that gave great importance to angelic or similar spiritual beings. In fact, throughout the New Testament there is an attack on angel worship; it is opposed to the worship of the Father and of his Christ. Revelation 22:8-9 is an example of just such a polemic.

The Father has placed all of creation beneath the feet of his enthroned Son. The ascended Christ is the definitive sign that he has conquered; his is victory over sin, over death, over the dominion of the devil, over all disorder. All things must pay him homage; every knee bends before him (Ph 2:9-11).

Ephesians reads: the Father "has made him, thus exalted, head of the church." Literally this can mean that the Father has given him to be head of the Church. Thus Christ exalted is the gift of the Father to the Church. As head, Christ is part of it; the Church is his body. It complements Christ as the body complements the head. The Church has received the authority to carry on the mission of Christ. The Church is the extension of the exalted Christ in the world today. In the Church Christ shows his power and his glory today.

Acts reminds the reader that the apostles had been instructed by the living Lord that once he had departed from their midst they would receive authority (v. 8) from the Holy Spirit to enable them to be witnesses "even to the ends of the earth."

As the people of God we are challenged this day to be proclaimers that Jesus Christ lives and gloriously rules the universe. And we must proclaim with the authority of his name.

P.J.S.

Seventh Sunday of Easter (B)
Acts 1:15-17, 20-26; 1 John 4:11-16; John 17:11-19

The word "radical" comes from the Latin *radix*, meaning "root." A radical, then, is not necessarily a wild-eyed liberal seeking the overthrow of the existing order. A radical is more accurately one who wants to get to the roots of a problem, one who wants to do away with false or unwholesome accretions or distortions.

In this sense the Old Testament prophets were radicals. They wanted to restore the covenant relationship between God and people as it had been from the beginning, at the roots of Israel's existence. They wanted to assure a true continuity between the roots and the present. Those roots had been forgotten by so many, and what God had intended was no longer recognizable.

Any historical institution needs this kind of solid continuity. There will necessarily be development. No one can relive a past historical experience in its totality. Every period has its own unique contribution to make to the institution. But there must always be that chain stretching back to the beginning. The radical element must always remain.

This is clearly the concern of the apostles, in our first reading, as they gathered to select a successor to Judas Iscariot. After all, they were "the Twelve," the new representatives of the new house of Israel (Lk 22:30). They were the twelve foundation stones of the new Jerusalem (Rv 21:14). The roots of the Church had to be restored.

The Twelve, as a group, were unique and *as such* were not to be replaced. Once their witness to the resurrection had been assured, their mission, if not their office, could be continued by others, as long as the link with the roots could be maintained.

In the Gospel reading we find another, more subtle, and more profound concern for continuity. Jesus desires that his followers be "consecrated" as he himself is consecrated. In 10:36 the word is used of Christ and is explained as a commissioning of the Son; the Father sends him into the world.

This opens up a magnificent vista on the lay apostolate. We can see that apostolate as another and important thread of continuity with our roots in Jesus. All the faithful, not just the clergy and religious, are like Jesus, "sent into the world." "As you (Father) have sent me into the world, so I have sent them (the disciples) into the world."

We are not questioning the special role of ordained ministers. The first reading, among others, assures us of the need for this structural element in the Church. It is a visible and radical sign of continuity in the Church as well as a special role of service to the faithful.

But here we stress, as Jesus does, the sharing of all his followers in his mission. They are to be protected by the Father's "name," that is, by the saving reality of his person, just as Jesus was. They are to share his (Jesus') joy, which is to do what the Father wants. They share the Father's "word," the "good news," which is Jesus himself.

Finally, Jesus says he consecrates himself "for their sakes." He is referring here to the terrifying mission of giving his life for others. And even this mission all the faithful may be asked to share.

This is radical Christianity. When the faithful recognize their mission to re-live the life of Jesus, they are touching their roots in the most profound manner possible. There is no deeper meaning to being a Christian.

Vigil of Pentecost (ABC)
See page 46

Pentecost (ABC)
See page 47

Trinity Sunday (B)
Deuteronomy 4:32-34, 39-40; Romans 8:14-17; Matthew 28:16-20

History speaks—and that statement tells us how God chooses to reveal himself to us. In the events that occur in our lives we can detect the voice of God revealing his will. True, the Scriptures are the inspired interpretation of those events and of his will. But God speaks first in history.

This means, among other things, that even such a profound doctrine as the Trinity, which we celebrate this Sunday, is the result of the divine activity in human events. The triune God revealed himself as such, not primarily in a proposition, but in the things that occurred to his people.

The reading from Deuteronomy does not, of course, speak of Trinity. But it does lay down the necessary foundation for such a truth. It speaks urgently and eloquently of the uniqueness of Israel's God. ". . . the Lord is God in the heavens above and on earth below, and there is no other."

This says monotheism, one God. Without that conviction the later revelation of three Persons in the one God would make no sense. Polytheism, or many gods, would exclude a Trinity.

But notice how the uniqueness of this one God was made known. It was by the things this God did for his people, in leading them out of the land of Egypt "by testings, by signs and wonders, by war, with his strong hand and outstretched arm. . . ." "Did anything so great ever happen before?" This God is unique; he is one; he is the only one.

The exciting piece from Paul's letter to the Romans shows us the Trinity "at work." Instead of saying, "There are three Persons in one God," Paul tells us what Father, Son and Spirit are doing in our lives.

He speaks of divine adoption, of sonship, of children of God. But he couldn't have known of such a possibility unless he had known of *the* Son, Jesus Christ. In the life of that man from Nazareth God revealed himself as Father and Jesus as only Son. Because he is true Son, it is possible for us to receive adopted sonship.

But again, how did Paul know about this overwhelming truth? He didn't climb up into an ivory tower and think it out. No, he saw it in the lives of Jesus' followers and in his own life. All were addressing

God as their Father in the same intimate manner ("Abba") that Jesus did. He must be their Father, then, and they must be his sons and daughters. God revealed himself in life, in history.

What was the power working in Paul and others to enable them to call God "Father"? Paul says it was God's Spirit. In other letters he speaks of "experiencing" this Holy Spirit in the form of special gifts, such as preaching, healing, consoling. Here he speaks of the Spirit as witnessing to our being God's children by enabling us to call him "Abba" ("Father").

In the Gospel reading we find the most formal presentation of the doctrine of Trinity in the whole New Testament. The disciples are told to baptize "in the name (note the monotheistic singular) of the Father, and of the Son, and of the Holy Spirit."

But this staid formula is intimately associated with the Christian life. In Baptism the Trinity of Persons begins to be a part of our life. When we recite the creed this Sunday, those three Persons must be real, not just names. Ultimately, it is in our own history, in our own lives, that we learn the truth of Trinity, because that is where God speaks.

The Body and Blood of Christ (B)
Exodus 24:3-8; Hebrews 9:11-15; Mark 14:12-16, 22-26

"This is the blood of the covenant which the Lord has made with you. . . ." When Moses pronounced those words at the foot of Mt. Sinai, they must have struck an awesome note in the minds and hearts of the Hebrew people standing about. They had just seen Moses splash half of the blood of the young sacrificed bulls on an altar that symbolized God. The rest of the blood he sprinkled on them.

That strikes us as a strange rite, indeed. But it had a powerful meaning for those people. The blood, as always in the Scriptures, symbolized life. Sprinkled on the altar and on the people, it symbolized a community of life shared by God and Israel. God, moved only by love, was making a covenant with them. He shared his life; they responded by keeping his law.

This religious experience was what constituted Israel as a unique people, God's special people. Though they did not realize it at the time, that covenant was an anticipation of another and new covenant, whereby a new people of God would be constituted, this time with no restrictions as to race or nationality. Blood was to be a symbol of the new covenant, too.

The new covenant is, of course, the one made by God through Jesus Christ with all people. And the blood of Christ, shed on Calvary, symbolizes the new life God shares with us.

The second reading describes the superiority of Jesus' sacrifice over that of the bulls' and of the new covenant over the old. The author says that Christ passed through a "more perfect tabernacle" and entered the sanctuary of heaven. He is referring to his passing from earthly life through suffering and death to a new life with the Father, a new life that would be shared with the new people of God.

In doing this, Jesus did something that was foreshadowed by what the high priest did in the Old Testament. The priest entered into the sanctuary in Jerusalem and sprinkled the blood of animals on the altar and the ark of the covenant. This symbolized the new life effected by the remission of sins. The author of our reading asks how much more efficacious is the blood of Jesus in cleansing our consciences.

Jesus did this "once for all," as our reading puts it. The sacrifice of Jesus was so radically effective that the Father accepted it as valid for all ages. Jesus does not have to shed his blood anew every time the eternal covenant is renewed.

Still, if all the people are to share this life of God through the covenant, there must be some rite whereby men and women of succeeding ages can effectively be made a part of the people of God. That is what our Gospel reading is all about.

One of the characteristics of biblical religion is the awesome realism of its liturgical celebration. We saw it in the first reading when the blood of life was sprinkled on the altar and people. In the Gospel reading it is present when Jesus takes bread and wine and constitutes them as his body and blood.

Jesus doesn't say, "This will remind you of, or will stand for my body and blood." They *are* his body and blood. Moreover, that blood is "the blood of the covenant." Jesus uses the same words Moses used. He is speaking of new life shared by a new people of God.

It is good to have a feast like *The Body and Blood of Christ*. It reminds us of the tremendous depths of our faith, of our need to surrender completely to this loving God of the new and everlasting covenant.

Second Sunday in Ordinary Time (B)
1 Samuel 3:3-10, 19; 1 Corinthians 6:13-15, 17-20; John 1:35-42

In the Hebrew language the word usually translated "obey" means literally "listen to." The same is true of the Greek word used in the New Testament. The psychological and spiritual significance of this literal meaning is considerable and worthy of our reflection. It will help us to appreciate our readings for this Sunday.

When we think of the word "obey," we think of someone doing exactly what one has been asked or told to do. Obedience is gauged by conformity to the spoken or written word. This is what is meant by "obeying the law." An exclusive emphasis on this leads to a dead legalism or conformism.

Underlying the biblical words is the thought of one hearing or reading the words of another and allowing those words to enter into one's mind and heart. Then, in accord with the truth and goodness of those words and in accord with one's openness to others, a person will act.

Note that the emphasis is not on the action. Rather, it is on the acceptance of the word. If the word is a "good" word and if the acceptance is genuine and wholehearted, the action will inevitably follow. That is why St. Paul could speak of true circumcision as flowing from the spirit, not the letter of the law (Rm 2:29).

In our first reading from the book of Samuel we hear of the young lad ministering in the temple. One night, while sleeping, he heard a voice calling out to him. Mistakenly thinking it was the aged priest, Eli, Samuel went to him to find out what he wanted. After the third time, Eli realized that the Lord was calling the youth and told him to "listen."

This Samuel did. It was not an order or command that the Lord gave to Samuel. It was the revelation of his plan for Eli's family. The next day the young minister reported the Lord's saying to Eli. Samuel had obeyed the Lord; he had listened to his words and accepted them.

At the end of the reading we hear that "Samuel grew up, and the Lord was with him, not permitting any word of his to be without effect." Because he had obeyed the Lord in accepting his words and allowing them to have free play within his being, so the Lord made Samuel's word effective, too. He would be obeyed or listened to by the people.

In the Gospel reading the word "obey" is not used. But the whole emphasis of the passage is on the attitude of openness to the Lord, of accepting his word and his person. When the Baptist pointed to Jesus and said to the two disciples, "Look! There is the lamb of God!", they "heard what he said, and followed Jesus."

This is obedience in the biblical sense. Andrew and John accepted the words that described Jesus and the act of following necessarily took place. It does not say that they heard the words and believed them. The very acceptance of the words into their hearts was an act of obedient faith. The action that followed was the result or manifestation of an obedience that had already taken place.

Obedience, then, is a matter of the mind and heart before it is a matter of action. In fact, the action that is done in conformity to the letter of the law but with an inner spirit of unwillingness and rebellion is not an act of true obedience.

But if we can say with the young Samuel, "Speak, Lord, your servant listens," and mean it, then we have already obeyed. We will do what is right.

Third Sunday in Ordinary Time (B)
Jonah 3:1-5, 10; 1 Corinthians 7:29-31; Mark 1:14-20

Schlemiel, a Yiddish term, describes one for whom everything turns out contrary to the way it was planned. Some say Jonah was a typical schlemiel. He appeared a born loser; his plans were constantly frustrated.

As the story has it, Jonah is called by God to preach repentance to the people of Nineveh, the capital of Assyria. But Jonah will have none of this; he finds it unthinkable that these ancient enemies of God's people should be worthy of a prophet's time and effort. So he flees on a ship bound for Tarshish, "away from the Lord."

But his escape plans are brought to naught. A violent storm threatens to break up the ship. Thinking Jonah responsible for the storm, the sailors cast him overboard. He is swallowed by a large fish and three days later spewed forth upon the shore, alive to preach in Nineveh.

Hearing Jonah's oracle of pending destruction of the city, the people do penance and turn to the Lord. Disgusted at this outcome, the prophet leaves the city and finds shade and rest under a wide-leafed plant. But even this simple pleasure is to be denied him. The plant is attacked by a worm and dies. Reflecting on his misadventures Jonah cried out, "I would be better off dead than alive."

The short book of Jonah, from which our first reading is taken, is a classic tale of human frustration, the story of a schlemiel. But it is also much more than that. It is the story of the victory of God's will against all odds. That is why the reading was chosen; it announces the repentance of a sinful people who could not "distinguish their right hand from their left."

Jonah, however, is not just an expendable foil in the hands of God. He is, despite everything, the indispensable instrument for the divine saving activity. He may be nothing, but by reason of God's choice, which obviously is not based on anything in Jonah, he becomes everything.

The Gospel reading presents us with an entirely different literary form. It is the account of Jesus' first public appearance in Galilee and his announcement of the presence of God's Kingdom. There is a resemblance to the story of Jonah inasmuch as the reaction to Jesus' preaching is to be repentance and faith.

But the Church, in choosing the reading, seems to have wanted emphasized the account of Jesus' call of his first followers, Simon, Andrew, James, and John. They, too, like Jonah, are not much by worldly standards. Mark states quite simply, "they were fishermen."

But Jesus chooses them. That is the decisive point. By reason of that choice they become "fishers of men." They will be the indispensable instruments of the Lord for the spread of the Gospel throughout the Mediterranean world.

There are a number of contrasts between the story of Jonah and the account of Jesus' appearance. The most notable one is between Jonah's first reaction to the call and those Galilean fishermen's reaction. The one was escape; the other was total acceptance.

The one major similarity, however, namely, the decisive call of the Lord, is what binds our two accounts together. When he calls, whatever we may have been before, we become conquerors of the world (1 Jn 5:4-5). And he has called you. That is as certain as is your reading of this column.

Fourth Sunday in Ordinary Time (B)
Deuteronomy 18:15-20; 1 Corinthians 7:32-35; Mark 1:21-28

Who is he? For this and the next twelve Sundays *in Ordinary Time* the Gospel reading will center on this question. Not until the twenty-fourth Sunday will the Markan reading provide a tentative answer to the question. The full disclosure by a Roman centurion comes only toward the end of Mark's Gospel (15:39).

Since Mark's Gospel is the basis for the third readings of this liturgical year, it would be well for us to get into the spirit of the drama he has written, to listen to his story as for the first time, and to experience the amazement of the crowds as Jesus makes his presence felt among them.

When we mention "his presence," that is not an idle expression. It is at the heart of the mystery of who Jesus is. Somehow that presence puts an indelible mark on the moment of encounter. It makes that moment meaning-filled, power-filled, grace-filled. When we hear the inspired words tell of his saving presence, we know something great has happened. It is not a fond memory of something past. It is not a hopeful promise of something yet to come. Rather, the "now" has been transformed.

We are attempting to explain what Mark means when he speaks of Jesus' "authority." Twice in this Sunday's reading does the word occur. In both cases it is associated with his teaching. The surface meaning would suggest that Jesus knew what he was talking about, that we can accept what he says just on his word alone.

Authority does mean that for Mark. But it also means much more. It signifies that mysterious, dynamic presence which gives meaning to the "now," as we tried to explain above. Note that the second time the word is used in connection with Jesus' "teaching," there is no teaching involved, in our understanding of the word. It refers to the cure of the demoniac.

So, whatever Jesus says or does is marked with this "authority." Those who experience it are caught up in amazement. "The people were spellbound. . . ." "All who looked on were amazed." "What does this mean?" Who is he?

The demon knows who he is. Mark has this supernatural being expose Jesus' identity right from the beginning. The bystanders, of course, would not have understood. But Mark's readers, including all of us, would be able to penetrate the secret in part. Our curiosity is aroused by this spirit's words. What do they really mean?

Recall that in the ancient world it was thought that if someone knew another's name, he or she could exercise power over the other. This was surely in the demon's mind. By calling Jesus "the holy One of God," he felt that Jesus would acknowledge defeat and retire from the scene. It didn't work. Only God can exercise that kind of name-power (Is 45:4). When others try to, it's only magic.

But the title is an interesting one nonetheless. "The holy One of God" evokes the title used by Isaiah of God, "the Holy One of Israel" (1:4; 5:19). Isaiah appears to have created this title after his mysterious encounter with God in his vocation vision (chapter 6). The shattering power of that scene, and especially the seraphim's cry of "Holy, holy, holy is the Lord of hosts" left the young prophet drenched with an overwhelming sense of the divine majesty. From that time on for him, God is "the Holy One of Israel."

Is this the sense Mark wants to leave with us as we encounter Jesus in his word? No doubt it is something like that. Now if we can open our minds and hearts to his saving presence, we will grow perceptibly through the year in our profound understanding of who he is.

Fifth Sunday in Ordinary Time (B)
Job 7:1-4, 6-7; 1 Corinthians 9:16-19, 22-23; Mark 1:29-39

"Evangelizing is in fact the grace and vocation proper to the Church, her deepest identity." Those are the words of Pope Paul VI in his Apostolic Exhortation, "On Evangelization in the Modern World." They are strong, challenging words. They tell all of us, who are the Church, that we must evangelize if we are to keep our identity as Christians.

Pope Paul's charge was evoked, in large part, by what the apostle Paul says to the Corinthians in our second reading. We can also find a grounding for it in the Gospel text.

Paul's words are particularly galvanizing. The opening verse of the passage reads literally this way from the Greek, "For if I evangelize, it is not a boasting on my part; for necessity is laid upon me. Woe to me if I do not evangelize!" What he is saying is that if he does not evangelize, it would be like not breathing. He can't exist without it.

That is why he goes on to say that he doesn't expect any recompense for his ministry. We know, as a matter of fact, that Paul did receive aid from his congregations (cf. Ph 4:14-16). What he means, above all, is that there can be no real recompense for evanglizing, just as no one gets paid for breathing. He simply has to do it, whether anyone gives him something or not.

We find this same note of compulsion in the Gospel reading, although it is not as explicitly stated as in Paul's letter. In the whole of the first chapter of the Gospel Mark uses the word "immediately" (at least in the Greek) some ten times. And just in the three verses that tell the story of the cure of Peter's mother-in-law, it is found twice, though translated differently. (The *New American Bible* gets in the spirit of things by adding one more in v. 31).

The disciples did not rush to tell him about Simon's mother-in-law. The mother-in-law did not rush to serve him. Rather, the use of the word expresses Mark's overwhelming sense of urgency in getting the message across. And, no doubt, he wants to say that Jesus himself was in a hurry to proclaim "the good news of God."

For Jesus evangelizing meant preaching the presence of God's reign. For Paul it meant preaching that the reign was fulfilled in Jesus Christ. And so preaching the gospel came to be most closely identified with evangelization.

But more profoundly we can say that evangelizing means bearing witness to a deep faith conviction. Both Jesus and Paul bore witness by preaching, as our priests and deacons continue to do today. But one can also bear witness to that good news by teaching it to others, by suffering, and by one's way of life.

In all of these cases we are saying, "Look! This is what the gospel makes me do. And I do it gladly because the word of the Lord lays this joyful burden on me." Thus the simplest Christian is able to tell others, just by a way of life, the good news. The simplest Christian can evangelize.

We do not evangelize in order that we might convert people. It is true that we would like to see the unchurched converted. But it is God who does the converting. We serve only as his instruments. But as his instruments, we are important, even necessary, all of us, for his work. For in evangelizing, as Pope Paul told us, we find our identity as Christians.

Sixth Sunday in Ordinary Time (B)
Leviticus 13:1-2, 44-46; 1 Corinthians 10:31—11:1; Mark 1:40-45

One of the features of Mark's Gospel, which is the principal source for the third readings of this liturgical year, is what scholars call the "messianic secret." By it is meant the frequent caution Jesus urges on those he cures. They are not to say anything about the cure to others. We have an example of the messianic secret in this Sunday's Gospel text. Jesus tells the cured leper to say nothing to anyone.

The ostensible purpose of this caution is to avoid a false understanding of Jesus and his mission. He was aware that many would interpret such miracles as signs of the messiah, but *as they understood that figure,* that is, in a political or nationalistic sense. We know that is how some did interpret them.

Mark has made use of this device for his own special purpose, since it appears so often in his Gospel. Scholars are not agreed on the details of that purpose. But we can be certain of some aspects of it.

First, it would have been quite understandable for Jesus to have actually urged caution at times. Second, Mark's "systematic" use of the secret as a literary device does add drama to his story of Jesus. Third, evidently it didn't always work. People didn't keep quiet. Our passage is a prime example of that.

Two weeks ago our commentary was about the mystery of Jesus' identity as Mark presents it. The second point mentioned above concerns that mystery. Here I would like to say something about the third point. "The man went off and began to proclaim the whole matter freely, making the story public." This former leper certainly wasn't bothered about any "messianic secret."

Last week we spoke of the sense of urgency found in Mark's Gospel. One of the signs was the frequent use of the word "immediately." Here we have another sign. Despite commands to the contrary, the good news will go out. It cannot be stifled.

This occurs elsewhere in Mark. Thus, unclean spirits would fling themselves down at Jesus' feet and call him "Son of God," despite his stern warning "not to reveal who he was" (3:11-12). And, after the cure of the deaf-mute, we read, "Then he enjoined them strictly not to tell anyone; but the more he ordered them not to, the more they proclaimed it" (7:36).

This kind of notoriety did lead to misunderstanding and, even more, to opposition from the authorities. Mark knew that, of course, but he doesn't condemn those who acted in this way. He seems to be sympathetic to their uncontrollable enthusiasm.

Is the principle that Paul sets us in the second reading, applicable here? He writes to the Corinthians, "The fact is that whether you eat or drink—whatever you do—you should do all for the glory of God." It would seem that it is applicable, at least in a broad sense.

The point Paul is making here is not the eating and drinking, though they provided the context for his principle, but the overwhelming importance of God's glory, the praise of his majesty. In whatever we do that must be, whether consciously or not, our ultimate purpose. That flows from the very nature of God himself.

This would seem to be behind the excited proclamation of the former leper, of the cured deaf-mute, even though against their will, of the unclean spirits. God's glory is all-encompassing. Even the "messianic secret" must give way before it.

Seventh Sunday in Ordinary Time (B)
Isaiah 43:18-19, 21-22, 24-25; 2 Corinthians 1:18-22; Mark 2:1-12

The axiom, "To err is human, to forgive divine," is true in a much stricter sense than most people realize. When one fully appreciates the nature of sin, one begins to see why forgiveness is one of the most proper activities of God.

The radical meaning of sin is rejection of God. Harming other people, committing adultery, seeking one's own glory at the expense of others—all these are wrong, but they are sins only because they necessarily involve a rejection of God.

In all these cases the offended party can forgive the wrong done, in the sense of not seeking revenge and of restoring friendship. But strictly speaking, he or she cannot forgive the sins. In sin God is offended, and he alone can speak for himself.

But there is added reason why God alone can forgive sins. In the biblical sense sin is not just the action committed or omitted. It is a totally new and radical direction taken by the sinner *away* from God. Through sin the sinner is set in movement toward a new destiny.

That is why the Hebrew word for sin includes also the consequences of sin. The whole movement of sin, with its necessary end of self-destruction, is envisioned in the word "sin." Jesus expresses this clearly when he says, "whoever does not believe is already condemned" (Jn 3:18). And so, in the final analysis, sinners judge themselves in the moment of committing sin.

Given this humanly irreversible movement initiated by sin, it follows that only God can step in and reverse the movement and forgive the sin. When God forgives the sin, he does not simply forget it. He wipes it out. And he *must* do this if the movement toward condemnation is to be reversed.

Perhaps we can appreciate now why the Scriptures are filled with pleas to God to forgive sins. One of the most powerful prayers for forgiveness is found in Lamentations where the Hebrew text reads literally, "Convert us, Lord, and we will be converted" (5:21). No human being can convert another, nor can we convert ourselves. Only God can bring us back to himself.

This could be a dreadful situation were it not for the fact that God is a forgiving God. He is one who wills to forgive the sinner if the sinner will accept this divine forgiveness. Notice the great emphasis on the divine initiative in our first reading. It is God who makes all things new, who wipes out, for his own sake, the offenses of his people.

In the Gospel reading Jesus forgives the paralyzed man's sins before he heals him. The paralysis is a sign of that deeper evil, and Jesus wills to remove that first, to reverse the movement toward condemnation. The healing of the paralysis is a far simpler matter.

In the context of what we have said the reaction of the crowd is understandable. They know full well that the reversal of the movement toward condemnation, the forgiveness of sins, is a properly divine act. "Who can forgive sins except God alone?"

What is just as wonderful as this forgiving act of Jesus is that God willed to continue this forgiving grace through his Sons's representatives in the Church. In the Sacrament of Reconciliation they do not, of course, forgive sins on their own; they extend absolution in God's name alone. This is at the basis of Matthew's statement, in his version of our story, that the crowd "praised God for giving such authority to men" (9:8).

Eighth Sunday in Ordinary Time (B)
Hosea 2:16-17, 21-22; 2 Corinthians 3:1-6; Mark 2:18-22

In the ancient world, covenants, or treaties between two parties, were usually solemn affairs. Ritual actions and rich symbolic language celebrated the new relationship between the two. Blood, the symbol of life, was a frequent part of the ceremony. They took their covenants seriously indeed.

Israel was no exception. When God initiated a covenant with this people, it was celebrated in a distinctly solemn manner. After the covenant code regulating Israel's conduct in her new life as God's people had been proclaimed (Ex 20-23), Moses took the blood of bulls and sprinkled it on an altar (symbolizing God) and on the people. This ritual signified the new life between them. Then Moses declared, "This is the blood of the covenant which the Lord has made with you . . ." (Ex 24:3-8).

In the light of such liturgical ceremonies we would expect God to be seen as a highly exalted figure who would be the object of absolute service by his people. And he was. The covenant form, modeled after treaties between a great emperor king and vassal nations, suggests that God was looked upon as the great King, sovereign of all (cf. Ps 95-99).

What is unique to Israel and her religious convictions is that she was able to introduce into this solemn framework of royal lordship the picture of her covenant God as a loving spouse. And she did this without losing any sense of the divine sovereignty. Our first reading from the prophet Hosea is a telling illustration.

Actually, the picture is even more powerful than might appear. What is presupposed here is that Israel, once bound in marriage to her divine covenant partner, had abandoned him. Like any common harlot, she had given herself to other gods. She had made a mockery of covenant love.

It is in that context that our passage is to be read. The Lord will draw her to himself again. He will lead her out to the desert where she had first loved him. The "valley of Achor," leading into the fertile plains of Palestine, symbolizes the new hope that Israel will enjoy.

The exuberant language of love and mercy, justice and fidelity in the last two verses signals the intimacy and the tenderness of the relation that God wants to share with his people. The only problem was whether their hearts were large enough to accept that kind of love.

So powerfully had Hosea painted this picture of mutual love between God and Israel that other prophets took up the theme after him (Jr 11:2; Zp 3:17; Ez 16:59-63). And Paul gave the theme a new depth of meaning by applying it to the love of Christ for his Church (Ep 5:22-33).

Jesus, too, as we might expect, was aware of this imagery and uses it himself. The Gospel reading speaks of the time when the bridegroom will be taken away from them. This is a reference to his death and is presented as a reason for the later fasting practice in the

Church. But the remarkable point is that Jesus is clearly presenting himself as a bridegroom. The implication is that his followers are the bride.

Did Jesus see himself as fulfilling the role of the Lord God in the Old Testament? That may be difficult to prove. But from the whole of the New Testament we know that Jesus is our sovereign Lord and that he does love us with the same love the Father had for his people. And the question Israel faced remains for us: are our hearts big enough to accept this love?

Ninth Sunday in Ordinary Time (B)
Deuteronomy 5:12-15; 2 Corinthians 4:6-11; Mark 2:23—3:6

One of the more beneficent effects of the Second Vatican Council was the recognition and repudiation of the spirit of legalism that infested so many of our religious observances. It is not that fasting, abstinence, and other similar practices were wrong; too often, however, they were observed solely out of fear of "breaking the law."

As frequently happens in the psychological aspects of changes of this kind, one extreme begets another. An almost compulsive need to observe the law led, in many cases, to total neglect of all that was good in the law. One example is the Sunday obligation. "Missing Mass on Sunday" was once considered a mortal sin except for the gravest of reasons, which were often interpreted without due regard for the overriding law of love. Now some think that any reason, even the most selfish is a valid excuse.

This phenomenon is not unusual. It is part of the dialectic of religious growth. But it does not mean that constant effort should not be made to achieve reconciliation of the two poles of thought. Often this is best done by an examination of the historical sources of the religious practice.

The word "sabbath" is in some way associated with a root Hebrew verb meaning to rest or cease from doing something. The origin and precise nature of the original Sabbath rest are lost in obscurity. But no exact parallel to the Jewish Sabbath has yet been found in other ancient religions.

Although in Israel the Sabbath was always given some religious meaning, the humanitarian aspect of it was more dominant in the earlier period.

Note that in the first reading for this Sunday the Deuteronomist emphasizes cessation from labor for everyone, even for animals. The religious motivation is the reminder that God had made their slavery in Egypt cease with the exodus.

In a later period the Sabbath rest was associated with the rest of God on the seventh day of creation, as narrated in the book of Genesis (2:1-4). This gave a much more profound, even cosmic, dimension to the observance, which led to the prescription of various rites in connection with the Sabbath.

This development, in itself, was quite legitimate. It was actually a recognition of the profoundly religious nature of all creation. But many were not able to appreciate the depths of this kind of recognition. For them the rites led to a legalism of good works. The rite became more important than the underlying reality.

That a legalism of this kind existed among a number of the Jews at the time of Jesus is too fully attested to be denied. We must, however, avoid the absurd extreme attributing it to all Jews of the time, just as we would hope that no one would accuse all Catholics of having attended Sunday Mass in a legalistic spirit.

The Gospel reading is illustrative of the kind of legalism that existed and of Jesus' attitude towards it. From other sources we know that thirty-nine kinds of work were forbidden on the Sabbath; of these preparing food and visiting the sick were two examples. We can understand, then, why some would consider plucking and rubbing grain and curing the sick violations of the Sabbath.

The reply given by Jesus to the objection posed by his opponents is, as usual, the most concise summary possible of his conviction. "The sabbath was made for man, not man for the sabbath." There is the principle; anything else is only commentary on it.

Jesus was not overthrowing the Sabbath. He would never have said that observance of the Sabbath depends on the whim of the believer. As a Jew, Jesus observed the Sabbath laws, to the best of our knowledge, in all their details. There was one notable exception: when the dignity of the human person stood in the way of the law. If that principle is observed, there never need be conflict between religious practice and deep human concern.

Tenth Sunday in Ordinary Time (B)
Genesis 3:9-15; 2 Corinthians 4:13—5:1; Mark 3:20-35

This Sunday's Gospel contains three literary units. In the first Jesus rejects the charge that he casts out demons by the power of the prince of demons. The second relates the saying about the unforgivable sin against the Holy Spirit. In the third Jesus explains who are his true family: those who do God's will.

The third saying provides a key to the interpretation of the whole. Jesus is told that his mother and brothers are outside seeking him. He replies that his mother and brothers are those who do the will of God.

Anyone acquainted with the Semitic penchant for paradox will recognize that this is no rejection by Jesus of his earthly relatives. It is, rather, a forceful manner of asserting a more profound bond among people than that of blood relationship. That deeper bond is the common acceptance of the Father's creating and saving will. Any other bond of unity is secondary to this.

The Gospels are unanimous in depicting Jesus precisely as the one who came to do his Father's will. For John this is almost a definition of Jesus: ". . . I seek not my own but the will of him who sent me" (5:30).

Similarly does John define those who belong to God's family. Some of the Jews claimed for themselves that relationship because they were descendants of Abraham. But Jesus replied that they only are of God who hear God's words and do his will. These are the true sons of Abraham (Jn 8:39-47).

It is in this same sense that Jesus defines his true relatives. Once man has recognized God's power radically at work in the world, then is he more radically related to that world and to all who are in it. Blood relationship cannot transcend physical nature. Accepting God's reign makes it possible to transcend all nature.

Returning now to the first unit, we note that, in New Testament theology, demons represent those powers that obstruct or try to destroy God's reign. If Jesus were acting by their power, then he would be acting against the very purpose for his coming. He would be working against the bond of unity he had come to restore. He would be abetting the enemies of his true family, the family of his Father.

Finally, in the saying about the sin against the Holy Spirit, we have a deeper explanation of the manner in which God builds up his family. Throughout the Scriptures God's Spirit is presented as that divine power at work in created reality bringing about salvation. God's Spirit is his saving power reconciling man to God.

Jesus says that any sin that man commits can be forgiven, even a sin against Jesus (Matthew 12:32). But to sin against the Holy Spirit here means to deny that the Spirit is at work. It means, therefore, to deny that God has any intention to save. Obviously, by doing this man places himself outside the pale of salvation. He rejects the one factor that is capable of having him repent of any sin.

The whole Gospel thus presents a rich theology of the true Christian family. That family is marked by the acceptance of God's will. And, more deeply, it is marked by an openness to the Spirit that makes the acceptance of God's will possible.

How strong is our faith? How deeply do we penetrate this secular reality of which we are a part and see God's Spirit at work? To recognize that Spirit is to be able to call God "Father" (Rm 8:15-16). It is to establish a relationship with others who recognize the same Spirit, a relationship that knows no earthly bounds whatever.

Eleventh Sunday in Ordinary Time (B)
Ezekiel 17:22-24; 2 Corinthians 5:6-10; Mark 4:26-34

This Sunday's Gospel is about the Kingdom of God. Jesus tells two parables, one concerning the seed that grows and is harvested, the other concerning the grain of mustard seed. The Gospel closes with the observation about Jesus' use of parables.

What immediately strikes us in these parables is the concept of growth. It is almost a mysterious growth. In the first parable the seed grows while the man who sowed it sleeps; he doesn't even know how it grows. In the second it is the small mustard seed that grows into a large shrub capable of sheltering the birds of the air.

When Mark wrote his Gospel he was keenly aware of the humble origins of Christianity and of its rapid spread throughout the Mediterranean world. There is little doubt he intended to underline that rapid spread in his recounting of these parables of Jesus.

But he was also convinced that this growth was not the work of people. It could only be adequately explained by the Spirit of God working in the world. It is true that apostles, evangelists, and prophets announced the Kingdom to all the different communities. But since Mark would have been aware of Paul's theology of the charisms of the Spirit, he would not have hesitated to see God at work in this phenomenon.

Modern critical analysis has made it possible to determine, to some extent, the purpose Jesus had in telling these parables. He would have intended, above all, to emphasize, not the growth, but the end result, the harvesting of the grain and the sheltering of the birds of the air.

In other words, Jesus, in his unique consciousness of himself as the final breakthrough of God's saving power in the world, would have focused on the significance of that breakthrough. Through him God's kingdom, or rule, was inaugurated. It could not but achieve its goal.

Here we find the principle for the tension that exists in all the New Testament writings. It is between what God has already done in Jesus Christ and what still remains to be done in humankind. It is the tension between faith in salvation achieved and hope in salvation yet to be achieved.

We need a theology of hope today perhaps more than at any time in our history. When nuclear bombs, injustice, inflation, and poverty seem about to overwhelm us, we need the conviction of the God of the future, the God whose reign of peace and justice will finally be established.

But that hope is barren without faith in a God who has made a promise and already fulfilled it, in an anticipated manner, in Jesus Christ (cf. 2 Cor 1:19-20). In fact, it is that anticipated fulfillment which makes our hope all the more intense.

This Sunday's Gospel confirms our hope. The Kingdom of God is in our midst. It is growing, even though we know not how. And Jesus Christ, who first uttered the parables, is himself our assurance.

But this is not a Gospel of complacency. Mark would have been the last one to claim that we need do nothing. He was writing for Christians who were giving their lives for the "good news" of salvation for all. For such as these the parables are a reminder that, in the face of apparently total human inadequacy, God's Kingdom is at work.

Twelfth Sunday in Ordinary Time (B)
Job 38:1, 8-11; 2 Corinthians 5:14-17; Mark 4:35-41

For this Sunday the Gospel reading is Mark's account of the storm at sea. Jesus, asleep in the stern of the boat, is awakened by his frightened disciples and calms the storm. The reading closes with the disciples' expression of wonder about who this man can be.

That closing expression provides the key to the passage and, in a sense, to the whole of Mark's Gospel. Who *is* this man? Throughout his Gospel Mark emphasizes the mystery of Jesus and his revelation. Mark, of course, is aware of Jesus' identity. He states it quite clearly in the opening verse of the first chapter: he is writing the Gospel of Jesus, the Christ and Son of God.

Mark is trying to evoke for his readers something of the sense of mystery that surrounded the Person of Jesus as he carried out his mission in Palestine. He wants us to experience that slowly awakening realization of the profound meaning of Jesus that was experienced by his followers in Galilee and Judea.

The act of faith in Jesus Christ is much more than a simple declaration that Jesus is the Christ and Son of God. It is far more than a creed recited on a Sunday morning. It is above all an encounter with a Person, an encounter that entails wonder, awe, puzzlement, doubt, amazement, and then, finally, a full-fledged confession torn from a heart that knows it has met God.

Mark seems to have designed his Gospel to reach two distinct climaxes, both of them confessions of faith. The first is Peter's confession of Jesus as the Christ, that is, as the one anointed by God and sent to announce the Kingdom of God (cf. 8:29). The second is the centurion's confession at the foot of the cross that Jesus is the Son of God (cf. 15:39). Both confessions come at the end of a series of incidents that veil the mystery while they partially reveal it.

Returning to our reading, we note the artful development of the story. It begins innocuously. Jesus decides to cross the lake to the other side. The disciples ready the boat. Mark adds the unimportant but interesting detail that "other boats were with him." It helps create the scene, but these boats are soon forgotten.

Quickly the storm arises. In a few telling words Mark describes the storm's intensity. With a touch that adds to the utter calm of Jesus, he mentions that he was asleep "on the cushion." The self-possession of the Master is contrasted with the absolute confusion of the disciples.

After stilling the sea, Jesus rebukes his followers for their lack of faith. They had not yet penetrated the mystery of this Person. They are filled with awe, a necessary prerequisite to the act of faith. In one sense, our passage is a capsule presentation of the entire Gospel of Mark. Only one element is lacking, the profession of faith. This would come only at the end when the veil was completely lifted.

Our own lives are repetitions of the Gospel incidents. At times we feel assured of ourselves and of our possession of the truth. We go about our tasks calmly. Then suddenly uncertainty strikes. We wonder that Christ can seem so unconcerned about the fate of his Church.

But Christ is present and the storm will subside. Our faith, however, must be strengthened by the incident. Our total abandonment to God must be renewed. The liturgical celebration is both the effective reminder of Christ's presence and the occasion of our inner renewal.

Thirteenth Sunday in Ordinary Time (B)
Wisdom 1:13-15; 2:23-24; 2 Corinthians 8:7-9, 13-15;
Mark 5:21-43

After all the Alleluias of the Easter season and of Pentecost, we come back again to the Ordinary Time of the liturgical year. But for Christians even Ordinary Time isn't commonplace. Every day is special, a time in which unique gifts from God are always being celebrated.

One of these gifts is life. While this includes our physical life, expressed in our breathing and moving about, it is also something more than that. It is a sharing in God's own divine life. It is a symbiosis, a "living with" God. Paul put it this way, "the life I live now is not my own; Christ is living in me" (Gal 2:20).

This is hardly commonplace life. It is a full life, joy-filled and God-entrusted. And that kind of life is what God's action among us is all about. "I came that they might have life and have it to the full" (Jn 10:10).

Obviously not all men and women have this life. They have either a deficiency in their physical life because of some sickness or malady, and this is terminated with physical death. Or they lack God's life; they have deliberately rejected his grace. This is a death more terrifying than the other.

Usually when the Scriptures speak of life and death, they mean them in both these ways, as both physical and spiritual. And it is the conviction of those same Scriptures that physical and spiritual death are not God's willing. God's will is for life, which was abundantly manifested in his Son's coming that we might have it "to the full."

The first reading for this Sunday could not be clearer on this point. ". . . God did not make death nor does he rejoice in the destruction of the living." That the author means physical death seems apparent. But that he includes spiritual death can be argued from a preceding statement where he had said that "a lying mouth slays the soul." Also, in chapter three he writes movingly of the immortality of the soul.

The author attributes the introduction of death to "the envy of the devil." Almost certainly he is referring here to the sin of Adam and Eve, instigated by the serpent (Gn 3). Here, for the first time, that serpent is identified as a symbol for personified evil, the devil.

A fascinating statement by the author is his final one, "they who are in his (the devil's) possession experience it" (that is, death). Here he is thinking only of spiritual death and says that those who have rejected God through sin are well aware of it. Their lives are already touched by the joylessness of death.

The Gospel reading is a glorious celebration of life. It tells of the restoration of the fullness of life to a hemorrhaging woman and to a young dying girl. To both, Jesus brings life and brings it gladly. Obviously physical life is the primary object of Jesus' concern here. But the Greek word Mark uses to describe the woman's saving faith is often used to include as well that richer life with God.

If we enjoy good health, we should be grateful to God and see it as one of his special gifts. But if we are in poor health, we can take comfort in the fact that we do share the far more precious life with God that never ends. We, too, can say with Paul that it is Christ who is living in us. And that is no commonplace gift.

Fourteenth Sunday in Ordinary Time (B)
Ezekiel 2:2-5; 2 Corinthians 12:7-10; Mark 6:1-6

The theme of Sunday's readings is the perils of the prophet. The readings deal either with the unpopular things the prophet must do or say or with the unfavorable reaction of the hearers to him. The prophet had to be called by God; it was not a life that he would have chosen on his own.

In the first reading we have one part of the call of the prophet Ezekiel. In the first part, not included here, God was seen in a vision abandoning the city of Jerusalem and the temple. This was a premonition of the destruction shortly to come on the Kingdom of Judah. The time was around the beginning of the sixth century B.C. The end came in 587.

It is said that "spirit" entered into Ezekiel. This means a special power coming from God enabling him both to hear the word of God and to communicate it to others. This is an indication of the extreme difficulty of the prophet's task. The word was one of doom; he would need "spirit."

He would need "spirit" above all because of the people to whom he would preach. They are hardhearted and rebellious, as the reading emphasizes. Israel's prophets had to be bearers of hard news; their people were such that they deserved only that.

Nevertheless, the power of God's word would be manifested, not necessarily in the conversion of the people, since that requires their free response. God may come down hard on them but he never forces anyone. The word's power is manifest in the fact that the people, rebellious as they are, still recognize it as God's word. They will know that a prophet has been among them. On the basis of that knowledge, let them choose.

If Ezekiel had his perils to face, no less did the Christian prophets, above all St. Paul. In his letter to the Corinthians he mentions the extraordinary revelations he had, but he was not permitted to rest easy with them. He had to endure "a thorn in the flesh." What this was is not known, no matter what the guesses might be. At any rate, it had a humbling effect.

In this respect Paul is like Ezekiel. The latter, too, had some kind of physical or psychic disability (some have named it epilepsy) that accompanied him most of his life. It was probably true that in both cases the disability evoked a theological principle that Paul enunciates: ". . . in weakness power reaches perfection. And so I willingly boast of my weaknesses instead, that the power of Christ may rest upon me."

Such a principle transcends rational argument. No one but a person of faith could ever formulate or accept it. But this is what made the prophets great. They accepted the perils they faced as the context in which human weakness was made strong by God's power.

The reading from Mark's Gospel repeats the same lesson. Jesus the prophet is not heard by his own people. They could not understand him. "They found him too much for them." This led Jesus to enunciate another principle, that of the prophet being without honor only in his own house.

What is the fruit of all these perils of the prophets? It is the survival of religion. Some estimate that if it were not for the prophets, despite all their perils, Yahwism would have died out in Israel. We, as Christians, know of course the power of the cross of Jesus. And we can ask how Christianity would have survived these two thousand years without the perils of a Paul and others like him. Ours is a hard faith and needs the strength of God to work in human weakness.

Fifteenth Sunday in Ordinary Time (B)
Amos 7:12-15; Ephesians 1:3-14; Mark 6:7-13

To be sent with authority is one of the significant events of life. No stranger in a foreign land is as highly respected as is an ambassador. Receiving him is to acknowledge the country that sent him. An affront to him is an affront to his people.

This concept of being sent with authority is built into the fabric of the human race. Once there is political or social structure, then some among the people must be delegated to represent the whole. It is impossible for a whole nation or group to represent itself before all other nations or groups.

We accept this concept without hesitation. What is fascinating is that God has made use of this human characteristic in his own dealings with us. As God, he could, unlike a created being, reveal himself directly to each human soul. He could be his own ambassador to everyone. It is fascinating that he chose to do otherwise.

He did send one unique ambassador to us in the person of his Son, Jesus Christ. But that did not exclude others. On the contrary, *the* apostle Jesus (cf. Heb 3:1) gives special meaning to those whom he sends as apostles. Because of him they know what indeed it means to be an apostle. "He who receives you receives me, and he who receives me receives him who sent me" (Mt 10:40).

In the Greek language there are three words for the act of "sending." But only in the one from which the word "apostle" is derived is the emphasis, not on the sending so much, although that is necessarily included, but on the relationship between the one sending and the one sent. The "apostle" truly *represents* the sender. The "apostle" acts with the authority of the sender. The passage we just quoted from Matthew makes sense only in that context.

What adds to the fascination of this word "apostle" is that it is rarely found in sources outside the Bible. The great Greek historian, Herodotus, used it only twice. The Jewish historian Josephus, who lived at the time of Christ, used it once. In the light of that, the eighty-one times it is found in the New Testament is noteworthy. The early Church felt the need to describe a unique office with a unique term. A Christian apostle is "one-sent-by-Jesus"—and that is unique.

It is no wonder, then, that the Gospels make so much of the mission of the twelve apostles. Our Gospel reading is just one of the records of that sending forth by Jesus. And in view of what we have said about the emphasis being on the apostle *as representing Jesus, as exercising his authority*, the details of the mission are secondary. For any who represent such a One, nothing should be surprising.

The reading from the book of Amos adds power to what we have said. Amos was an Old Testament "apostle." He emphasizes that even over his prophetic office. That he was sent by God is more important than what he said.

This is brought out even more strongly by the fact that Amos was sent by God from the southern kingdom of Judah to the northern kingdom of Israel. The high priest Amaziah told him to go on back to his own land to "earn his bread." But Amos held his ground. He couldn't do otherwise; God had sent him.

In the Christian community some are "sent by Jesus" for a special mission. For them the responsibility is awesome but the assurance of grace is certain. For all, the need to recognize and affirm those who are sent should be accompanied by a keen sense of sharing in the mission itself.

Sixteenth Sunday in Ordinary Time (B)
Jeremiah 23:1-6; Ephesians 2:13-18; Mark 6:30-34

The sheep image is out—or so we're told. A mindless lot, sheep spend all their time nibbling at the grass and pushing up against one another so they don't get lost. That is hardly the image to describe the modern, sophisticated, free-thinking American.

The shepherd image, on the other hand, despite its necessary tie to that of sheep, fares much better. The shepherd is usually identified as a strong resourceful, dedicated person who makes special efforts to protect and feed his charges. Tradition has treated the shepherd image well.

Shepherds and sheep are important images in our first and third readings. In line with a long tradition that had pictured kings and pharaohs as shepherds, Jeremiah depicts God as the true shepherd of his people. Completely disappointed by the earthly monarchy that had, almost without exception, brought disaster on the people, the prophet sees that only God can do what must be done. And he will do it.

What is important in this total picture is the image of shepherd as applied to God, not the image of sheep as applied to people. For it is a new *Shepherd* that is taking over, not a new flock that is replacing the old one.

In other words, the total image is determined by the divine Shepherd, not by the human flock. Or, the shepherd-sheep imagery would never have been adopted by the prophet if the prior image had not been that of the divine Shepherd. It is, after all, the condition of the leader that determines that of the led, not vice versa.

This is not just wordplay. This has to do most intimately with the question of our relationship to God as well as with that of an appropriate imagery. To put it bluntly, God is not determined by who we are; we are determined by who God is. If that is true, then any imagery describing our relationship to God must be determined primarily by the reality of God.

Applying that to our readings, we must say that if we are depicted as sheep, it is only because God is first of all our Shepherd. This then does something to the image of sheep. In this context sheep can only be defined as those who are completely known by their Shepherd, as those who enjoy a total providence, as those who, because of that, can have absolute trust in their Shepherd.

Trust, sense of security, total providence, intimate relationship— these are the characteristics indicated by the sheep image in our readings. And what of the mindless, grass-nibbling, pushing animals that our imaginations conjure up? Those characteristics are not applicable here.

Is the image, then, defective? Every image is, when it deals with the divine reality. Few sophisticated Americans would want to be considered slaves. Yet Paul, who was as sophisticated as any educated person, called himself without hesitation a slave of Jesus Christ. As the sheep image, so the slave image is justified solely by its connection with the divine reality, the lordship of Jesus.

All this comes across beautifully in the figure of Jesus in the Gospel reading. The people are coming and going, hastening on ahead, a vast crowd, "like sheep without a shepherd." Then Jesus takes over, a Shepherd. ". . . he began to teach them. . . ."

The reading is not long enough to tell us what happened. But we can guess. There will be orderly arrangement, satisfaction of hunger, complete security. The true Shepherd is at work.

Seventeenth Sunday in Ordinary Time (B)
2 Kings 4:42-44; Ephesians 4:1-6; John 6:1-15

The ordinary Hebrew word for "bread" (*lechem*) is used some 287 times in the Old Testament. The ordinary Greek word for "bread" (*artos*) is used some 95 times in the New Testament. I suspect that in a comparable piece of contemporary American literature of comparable length the usage would be significantly lower.

Because of the vast variety of foods available to us, bread is not the staple that it was to the biblical world. Because of that, it has lost much of its symbolic value. We should keep that in mind here.

Symbolic value is important in considering the first and third readings this Sunday. By saying this we are not making any judgment on the historical nature of the events. Like the biblical authors, we simply wish to transcend the ordinary and see what is of higher meaning, the ultimate divine purpose in these events.

The first reading is from a series of stories about the prophet Elisha. The immediate context revolves around food for the prophet's companions. A famine is mentioned in v. 38, which prepares the way and provides the atmosphere for understanding God's saving action. In the story immediately preceding ours the "man of God" renders some poisonous food harmless. We are in the world of the sacred.

In our story twenty loaves are made to serve a hundred men and "there were some left over." What is stressed is not the physical satisfaction of hunger, but the sacramental, and therefore spiritually nourishing, nature of the meal. Twice there is reference to the Word of God: "thus says the Lord," and "as the Lord has said."

When the Lord speaks, a new dimension is added. Bread now becomes what it is intended by God to be in its most profound sense, a means of satisfying the spiritual hunger of the human person. Of course "there were some left over," because sacraments are always in themselves wholly satisfying.

The symbolic value of the Gospel story is even more pronounced. Here the sacramental character of the bread is seen inasmuch as the multiplication of the loaves is made the introduction to the discourse on the bread of life, that is, on divine revelation (bread come down from heaven) and on the Eucharist (Jesus' flesh and blood). The chapter is a story of a sacrament.

All the evangelists have the account of the multiplication of loaves. Mark and Matthew even have two accounts. This fact and the manner in which the story is told, tell us two things. First, it is one of the earliest traditions about Jesus that was preserved. Second, from the time it was first told in the Church it was given a Eucharistic significance. It has a sacramental character.

Once again, as in the Elisha story, "there were some left over." Even more so in this case, since it points to the eminently satisfying nature of the Eucharist. We would expect there to be at least "twelve baskets full of pieces left over. . . ."

The Church intends us to reflect on the Eucharist in these readings. The Gospel story is, in fact, the first of five readings we will be given from John's sixth chapter, the Eucharistic chapter. And the lesson that comes through most powerfully here is how satisfying that "bread of life" is. Received in faith, it nourishes faith, so much so that those who share this Eucharistic meal can say that they had "as much as they wanted." What more could there be?

Eighteenth Sunday in Ordinary Time (B)
Exodus 16:2-4, 12-15; Ephesians 4:17, 20-24; John 6:24-35

Bread is food. That simple statement can have a depth of meaning which those of little faith (Matthew 16:8) fail to grasp. Only the open mind and heart can manage the notion that food for the soul can also be called bread.

Several times Jesus had to rebuke his disciples because of their inability to understand the deeper meaning of spiritual bread. He talked about the "leaven of the Pharisees and the leaven of Herod" and they thought he was referring to the fact that they only had one loaf of bread with them in the boat (Mk 8:14-21). A narrow mind doesn't admit of broad ideas.

These remarks are prompted, of course, by the Gospel reading. Jesus clearly states there that his followers "should not be working for perishable food (physical bread) but for food that remains unto life eternal." This is a typical Semitic statement in which the absolute denial of one part serves to reinforce the affirmation of the other part. In other words, Jesus isn't condemning manual labor to gain a living; he is saying that it cannot be compared to the higher goal of life.

Jesus identifies this higher goal as "food," as "the bread of life," as "manna." What does he mean by this? Later on, as we'll see in the following weeks, he means his own flesh and blood. But here he is talking about believing in him, about accepting his words. Bread, or manna, is identified with the revelation that he brings from the Father.

There is a precedent for this understanding of food as the Word of God. In the book of Isaiah (c. 55) the faithful ones are told not to spend their money on bread that cannot satisfy. Rather, they are invited to buy the food that costs nothing, but that delights them "in fatness." The entire chapter shows that the author is speaking of the Word of God.

Our first reading, from Exodus, records how God provided the Israelites in the desert with manna. Was he thinking, too, of God's revelation, of his words of wisdom? Not likely. Physically hungry Israelites would need physical sustenance before they could appreciate the deeper meaning.

But the Church has this deeper meaning in mind when she gives us the reading as the counterpart of the Gospel reading. And she, too, has a precedent in proposing this meaning. In the book of Wisdom, composed much later than Exodus, the author speaks of the manna in the desert as "your word that preserves those who believe in you" (16:26).

So, God first shows his living concern for his people by satisfying their physical hunger. But he wants them to know a deeper hunger, a hunger for his Word. The manna that satisfied the physical hunger now becomes the "bread of life," the true bread from heaven" that Jesus brings to those who believe.

The human spirit will never be completely satisfied by the "leaven of the Herods," that is, by all the good things this world's wealth can provide. It wants more than that, even when it doesn't know what that "more" really is.

This is why the Church has always been concerned not only to "preach" the Word that will change minds and hearts, but also to "teach" the Word that will lead those minds and hearts to maturity. From the sermons of the Fathers to the manuscripts of the monks to the stained glass windows of the Middle Ages to the catechisms of our modern age, the one concern has been to feed the faithful with the "bread of life." Christian education is not just an incidental charge of the Church; it is at the heart of her mission.

Nineteenth Sunday in Ordinary Time (B)
1 Kings 19:4-8; Ephesians 4:30—5:2; John 6:41-51

"Praised be our Lord and Savior, God the Father!" That doxology, or praise-formula, is not in the Bible. Yet the idea behind it is supremely biblical. Most of our readers would probably be surprised to learn that the title "Savior" in the New Testament is applied just about as often to the Father as to Jesus Christ. The doxology is orthodox.

The idea behind it is that throughout the Scriptures God the Father is portrayed as the initiator, not only of creation, but also of salvation. Even his creative activity is seen in the larger context of his saving activity. He is first and foremost a saving God, a Savior. "It is I, I the Lord; there is no Savior but me" (Is 43:11).

The reason for our slight uneasiness about the doxology is that we are so accustomed to hearing Jesus proclaimed as Savior. It is the common profession of every one of the major Christian church bodies. With the people of Samaria we, too, hold that this Jesus "really is the Savior of the world" (Jn 4:42).

If the title "Savior" is applied to both Father and Son, it cannot be in the same way. The Father is the Savior in the primary sense as initiator and goal of all saving activity. The Son is Savior as one "sent" by the Father (1 Jn 4:14), as the "mediator" of salvation (1 Tm 2:5), as the one "through whom" God has given us the victory (1 Cor 15:57).

All this has an important bearing on our Gospel reading. We saw in last week's reading that in the first part of this discourse (vv. 35-50) Jesus is speaking of the "bread of life" in the sense of what he reveals by his teaching. The bread, or manna, is revelation.

Some of his hearers are astounded at such claims. They know Jesus only as a carpenter's son. But Jesus insists on his claims and cites the Father as the source of his revelation. It comes from him and is destined to reveal him. Moreover, no one can even come to Jesus "unless the Father who sent me draws him."

John, otherwise, emphasizes the uniqueness, the divinity, of Jesus. Jesus is the preexistent Word of God (1:1). He is one with the Father (17:22). He is the "I am" (8:58), just as was the Father (Ex 3:14). Yet it is the same John who insists on the Father as the ultimate source of all life, truth, and salvation. Our reading confirms this forcefully.

The importance of this for us is the effect on our attitude to Jesus and the Father, and, consequently, on our prayers. In Jesus, the Father's saving love, already manifested to Israel, is now revealed as a Person. He is the incarnation of that love, the Word-made-flesh whose total humanity leaves no doubt about the Father's desire to be with us: "Whoever has seen me has seen the Father" (Jn 14:9).

Pentecost had shown us the Spirit as the divine power working within us, helping us to accept Jesus as the unique mediator of the Father's salvation. Only in the Spirit, Paul reminds us, can we proclaim that "Jesus is Lord!" (1 Cor 12:3).

And so the whole content of our Christian faith can be summed up in the formula: to the Father, through the Son, in the Holy Spirit. That is why our opening outburst of praise is orthodox: "Praised be our Lord and Savior, God the Father!"

Twentieth Sunday in Ordinary Time (B)
Proverbs 9:1-6; Ephesians 5:15-20; John 6:51-58

"I want to be with you." If not spoken in a mawkishly sentimental way, those are among the most powerful words that one person can say to another. What is extraordinary is that God has, effectively, said that to his people throughout the Scriptures.

First we must make it clear that God's wish to be with his people is no sign of weakness on his part, no sign of any dependence on such association for his fulfillment. As transcendent Lord and creator of all things, he is totally self-sufficient.

All we need do is read some of the biblical descriptions of theophanies, or divine manifestations, to be reminded of his absolute majesty and glory. The Sinai appearance (Ex 19), for example, when absorbed into one's mind and heart, evokes a strong sense of mystery and awe. Or we can recall the highly emotive reaction of the young Isaiah when he experienced the thrice-holy God's call to him (6:1-5).

It is essential that we hold firm to this notion of God. For it is precisely his transcendence, his awesomeness, his being the all-powerful "Other" that makes his desire to be with us so shatteringly real. It is no pagan Baal, nor even some "heavenly being" who wants to be our companion on the way. It is the Lord.

The theme of God's "being with" his people is as old as the Scriptures themselves. In Genesis 3 we read of God's "moving about in the garden." He obviously wants to be with the ones he had created. But the barrier to his presence had been raised by sin. God's wish was, for the moment, frustrated.

The reminder of the Old Testament provides ample witness to God's intent to remove that barrier and to be with those he loves. The patriarchs, the people Israel in the desert, Hosea and his image of the husband-God, Isaiah and his "Immanuel" (the word literally means "with us is God")—all are testimonies to this remarkable divine hunger.

By the time the author of our first reading was writing, the theme of God's "being with" his people was well established. He presents it now in a new form, under the symbol of Wisdom. In the later Old Testament period God was personified as Wisdom, not only because of his marvelous creative activity but also because of his bringing to his people correct norms for living.

Here Wisdom invites "whoever is simple" to come to her banquet. "Come, eat of my food, and drink of the wine I have mixed!" To share a meal with others is the truest mark of hospitality. Such is the Lord's wish.

In the New Testament Jesus *is* "Immanuel" (Mt 1:23). He is the incarnation of God's love, the living realization of his presence. He is with his people now in a wholly new way.

To be with Jesus is to be with God. We are with him, as Paul reminds us, when we allow him to come to us in faith. Then, Paul says, "I live now, not I, but Christ is living in me" (Gal 2:20). Scholars refer to this as a symbiosis, or literally, a "living with."

Our Gospel reading assures us that this is what the Eucharist effects in us, a symbiosis with the Lord. The one "who feeds on my flesh and drinks my blood remains in me, and I in him." Presupposing the faith that opens the door to the Lord, the Eucharist is the most intimate manner in which Jesus fulfills that ancient divine wish, "I want to be with you."

Twenty-first Sunday in Ordinary Time (B)
Joshua 24:1-2; 15-18; Ephesians 5:21-32; John 6:60-69

The Old Testament and Gospel readings for this Sunday are unusually complementary. Both have to do with one of the most profound realities of life—human freedom. Both present this reality in the most dramatic fashion possible—the freedom to accept or reject God.

The passage from Joshua, read in its whole context, is unsurpassed in sheer drama. The tribes of Israel, now in the land of promise, are depicted as having at last defeated their enemies. They stand, *en masse*, before their leader Joshua who recounts all the adventures of their people from the time of Abraham, some five hundred years previously, down to the present.

The thread that binds all these adventures together is the hand of Yahweh. He led their forefathers into the land of Canaan and down into Egypt, brought the people out of that land of bondage, through the wilderness, and now once again into the land of promise.

That is your history, Joshua tells them. Now, choose the gods that you will serve! Do you want the gods of your ancestors "beyond the River" (the Euphrates)? Or do you want the Amorite gods who once "protected" this land you have conquered? Or will you serve Yahweh?

It is clear what Joshua expects of them. If they accept the history that he has just recounted, how can they help but choose Yahweh?

He brought them here and made it possible for them to have a choice. Joshua's own resounding cry of faith serves as an example to all the others: ". . . as for me and my house, we will serve the Lord!"

We might well wonder whether John had that scene in mind as he recorded the climactic exchange between Jesus and his disciples after his discourse on the bread of life. He had referred to his teaching as the true manna that comes down from heaven. He had spoken of his own flesh and blood as the food that gives eternal life. He asks his disicples whether they believe this.

That some should say, "This sort of talk is hard to endure!" is understandable enough. That some of his disciples should turn away and no longer follow him is sad but not wholly unpredictable.

Then, like Joshua to the twelve tribes, Jesus turns to the twelve apostles, "Do you want to leave me too?" Just as the twelve tribes told Joshua that they could hardly reject the Lord who had done all those things for them, so Peter asks how they could turn to anyone else for words of eternal life. "We have come to believe; we are convinced that you are God's holy one."

What is remarkable about both these passages is the radical freedom humans are seen to enjoy. We are free to accept or reject the ultimate source of our being, the ultimate destiny of our lives. No freedom can be more radical than that.

The question is frequently asked today whether there is a hell. To some it seems to be incompatible with a good God. But is it? Hell is not God's creation. Hell, which in its deepest meaning is absolute loneliness, is a human creation. Hell is the condition of those who choose not to live with God. It is always a free choice.

Hell is the strongest argument for the depths of human freedom. If there were no hell, then we really would not be free to reject God. Just the possibility of hell says what kind of awesome power the Lord has given us.

But that same awesome power makes it possible for us freely to choose God, to serve the Lord, to accept the words of eternal life, to choose "life and good," not "death and evil" (Dt 30:15). The life we live tells God which choice we have made.

Twenty-second Sunday in Ordinary Time (B)
Deuteronomy 4:1-2, 6-8; James 1:17-18, 21-22, 27;
Mark 7:1-8, 14-15, 21-23

"For what great nation is there that has gods so close to it as the Lord, our God, is to us whenever we call upon him?" That cry of faith, from the first reading, is the basis of biblical monotheism. We believe in the one and only God, not because of philosophical reasoning, but because of the way he has revealed himself to us. Accepting him in what he has done for us, we accept him as unique.

This is one of the great themes of the book of Deuteronomy. The readers are constantly reminded of how this God has acted in their favor. "Not with our fathers did he make this covenant, but with us, all of us who are alive here this day" (5:3). The Lord "brought us out of Egypt with his strong hand and outstretched arm, with terrifying power, with signs and wonders; and bringing us into this country, he gave us this land flowing with milk and honey" (26:8-9).

In the context of the one God's self-revelation in history the Deuteronomist sees "the statutes and decrees" which Israel is to follow in order that she might live. In other words, we do these things because of the kind of God we follow. Our lives, our moral conduct, reflect the nature of the one Lord of history.

In another passage the same Deuteronomist says that this word of *torah*, or directions for living, is not something hard, nor up in the heavens, nor across the sea. Rather, this word "is something very near to you, already in your mouths and in your hearts; you have only to carry it out" (30:11-14).

What I am trying to show here is that the Deuteronomist is quite close to the teaching of Jesus, which we will consider shortly. He does not manifest that over-emphasis on the letter of the Law which characterized a later generation and which both Jesus and Paul condemned. In this later development Law became an absolute, something hard and rigid "out there." Minute prescriptions had to be followed, not the Lord behind them.

As we learn from the Gospel reading, Jesus says that the minute prescriptions can even be ignored for some higher good. The discussion was occasioned by the fact of Jesus' disciples eating with unwashed hands, which was contrary to the Jewish ritual prescriptions of the time. Such a prescription, Jesus implies, may not at times be in accord with the personal Lord's will.

He follows this up with what some consider to be one of the most radical statements in the Scriptures. We are defiled not by what comes into us from the outside, but by what proceeds from within the hearts of individual men and women, by those actions that reveal our evil intentions and self-will.

The radical nature of the statement consists in the denial that anything in creation is "sacred" or "impure" *in itself*. All these external things are part of God's creation and are good. They are evil when we misuse them to another's or our own harm. The human person, made in the image and likeness of God, is the measure of moral values.

That is, the human person *as intended by God*. This is a clear presupposition both of the Deuteronomist and of Jesus. Ultimately, God alone establishes all values. But they can only be manifested in human values, not primarily in objective law. A law is good if it is good for the person.

God has revealed himself in history as a loving, saving God. If we respond to this God and accept his love, we will act properly. When we can say with conviction that no other god has shown himself as our God has to us, then we will follow his "statutes and decrees," because we know they are for our good.

Twenty-third Sunday in Ordinary Time (B)
Isaiah 35:4-7; James 2:1-5; Mark 7:31-37

The Scriptures are filled with symbolic language. The stories frequently have a meaning deeper than what appears on the surface. The presence of this deeper, richer meaning speaks forcefully of the presence of God. For God can never be "defined" in finite human words; he can only be hinted at or suggested by an exhuberance of language.

It is important that we appreciate this insight. Otherwise, we will miss so much of the real depths of biblical teaching. Our first reading is a prime illustration. It was written while the people were in exile in Babylon. All seemed lost. The people experienced the absence of God in the misery in which they lived.

But our author had firmer convictions. He knew that the saving Lord was no absent God. He knew that God was close at hand and that he would soon reveal his saving arm. He expresses this conviction in an outburst that surely cannot be limited to the literal meaning of the words. He is speaking of the end-time when the fullness of the divine healing will be manifest.

The blind will see, the deaf will hear (the Gospel too tells us this), the lame will walk. But when the author goes on to say that "streams will burst forth in the desert, and rivers in the steppe, the burning sands will become pools . . . ," we know that he has something more in mind than just physical wholeness.

We can know what that "something more" is, when we realize that the physical defects are the result of sin, of alienation from God. The restoration to wholeness, then means not only the physical cure; it symbolizes also the destruction of evil, the renewed presence of the saving God.

It means that the blind can see, not just with their eyes, but also with their minds and hearts. It means that the deaf can hear, not only human words, but also the Word of God. It means that the lame can walk, but also they can follow in the way of the Lord.

This is what wholeness means. A wholeness of the body without a wholeness of the spirit is a broken wholeness. The evil that the Lord overcomes is not just the evil of broken limbs, but also of broken hearts. That is why Jesus forgave the paralytic's sins as he cured his sickness (Mk 2:1-12). And that is why every narrative of a physical healing points to a deeper healing.

We are prepared, then, to see the meaning of the Gospel reading for us. The deaf man, with a speech impediment, is brought to Jesus. The Lord cures him of both deficiencies. Moreover, he charged the witnesses to tell no one of the miracle. But "the more he ordered them not to, the more they proclaimed it."

Why this apparent disobedience? The answer may lie in the word "proclaim." Jesus wanted no false messianic ideas bruited about, no claims that he was a political savior or migrant medicine man. They,

on the contrary, including especially the deaf and dumb man, were
"announcing the good news" (the meaning of "proclaim"). Their
ears were opened to hear God's Word and their tongues were
loosened to proclaim it. Something more had happened than just a
physical healing; that is what Mark is saying.

When the story of the healing is read to us on Sunday, it is surely
not the whole purpose of the Church to tell us that Jesus can work this
kind of miracle. The reading, in this case, would have little direct
meaning for the majority of us. But that Gospel is *for us*, for all of us
who hear it. It is telling us that we who hear that Word can have our
spirits lifted. We can now "proclaim" the good news of Jesus Christ.

Jesus cures us by his Word. He opens our ears and loosens our
tongues. Are we listening—and then proclaiming?

Twenty-fourth Sunday in Ordinary Time (B)
Isaiah 50:4-9; James 2:14-18; Mark 8:27-35

All biblical scholars agree on one point. The Gospel reading for this
Sunday is at the heart of Mark's account. It serves as a hinge for the
whole Gospel. It provides the grand climax for all that went before
and the introduction to all that follows. It is the latter role that the
Church emphasizes today, as the first reading confirms.

Let's first consider its role as climax. This will help immeasurably
in appreciating its role as introduction. In all that preceded this
passage Jesus had been presented as a miracle worker *par excellence*. He had healed blind men and deaf-mutes, fed thousands,
walked on water, quelled a storm at sea, and expelled demons.
Nothing was beyond his powers.

The reaction of the crowds was understandable. They were
"spellbound," "amazed," "awestruck," "astonished." With such a
succession of events and their effect on the people, Mark was clearly
building up to something. Our reading tells us what it was.

Jesus asks his disciples what the people were saying about him.
The answers are not unexpected: Jesus is one of the great figures of
the past brought back to life—Elijah, the Baptist, one of the prophets.
When the disciples are asked for their estimation, it is the irrepressi-
ble Peter who bursts forth with, "You are the Messiah!"

That is what we would expect. God's anointed One had been long announced. He would be a true *Wunderkind*, One obviously sent by God to save his people. And no one had ever filled the bill as perfectly as had Jesus. Peter knew that he *had* to be the Savior, the one to crush the Roman might and make the name and power of King David live again.

But as surely and as forcibly as Mark seems to justify this confession by what he had written, just as surely does he seem to repudiate it by what follows. This Savior-Messiah will suffer, be rejected, and be put to death. Moreover, his true disciples would not bear the laurel wreaths of military victory but the bloody crowns of martyrdom. Peter may have had visions of a procession around the famous coliseum in Rome, but it wasn't to be the kind he had in mind.

It isn't just in our passage that Jesus speaks of his coming passion and death. Twice again in Mark's Gospel (9:31; 10:32-34) are we told about this ignominious end of the Savior-Messiah. The passion account itself consumes a disproportionately large amount of space in the whole Gospel. And, the final, climactic confession, by the Roman centurion, "Clearly, this man was the Son of God" (15:39), is made at the moment of death.

Apparently Mark felt his readers needed this shock treatment. It is possible that they were too exclusively insistent on Jesus as a wonder-worker. They may have thought that to be a Christian means only that you have your own personal miracle man.

Certainly Mark isn't denying that Jesus is a Savior and that he did and does work miracles. But it's just as certain Mark is saying that Christianity is nothing without the cross. If you want to be a follower of Jesus, he is saying, prepare for your cross.

Nothing has happened in the Church's two thousand year history to disprove Mark's thesis. So confess with all the boldness of Peter that Jesus is the Christ, and then be prepared to take up your cross and follow him.

Twenty-fifth Sunday in Ordinary Time (B)
Wisdom 2:12, 17-20; James 3:16—4:3; Mark 9:30-37

A young boy asks his five-year-old sister if she would help him deliver the morning papers. Her reply is, "No. I plan on being a newspaper *publisher.*'' The humor lies partially in the determined expression of such a lofty ambition by a five-year-old child. She is hardly the kind of figure Jesus had in mind when he spoke of children to his disciples.

"If anyone wishes to rank first, he must remain the last one of all and the servant of all." That would seem to be the key saying in a series of remarkable sayings in the Gospel reading. The kind of "first" that Jesus is speaking of here is not that of the business world or that of any of the other worlds that make the human enterprise. The "first" he is speaking of is in the Kingdom of God. And that is a "first" that is never achieved; it is the effect of amazing grace.

The presuppositions and implications of all this are complex; we cannot explore them all exhaustively here. But let us put the principle as simply as possible and then reflect on it in the light of our reading. The principle is: God makes us all that we are by his love. We must be as open to that love as a slave is to the master's bidding. Or, to use Jesus' other figure, as open as a child is to a brand new world.

Here the working concept, on the human side, is responsible openness, acceptance. That can be expressed in many different ways. The most striking way, the one illustrated above all by Jesus, is acceptance of the Father's love that asks the obedience of death. As we heard in last Sunday's Gospel, that is what no human person could conceive of, only God.

That is total acceptance, total openness, and total self-giving. And what is the "first" that Jesus becomes by being this kind of servant? As Jesus puts it, "after three days he will rise." This refers to a new life in total union with the Father. Most scholars think this is a Markan addition made in the light of Easter Sunday. Probably so. Still, Jesus would have known that his suffering and death were a response to love that would lead to life.

The "child" saying in the reading does not explicitly refer to openness to and acceptance of God's love. Rather, Jesus here seems to extol the child as one of the "poor ones of Yahweh," that is, the humble ones of the earth. Jesus' disciples are urged to receive them in his own name. In receiving such humble and "unimportant" people they would show their awareness of where God puts value, of the kind he considers to be "first."

All of this probably sounds orthodox enough. But it poses problems. The biggest problem (and one that we like to ignore since we've already done well enough in discovering a radical "truth") is what we're going to do about it. No homilist can resolve that problem for anyone but himself.

Another, perhaps lesser but surely looming, problem is what this means as far as our worldly ambitions are concerned. Shouldn't there be those who strive to be newspaper publishers? Surely the world cannot survive with delivery boys alone. Christianity cannot be that impractical.

The biblical response is that of course all those areas of human endeavor are important and worthy of our efforts. What Scripture proposes is a vision so broad that it embraces all these areas, roots so deep that they give a special kind of life to all human talents, a love so strong that nothing escapes its mark.

With that vision we can, even if we are president of a giant corporation, be what Jesus asks us to be, "last one of all and servant of all."

Twenty-sixth Sunday in Ordinary Time (B)
Numbers 11:25-29; James 5:1-6; Mark 9:38-43, 45,47-48

The less official the task, the more officious its exercise. That bit of homespun wisdom is verified in the first and third readings of this Sunday. The real leader is interested in proper results. The lesser officials are more interested in the manner in which they are obtained and in exercising authority in obtaining them.

The first reading is easily summarized. The gift of prophetic utterance, restricted to Moses, is now, by the Lord's favor, shared with seventy elders of the people. It is discovered that two men, who had not been present at the place where the gift was shared, are nonetheless engaging in prophecy. When Joshua complains about this to Moses, he does nothing, thankful only that two others share the gift.

The book of Numbers is highly structured and, in fact, envisions a highly structured society. This is what we would expect from the priestly group responsible for the book. A strongly hierarchical flavor emerges from the reading of these chapters.

The desert-like conditions in which the people lived at the time no doubt required such a structure. Survival itself demanded it. In that context it is remarkable and surely commendable that the priestly authors could, as they do by recounting the story, appreciate the Lord's working outside the structure.

While the institution is an essential part of present human existence, it is not the final destiny of that existence. The Lord can tell us that by operating at times outside its context. Moses recognized that. So did our priestly authors. We are indebted to them for this important insight.

Jesus must have been aware of the incident recorded in the book of Numbers. The story in the Gospel reading is an almost exact parallel to it. John complains that someone "not of our company" is expelling demons in Jesus' name. The disciples tried to stop him but Jesus said to let him be.

Moses had permitted the prophesying because he knew it was God's working. Jesus permits the expulsion of demons in his name because he recognized it as "a miracle" and therefore of God. Maybe the man wasn't "of their company" but he was certainly doing something good. And there's too much evil in the world for us to be concerned with what we see as a less than perfect good.

I have checked carefully the Second Vatican Council's *Decree on Ecumenism* to see if these passages are used there. Although I could not find them, no one can doubt they would be especially appropriate in that context.

This is especially important for Roman Catholics. We have always believed, and still do, that all the means of salvation are to be found in our Church. Too often in the past this has been understood to mean that none are found in other Christian communities. The *Decree on Ecumenism* says otherwise. And our two readings tell us why. God doesn't work where he finds good; good is found wherever God is working.

Let's return to the homespun wisdom with which we began this column. In all of us is a tendency to officiousness with regard to possession of the truth, especially religious truth. We are tempted to look down on those "not of our company," to consider them less favored. But the Word tells us, not to compromise our faith convictions, but to acknowledge that the Spirit blows where he will.

Twenty-seventh Sunday in Ordinary Time (B)
Genesis 2:18-24; Hebrews 2:9-11; Mark 10:2-16

The theme is obvious. So obvious that it's difficult to find something striking to write about the subject. The temptation is to say simply, "Well, that's the way it is. What are you going to do about it?"

The subject is marriage and divorce. The biblical teaching is so straightforward that it is difficult to see how any Christian can claim to be a follower of Jesus and still accept the possibility of divorce and remarriage. Marriage is forever. That is what Jesus seems to be saying.

True, he admits that Moses allowed exceptions. But that wasn't what God intended from the beginning. ". . . God made them male and female . . . and the two shall become as one. They are no longer two but one flesh. Therefore let no man separate what God has joined."

". . . what God intended from the beginning." That is verified by the first reading and is unquestionably the reason why the Church has given us Genesis 2 as that reading. There it says plainly that the man leaves his father and mother and clings to his wife, "and the two of them become one body."

When we realize that this section of Genesis was most likely written in the aftermath of Solomon's disastrous "marriage encounters," we can appreciate all the more the inspired author's insistence. That, surely, was not what God had in mind when he made man and woman.

But. Yes, there is a "but." We do live in a world where there is sin. True, Jesus, in a real sense, had made the world whole again by his death and resurrection. And so he can call for that kind of living that his Father had envisioned from the beginning. At the same time, it is a world still reeling from the onslaught of sin. The beast has been vanquished, but its quivering carcass is still inflicting considerable damage.

This means that provision will have to be made for the ravages of sin. Already Paul had made such provision in the case of a Christian married to a nonbeliever. If the latter refused to live peacefully with the former, let them be separated (1 Cor 7:15). This is known as the "Pauline privilege" and has been used by the Church down through the centuries.

Matthew, too, admits of an exception in his Gospel (19:9). Some scholars think he is referring here to marriages within forbidden degrees of blood relationship before conversion. In any case, the Church today declares many marriages invalid because of some impediment present at the time of the marriage. In these cases civil divorce is permitted and remarriage possible.

Nevertheless, the principle enunciated by Jesus remains the norm. The covenant sealed by the two parties is not to be broken. In the light of Jesus' general stance on Kingdom morality, it would seem far better to foster means of preserving the marriage union than to seek reasons for exceptions to the norm. The Christian must bear a special kind of witness to a world where marriage is a convenience, not a sacrament.

We might wonder why the Church has included the passage on the little children in this reading. It must be for some deeper reason than that children are the expected fruit of happy marriages. More likely it is that to accept Jesus' teaching on marriage requires the openness of children and a sense of dependence on God's strength matching the child's sense of dependence on parents.

Whether or not that is the reason for the passage's inclusion, no one can doubt that such trust in God's help is necessary. With it the impossible can become possible.

Twenty-eighth Sunday in Ordinary Time (B)
Wisdom 7:7-11; Hebrews 4:12-13; Mark 10:17-30

Is Christianity practical? That kind of question is provoked by the Gospel reading for this Sunday. Jesus tells a rich man to sell all he has and give it to the poor if he wants to "share in everlasting life." But if every Christian did that, what kind of world would we have? The question is not rhetorical.

Not all New Testament writings demand that kind of abandonment of goods in order to be a Christian. James, whose letter is one of the most down-to-earth products of the young Church, speaks with no obvious embarrassment of the presence of a wealthy person in the Christian assembly (2:2). He berates the rich later on, but it is for their injustices to the poor.

A recent study on the social condition of the early Christians argues that, except possibly for the first few months of Jesus' earthly ministry, believers in him came from all strata of society, although the majority were from the poorer classes. The point is that total renunciation of wealth and property did not appear to be a *necessary* condition for being a Christian.

We are not saying this to water down in any way the radical nature of Christianity. Jesus did ask of some the leaving of all things. And many Christians throughout the history of the Church have understood their own calling in that way. Since such renunciation is the Gospel theme, we can ask what is its motivating force.

The first reading guides us to an answer. It is from a book called "Wisdom of Solomon." Although written less than a hundred years before Jesus' time, it was attributed to Israel's third king because of his legendary wisdom.

And Wisdom (with a capital "W") is the issue in the reading. A personified divine attribute, Wisdom is said to be the gift Solomon prayed for above all others. (The reference is to the story in 1 K 3:5-15 where, in a dream, God bade the king to ask for any gift he wished. He chose "an understanding heart," which our author equates with Wisdom.)

Wisdom, for our biblical author, is a wholly transcendent quality, immeasurably surpassing any other possible good the human person could enjoy. He expresses this by saying that even gold is, in comparison, "a little sand, and before her, silver is to be accounted mire." In possessing Wisdom, the author is convinced, Solomon possessed everything.

What Wisdom was to the Old Testament author, the Kingdom of God was to Jesus. The Kingdom was the situation of peace and justice and of total communion with the Lord. Inaugurated here on earth in the saving acts of Jesus, it would be fully established in the end-time when God's presence to and with his people would be perfected.

When the rich man asks how he can "share in everlasting life," both Jesus and Mark understand this to be equivalent to the Kingdom. And Jesus' reply is, in effect, that the man must regard the Kingdom as Solomon had regarded Wisdom, something absolutely surpassing any human or earthly value. And, *in his case*, Jesus said that he must express this by the actual renunciation of his wealth.

Can others have this longing for the Kingdom and still retain their wealth? Jesus only says that possession of material wealth makes it more difficult. But "with God all things are possible."

Is Christianity, then, practical? If "practical" means how to increase your bank account, the answer is obviously "no." If it means living fully in the way that really counts, it's the ultimate in practicality. Unfortunately that is not the common definition of "practical."

Twenty-ninth Sunday in Ordinary Time (B)
Isaiah 53:10-11; Hebrews 4:14-16; Mark 10:35-45

To live forever! The literature of the human race is filled with stories of man's search for immortality. Since death is the denial of life, death must be the most meaningless of human events.

Most of the world's philosophers would accept this appraisal. But the Scriptures say something else. They do not deny the truth of the human longing to live forever. Nor do they question the horror of death. They do, however, add another dimension to both life and death.

From the opening chapter of the book of Genesis life and death are seen in the large context of a relationship with God. Life is not just the knowing, loving, and moving of the human person; life is, supremely, being with God. It is, as Genesis would put it, walking with him "in the garden at the breezy time of the day" (3:8).

Death, too, is not just the stopped heart and arrested brain; death is, supremely, being without God. Or, again as Genesis would put it, it is hiding from him because of the shame of sin (3:8-11).

With this deeper perspective the Scriptures can envision physical life and physical death in a way that an unbeliever never could. Israel struggled long and hard in her attempt to understand this new way before she was able to articulate its meaning clearly. Our first reading for this Sunday is a giant step in that direction.

It is part of a poem that we have encountered several times in our readings. It tells of "Yahweh's servant," who serves by dying for others. From 52:13 to 53:9 we read of this amazing One who is "led like a lamb to the slaughter," who is "pierced for our offenses, crushed for our sins. . . ."

Now, in our reading, we learn that, in giving his life, "he shall see the light in fullness of days. . . ." The author may have been thinking of the survival of Israel after the exile in Babylon, a survival that would involve the servant's "descendants in a long life. . . ." But the early Church understood it as Jesus' risen life after his sacrificial death.

This, then, is a new way of understanding physical death. It is no longer the end of all life. Rather, death, especially when accepted as a sacrifice for sin, leads to "fullness of days." Other texts would describe that fullness in a variety of ways. Here we are concerned only with the reality of a new life itself.

We must understand the Gospel reading in its longer context. Jesus had just made the third prediction of his coming passion, death and resurrection. He had just reaffirmed this new way of seeing physical death. It is an act of service leading to a full life with the Father.

But the disciples find it hard to grasp this. They want only to share Jesus' glory; they want only to rank first in the kingdom. But Jesus insists that there is no greatness, no ranking first unless there is the giving of one's self, even the giving of life "in ransom for the many."

Living for others leads to life in its fullness, to immortality. Then death, in the fullness of its meaning, is truly overcome. Then there will be no hiding from God out of shame, but a walking with him forever.

Thirtieth Sunday in Ordinary Time (B)
Jeremiah 31:7-9; Hebrews 5:1-6; Mark 10:46-52

Mark 10:46 begins with this curious statement: "And they came to Jericho; and as he was leaving Jericho. . . ." The first part suggests that the city will be the scene of some event in Jesus' ministry. The second part denies any significance to the city as far as Jesus' ministry is concerned; he comes to it only to leave it.

Scholars argue, on good evidence, that the curious statement can be explained by different stages in the transmission of the story. The story, as Mark received it, began with the mention of Jesus leaving Jericho. But in his account Mark had not yet said anything about Jesus being in Jericho. He therefore had to add the first statement, which the lectionary has omitted.

Unquestionably the scholars are right. But we can use the curiosity to illustrate an important theme in Mark's Gospel. For this evangelist Jesus can accurately be described as "a man in a hurry." He is totally possessed by his vision of the Kingdom, and he is in a hurry to proclaim its message, to exercise its power in forgiving sins and healing broken bodies, to fulfill its meaning in his coming death and resurrection.

One of the clearest of the telltale signs of this Markan theme is his frequent and unexpected use of the word "immediately." For example, in his story of Jesus' cure of Simon's mother-in-law we learn that Jesus came "immediately" from the synagogue and that the disciples "immediately" told him about the fevered woman (1:29-31).

In these and other cases Mark is not intending the word in its ordinary sense. Rather, it lends a spirit of breathlessness to the account. Look! the Kingdom is at hand! Strange and marvelous things happen!

In the light of this emphasis, then, Mark felt no embarrassment in saying that Jesus came to Jericho and adding immediately that he left it. Jericho is of no importance to Mark. He gets Jesus out of it as quickly as he got him into it.

But he needs the mention of Jericho because his story is linked to it. And the story is important; it's another record of Kingdom power. Note the sense of urgency in the story. The blind man cries out insistently to Jesus. Nor can the crowd's rebuke still him. Rather, he cries out "all the more." When Jesus calls him, he "throws off" his mantle and "springs to his feet." Finally, on Jesus' words, the blind man "immediately" receives his sight.

We can sense something of this same urgency in the first reading.

It is from Jeremiah's "Book of Consolation" (cc. 30-33) written for the dispirited people in exile. The prophet conveys this urgency by an exuberance of language. The people are told to "sing along," to "raise shouts," to "proclaim, give praise." God will comfort his people; he is coming to "bring them back."

But all that is propaedeutic, preliminary to the reality. With Jesus the Kingdom is here. There is no mistaking it in Mark's Gospel. It is as though he had written it with an exclamation point after every sentence.

What is more, the Kingdom presence does things to people. They are "amazed," "astonished beyond measure," "utterly astounded." What is most important, however, is that some, like the blind man in our story, "followed him on the way." The "way," for Mark, is not the road from Jericho. It is the way of Jesus, the way of the cross, the way of love and service to others, the way we all must travel as Christians. We can't stay long in Jericho; there's too much to do elsewhere—immediately.

Thirty-first Sunday in Ordinary Time (B)
Deuteronomy 6:2-6; Hebrews 7:23-28; Mark 12:28-34

Is love enough? Jesus apparently says that it is. The scribe asks him which is "the first of all the commandments," and the reply is love. This could suggest that other things are necessary but none is as important as love of God and neighbor. In that case, love would not be enough.

Good reason exists, however, for thinking there is more to it than that. We know, from other sources, that Jewish teachers at the time of Jesus were frequently asked to propose a "one line" summary of the Law. What commandment could be said to contain all the others?

We can understand this concern. By Jesus' time some industrious rabbi had figured out that the Mosaic Law contained more than 600 precepts. If they all had to be observed for salvation, it would seem that the first necessary step to salvation was a good memory. Clearly, a "Reader's Digest" version of the Law would be something eagerly sought. In fact, one rabbi was asked to sum up the Law while standing on one leg. That would ensure brevity!

Given this propensity at the time for *summaries* of the Law, we can be sure this is what the scribe was asking of Jesus. Not just the greatest, but also the all inclusive commandment is what he wanted.

Jesus does provide such a summary. But he does so with two commandments, not just one. In our reading this is evident from the fact that Jesus refers to "the first" and "the second." Love God *and* neighbor. So, love *is* enough if it includes both kinds, Jesus is saying.

It is important to note that he mentions both loves. They are not the same, as some have claimed. These people would say love of neighbor is enough. Love of God is just an outmoded way of saying love of neighbor. You can't even see God, so why waste time trying to love him when our fellow human beings need all the love we can give them? Some proponents of a "liberation theology" have argued in this way.

Our first response is that Jesus very deliberately mentions both loves. By saying "first" and "second" he indicates a separation, not an identification. He could very well be responding to a form of secular humanism that would call love of God obsolete. No, he says, not only is love of neighbor not enough; love of God is also necessary and it is "first."

We must also say that the two cannot be identical because of the difference in the objects of love. Love of the infinite, totally transcendent Lord is a wholly self-surrendering love. The totality of this love is demonstrated in the words, "with all your heart . . . , soul . . . , mind . . . , strength."

But something else is even more important. Jesus begins his summary by saying, "The Lord our God is Lord alone!" In saying "Lord" he is not just saying "infinite creator." He is saying "loving, saving God," the One who reached into our lives with the most magnificent display of love one could imagine. That is the meaning of "Lord," both for the Deuteronomist in our first reading and for Jesus in the Gospel.

Jesus quotes this passage here because he knows that the commandments to love God and neighbor flow from the energizing, empowering love that the Lord has for us. Becuse of that enabling divine love, Jesus can say, "Therefore you shall love. . . ."

Is love enough? If we mean *only* our love of God and of neighbor, it is not only not enough; it isn't even possible. But in accepting God's love of ourselves, then our love of God and neighbor is possible and is more than enough.

Thirty-second Sunday in Ordinary Time (B)
1 Kings 17:10-16; Hebrews 9:24-28; Mark 12:38-44

Totus tuus. Those Latin words mean "totally yours." They were allegedly inscribed on a card accompanying a rosary Pope John Paul II, in the course of his first visit to the United States, gave to a young woman in a wheel chair. This expressed the Holy Father's desire to give himself wholly to all he met.

Such total self-giving is characteristic of biblical religion. It is not to be understood as a purely human initiative. Rather, it is the expected response to the redemptive love of God. It is he who loves first. Then, empowered by that love, we can love God and neighbor in turn. This was the theme of last Sunday's readings.

The Scriptures do not explicitly mention the prior of love of God every time it mentions the human response. Often the total self-giving of the believer is alone recorded. But God's initial love is always a presupposititon. Our lives are, or should be, one large "thank you" to a loving God. And the "thank you" must be expressed wholeheartedly.

The Gospel reading exhibits this theme. The widow who gave her "two small copper coins" gave "all that she had to live on." This was her version of "totus tuus"to God. Because it was that, it was worth much more than the huge donations of the wealthy.

We need not ask whether a Jewish widow actually did give her "last cent" to the temple treasury. (If she did, she probably would have been back the next day seeking a bite to eat!) What Jesus is emphasizing is precisely the spirit of "totus tuus." When we give whatever we give to the Church or to some charity, can we say with sincerity "totus tuus" to God or to our neighbor?

The Old Testament reading was chosen for obvious reasons. A widow is asked to sacrifice the last bit of food she has. This is surely another form of "totus tuus" addressed to God and to the prophet

Elijah. It is even more pronounced here inasmuch as the widow is a pagan, from Zarephath in Syria. She can speak only of "your God" to Elijah. And yet she gives.

Here, too, we have a display of the divine "totus tuus" in the form of a miraculous provision of flour and oil "until the day when the Lord sends rain upon the earth." Thus the Elijah story caps the total gift of the widow with a total gift from God. But the emphasis, as in the Gospel story, is on the completeness of the human gift.

What is it that sparks this kind of total self-giving? We have already said, of course, that it is a "thank you" to God for his unending love. But we can detect also a sense of "once-for-allness" in these stories. It is as though this were the only chance that the widow of Zarephath or the widow of Jerusalem would have to give their gift. It's a case of "now or never."

This "once for all" character is especially marked in Christianity, and the author of Hebrews brings it out most clearly. Christ "has appeared at the end of the ages to take away sins once for all by his sacrifice." Jesus is the Father's "totus tuus" to us. When we respond, it must also be in the once for all spirit of "totus tuus."

That is why reincarnation doesn't make sense in Christianity. That doctrine says, in effect, "You don't really have to try too hard. You'll get another chance." In Christianity God has given his all once for all. We are asked to respond in the same way. As our second reading puts it, ". . . it is appointed that men die once, and after death be judged. . . ." That is why we say right here and now to God, "Totus tuus, Lord!"

Thirty-third Sunday in Ordinary Time (B)
Daniel 12:1-3; Hebrews 10:11-14, 18; Mark 13:24-32

Hope is a uniquely biblical virtue. In general, it is the confident expectation of a happy outcome. In the biblical sense it is the confident expectation of the eventual establishment of God's Kingdom, of his reign in peace and justice among his people. The hopeful individual expects to be a member of that people.

What is it that makes hope so uniquely biblical? It is, first of all, the strong faith conviction that God has already "shown his hand." He has done this in the history of his people. Moreover, it was a saving hand, a manifestation of a love that would not be thwarted. With a God like that in command, how could there be anything but a happy outcome for those who accept him?

And so we find throughout the Bible a twofold view, one toward the past in faith, one toward the future in hope. Israel celebrated the mighty acts of God in the exodus, that time when he brought them out "with his strong hand and outstretched arm." Because of that, the prophets could speak confidently of the future when there would be "no harm or ruin on all my holy mountain, for the earth shall be filled with the knowledge of the Lord. . . ."

Similarly, Christians celebrate the Paschal mystery of Jesus Christ whereby "God has saved us and has called us to a holy life. . . ." Because of that, "it is all the more certain that we shall be saved by Christ from God's wrath." A saving past, marked by God's love, insures a saving future, marked just as surely by God's love.

It is important to keep this twofold view of biblical religion in mind because our two major readings for this Sunday, from Daniel and Mark, deal solely with the future. Both presuppose that this future is a necessary consequence of a past, a past of divine activity. Let us look briefly at each.

The book of Daniel was written at a time "unsurpassed in distress" for the Jewish people. A pagan emperor, from Syria, was trying to force his pagan customs on God's people. The temple had been taken over and used for pagan worship, and many Jews were made to apostatize (cf. Dn 11:31-32).

Many of God's people could see no saving future for them at all. Life was bleak and dreary. But there *had* to be a saving future because God is a saving God. In this context and in this conviction our author wrote what we hear this Sunday. They "shall live forever" and "shine like the stars."

Here, for the first time in biblical history, we have the expression of a transcendental goal, of a saving future that eclipses ordinary time and history. What made such an overpowering hope-expression possible, even necessary, was the faith conviction of a saving, loving God.

The Gospel reading applies the same principle. Jesus speaks of the Son of Man coming in power and glory. He is coming, of course, to mark the definitive reign of God, to bring salvation's consummation to all his people.

The Church reminds us of this hope not as a harmless placebo to help us forget our present ills. On the contrary, this surpassing hope is to give deeper meaning to the present. For he who is coming has already come. It will be a final divine "yes" to a world already touched by his saving hand.

What we must do is live as though we believe it. For Jesus will come, precisely, for those who await him. He will come for those who hope because they believed.

Christ the King (B)
Daniel 7:13-14; Revelation 1:5-8; John 18:33-37

"So, then, you are a king?" The question, directed by Pilate to Jesus, was straightforward enough. He wondered how this apparent criminal could possibly claim the lofty title of king. But Jesus' answer is elusive. His kingship "does not belong to this world." Or, as some translate, his kingship "is not from the world." If Pilate was baffled, he was not alone.

Kings don't fare too well in the Bible. It's true that at times we'll find some glorious things said about David and his dynasty. A number of "royal" Psalms were composed to extol his reign or that of one of his successors. "You are the fairest of the sons of men; grace is poured upon your lips; therefore God has blessed you forever" (Psalm 45:2). That is pretty glowing tribute to a human monarch.

But the actual experience of kings usually gave the lie to such praise. Proclaimed, almost invariably, on the day of coronation, the poems expressed a hope more than a reality. And the hope was often quickly dashed. So the royal Psalms, in due time, came to be understood of an ideal king who would appear at the end of the ages, of someone who could represent more than this seamy world of *Realpolitik*, the real world of political power.

Israel had also a strong anti-king tradition. Human kingship appeared almost inherently bad. When the psalmist wrote, "Kings in their splendor he slew," many a reader would have responded, "Right on!" If you want a good list of reasons for feeble support for monarchy, read 1 Samuel 8:10-18. Enough is there to chill the hearts of most royal enthusiasts.

Still, somehow, the notion of kingship was never totally abandoned. As we have already pointed out, the imagery was transferred, gradually, to an end-time figure. This allowed for the retention of a royal idealism.

Also, God himself was hailed as king, which gave Israel more than sufficient grounds for thinking good thoughts of kingship. It is not certain how old the concept of the Lord's kingship is, but it does pervade a good number of the biblical books. In fact, the realization of the greatness of the Lord's kingship had much to do with Israel's disillusionment with human kings.

One more important factor conditioned the biblical notion of kingship. It was suffering, a kind of emptying out of one's very self, a being stripped of earthly glory and power. Once this was experienced and accepted, effective and royal service of others was possible.

Israel discovered this in exile. At least the author of Isaiah 40 to 55 discovered it. And he described it magnificently in the "suffering servant" songs of that book (cf. 52:13—53:12). Through suffering to kingship became the working principle.

Evidence? The first and third readings for this Sunday. Daniel's "son of man" is Israel, suffering now under the persecution of a Syrian king. But this "son of man" will receive "dominion, glory, and kingship; . . . his kingship shall not be destroyed."

And Jesus' throne is his cross. From that throne, as John sees it, he will reign in glory over all peoples. Of course Pilate was baffled by Jesus' answer. He wouldn't understand that kind of kingship. Where is the worldly power, the political power, the military power? Jesus' power is that of self-surrendering love. It's the only kind that makes for effective rule.

Some want to drop this feast; "king" is too worldly a title. Let's keep it and let worldly rulers know what true kingship can be.

THE WORD ALIVE

Cycle C

What do we have in common with the Christians of ancient Thessalonica? One reasonable response would be a question as to who they were and what they believed that might be of interest to us.

Thessalonica was a fairly important city in the northeastern part of what is today modern Greece. It was the second city in Europe to be visited by Paul on his second missionary journey about 49 A.D. A good number of its citizens embraced Christianity after hearing Paul preach to them. In his two letters to them written about a year or so later, Paul expresses his gratitude to them for their faith in Jesus Christ.

Here is part of what he has to say to them: ". . . you became an example to all the believers in Macedonia and Achaia"; ". . .your faith in God has gone forth everywhere. . . ." (1 Th 1:7-8). Would Paul have been able to write something similar about the faith of the church in Cincinnati, in New Orleans, in Honolulu? Do we have this kind of faith in common with those ancient Thessalonians?

But something else is special about their faith. We know about it from the two letters Paul wrote to them. In our second reading for this Sunday, from the first of those two letters, it is mentioned, though only in passing. He prays that their hearts might be made blameless and holy "at the coming of the Lord Jesus with all his holy ones."

The Lord's "coming" refers to his second coming in glory at the end of time. The Greek word for it is *parousia*. A common belief among the early Christians was that Jesus would come again, this time to mark history's fulfillment and the definitive establishment of

God's Kingdom. The belief was rooted in Jesus' own words, such as are found in the Gospel reading.

What distinguished the Thessalonican faith in this regard was the intensity of their longing for the *parousia*. Doubtless this could be traced back to Paul's own preaching to them, since he also shared that longing. But with these Christians some problems surfaced concerning the *parousia*.

One was their concern about their fellow-Christians who had died. Would they also share in the glory of "that day"? Paul had to assure them that they would. He also had to remind them that being alive or dead at the time of the "coming" was not the important thing. Rather, the bottom line of the Christian hope is that all would be "with the Lord forever."

Another problem was their conviction that the parousia would occur soon, certainly in their own lifetime. Paul probably shared that hope (cf. 1 Th 4:17), but he knew that the *time* of the coming was not essential to the Christian faith. Jesus himself had said that he did not know the "exact day or hour" (Mk 13:32). So Paul had to calm their ardor in this respect.

Still, the expectation of the *parousia* remained for them and remains for us a real part of the Christian faith. If we believe that the Son of God came in human flesh, then we must believe that he will come again. If we rejoice in that first coming, we must rejoice also in the second.

We do not have to share the Thessalonian Christians' expectation that we will witness the *parousia* "in the flesh." But we must have in common with them the hope in his coming. If we have that hope, then we will appreciate what both Jesus and Paul say about "being ready." Inevitably all of us, alive or dead, will meet the Lord. May it be a joyful reunion.

Second Sunday of Advent (C)
Baruch 5:1-9; Philippians 1:4-6.8-11; Luke 3:1-6

Who in the world is Baruch? The question is not surprising. Readings from the book attributed to him occur only on the Easter Vigil and on this Sunday of Cycle C.

Biblical scholars would give high marks to the *historical figure* known as Baruch. Jeremiah's secretary, he twice wrote down the oracles of the prophet. The second draft was necessary after the king of Judah had destroyed the first one. Had it not been for Baruch's diligence, the world might well have been deprived of some of its most moving religious literature.

The *book* of Baruch is another matter. It was almost certainly not written by Jeremiah's secretary. Rather, it seems to have emerged from the somewhat turbulent era before the coming of Jesus Christ. That it was attributed to Baruch is testimony to the esteem in which he was held.

But there is more than that. The author (or authors) doubtless saw the contemporary scene as a reflection of the age of Jeremiah. There were threats from without and from within. A new Baruch was needed to record the prophetic message, warning the people of their sins and encouraging them with oracles of hope. The book does just that.

This Sunday's reading is the last half of a poem addressed to the new Jerusalem of the end-time, not to the famed city of Judah. She symbolizes the end-time people who "will be named by God forever the peace of justice, the glory of God's worship." If at all possible, read the poem reflectively before the Sunday Eucharist. Let the power and beauty of its words of hope fill your mind and heart; make these words be words for today.

We are justified in doing that. The fact that a second century B.C. author took a sixth century B.C. setting and made it the background for his own day tells us so. It shows we can take this second century B.C. book and make it a word of hope for a twentieth century A.D. people.

We can do this for a simple reason. This book is God's Word, and God's Word is for all time. More than that, it describes God's saving action for his people. That saving action is realized in quite specific times and places. But once realized then and there, it becomes a possibility, even a certainty, for those whose hope is firm, in every time and place.

The Gospel reading, from Luke, helps us to appreciate this even more. It is the account of John the Baptizer appearing in the land and

announcing the coming salvation. Surely the Church combined the
Baruch reading with this one because of the similar theme of hope
and approaching salvation. There is even a sameness in the descrip-
tive imagery. In Baruch we read that "every lofty mountain (will) be
made low." In Luke the Baptizer announces that "every mountain
and hill shall be leveled."

More significantly, Luke has tied this Baptizer even to a precise
time and place. Read the first two verses. They speak of Tiberius
Caesar, Pontius Pilate and Judea, Herod and Galilee, and tetrarchs
and high priests. Luke is saying that it really happened among real
people and in real places.

But because of the nature of God's word and God's loving action,
the Church tells us in this liturgy of the Word that it really happens in
our time too, among our people, in our cities. We could just as well
read, "In the third year of President Carter, when James M. Rhodes
was governor of Ohio, during the papacy of John Paul II, the word of
God came to the people of Ohio." The Gospel, the Word of the Lord,
will be forever here-and-now.

Third Sunday of Advent (C)
Zephaniah 3:14-18; Philippians 4:4-7; Luke 3:10-18

Patient anticipation. That's a strange combination of adjective and
noun. One might well expect something like anxious anticipation, or
eager anticipation. To anticipate with patience seems unusual. Yet
that is what the Gospel reading tells us this third Sunday of Advent.

For the First Advent Sunday the theme of hope, an obvious one for
the season, was introduced. On the second Sunday we saw how the
Baptizer's words of hope can be applied to our day. The Word of God
is for all time; it is for us. On this third Sunday we learn how to handle
our hope, namely, patiently.

The reason we suggest this qualification is found in John's reply to
those who asked him what they should do to prepare for the coming
One. He tells them that they should act in a normal manner in their
dealings with others. He asks nothing beyond what the Law would
require. The "normalness" fairly leaps out at the reader. Act kindly.

Act justly. In a word, "Keep calm as a faithful member of God's people."

This is in marked contrast to the agitated state of the people themselves. Luke notes that they "were full of anticipation." The New English Bible probably catches the spirit more precisely by translating, "The people were on tiptoe of expectation."

Also in marked contrast to John's "normal" admonitions are the words that these same people would soon be hearing from the lips of Jesus: "Blessed are the poor. Love your enemies. Do good to those who hate you. Go, sell what you have and give to the poor, and come, follow me. Take up your cross daily." But only the coming One, only the One whom John called "mightier than I," could say words like that, could ask for that kind of commitment.

John knew, then, that this "mightier One" would ask more of the people. He felt, however, that the best he could do was to prepare them for the greater call by being true to their present call. "Do what is expected of you." Thus will you patiently anticipate "He-who-is-to-come."

As Christians, we have heard that higher call and made that deeper commitment. We have surrendered in faith to Jesus Christ. We have, as Paul expresses it, put on the Lord Jesus Christ, the "mighty One."

That is why Paul can speak as he does in our second reading: "Rejoice in the Lord always! I say it again. Rejoice!" Can you imagine John the Baptizer making that kind of proclamation? It shows that something definitive has occurred and that we have been affected by it. One of the major missions of the Church has been to let the people know about it. This is what we call evangelization.

Are John's tempering remarks no longer viable then? Is there no more room for "patient anticipation"? Of course there is. Despite our rejoicing and our alleluias, we still look forward to the Lord's coming in glory. Or, to put it as Paul does in his letter to the Roman church, "Our salvation is closer than when we first accepted the faith" (13:11).

This means that, while retaining our deeper commitment and hope in the Lord's coming, we should not act as though we knew "the day or the hour." We don't go climbing mountains to await in suspenseful anticipation his coming. We don't carry banners trumpeting the message, "The end is near!" Rather, with patient anticipation we let the world know what it means to be a Christian here and now.

Fourth Sunday of Advent (C)
Micah 5:1-4; Hebrews 10:5-10; Luke 1:39-45

John meets Jesus. The Old Testament encounters the New. On that note the Advent season draws to a close. Through these two infants, still in their mothers' wombs, we are provided with a foretaste of the coming Christmas season.

It is important that we appreciate the full significance of what Luke is recording for us here. It is not unlikely that the evangelist was in possession of some family memoirs concerning the child Jesus. He has used them as the basis for a magnificent theological tableau that both penetrates the mystery of Jesus' person and anticipates the mission he would be carrying out some years later.

In doing this Luke has made use of a number of Old Testament themes, a couple of which we shall see in our reading for this Sunday. In that way he shows both the close connection between the two Testaments and the profound way in which Jesus Christ gives the fullest of meaning to all that had gone before.

John the Baptizer plays an important role in Luke's theology. He is the culmination, the final and climactical representative of the Old Testament message. He closes one period of history and opens the door to another.

After our scene, Luke never records a meeting of John and Jesus. He is, however, aware that John was still alive during Jesus' ministry. For example, he tells of John's sending of two of his disciples to Jesus to ask about his mission (7:18-23). But they do not appear together. Jesus' time is his own, uniquely and exclusively. He alone is giving a new meaning to history.

Even at Jesus' baptism, which, of course, Luke knew was performed by John, he is careful not to mention him by name. He simply says that Jesus was baptized (3:21-22). In fact, in the verse just preceding the mention of Jesus' baptism Luke notes that Herod "shuts up John in prison." John must not be seen as intruding on Jesus' time.

The reason for this literary maneuvering on the part of Luke is the arch significance of Jesus. While fulfilling all that went before, he also gives totally new meaning to all that will come after. Jesus, in the brief span of time on this earth, is in reality the middle of all time, of all history.

In the light of the theology Luke presents, we can appreciate our passage all the more. The meeting of the two figures, the only one that Luke will record, is deep in meaning.

Note that Mary takes the initiative in going to Elizabeth's home. The Greek phrase translated "in haste" can also mean "deliberately" or "thoughtfully." While it is naturally proper that the younger woman visit the older one, is Luke perhaps saying, "That is Jesus' work; he is the gift brought to others"?

Again, Elizabeth calls Mary "the mother of my Lord." This recalls the exalted place held by the Queen mother in the time of Judah's king (1 K 2:19). Mary is, in truth, a Queen mother. Also, the title of Lord was given to Jesus by the early Church at the resurrection. So, his risen lordship is already anticipated.

Finally, the infant John is said to "leap" in Elizabeth's womb on the occasion of the visit. Surely Luke was thinking of "King David leaping and dancing before the Lord" as the Ark was brought to Jerusalem (2 S 6:16). If this meeting of John and Jesus provoked these profound reflections by Luke, how shall we prepare for this "One who is to come"?

Vigil of Christmas (ABC)
See page 9

Christmas Midnight Mass (ABC)
See page 11

Christmas Mass at Dawn (ABC)
See page 13

Christmas Mass during the Day (ABC)
See page 14

Holy Family (C)
Sirach 3:2-6, 12-14; Colossians 3:12-21; Luke 2:41-52

Respect for the human person is the cornerstone of a human society. Where no respect for the human person exists, there can be random killing, rape, torture, and repression of all kinds. These are the signs of its absence.

Respect is both cause and effect in a good Christian family. It is the necessary requirement for the development of loving bonds within the family, and a good family will engender respect for all other persons in the human society.

Our three readings for this Sunday address themselves to respect for persons as the requirement for a good family. The reading from Sirach uses two Greek words several times in speaking of the children's attitude toward their parents. A closer look at both of them will help us appreciate the author's intent.

The one word, as used in secular literature, means primarily to hold an opinion or make a judgment. But in biblical usage it means almost always to glorify or extol. The noun is used of God's glory, the outer resplendence of his inner being.

Children, thus, are asked to recognize the worth of their parents and so to honor or revere them, as the New American Bible translates the word. What is more, the opening verse of our reading states that the Lord himself has given this worth to the father, setting him "in honor over his children."

The second word is somewhat similar but adds a note of awe to the children's attitude. The New American Bible uses the same word, "honor." The Good News Bible, Catholic Study Edition, has "respect," which is a bit closer to the Greek. Respect and reverence go hand in hand.

The author of Sirach observes that children who have these attitudes toward their parents "will live a long life." He borrows that, of course, from the Decalogue where the fourth commandment, the honoring of parents, mentions that precise reward. Strikingly it is the only one of the ten that has a reward explicitly attached to it, a mark of its importance in Jewish eyes.

Of course, in the Christian faith that "long life" takes on a new dimension. In the New Testament, life is something that does not end with physical death. Rather, it is "eternal," a life begun here on earth and continuing after death because it is life with God. This kind of life has respect for parents as a supposition.

In his Colossian letter Paul offers a beautiful picture of Christians living in love and respect for one another. The passage concludes with specific injunctions for the members of a family. Paul observes that all of this is possible if the rich word of Christ dwells in them.

Is it not this rich word of Christ that dwells in Mary and that accounts for the reverence and mutual respect that mark the Holy Family? After the scene in the temple precincts, this family returned to Nazareth. But Mary, Luke tells us, "kept all these things (or "words") in memory." The evangelist must have had some reason for making that observation.

Once before, Mary had accepted a "word" from on high and because of that she became the messianic Mother. This provides a concrete suggestion for our own growth in respect for others. It is that each family read, once a day, a passage from the Gospels. A respectful reading of that Word can implant in all a sense of wonder for the persons round them.

Mary, Mother of God (ABC)
See page 18

Epiphany (ABC)
See page 20

Baptism of the Lord (C)
Isaiah 42:1-4, 6-7; Acts 10:34-38; Luke 3:15-16, 21-22

Good evidence indicates that in the latter part of the first century a number of people considered John the Baptizer to be the Messiah. That seems strange to us who consider the word "Christ" (which is the Greek word for the Hebrew word "Messiah") to be the second name of Jesus. The name of "John Christ" is as foreign to us as the name "Jesus Christ" is familiar.

There were varying reasons for this religious aberration. One of the more prominent was the fact that John baptized Jesus, a surface indication of superiority. But what is important for us to reflect on today is that, despite the presence of this movement, none of the evangelists fails to mention Jesus' baptism by John. It was too important an event in the ministry of Jesus.

Part of the importance lies in the fact that the baptism was the first public event in Jesus' ministry. The events recorded in the infancy narratives of Matthew and Luke were "family affairs" whose significance for his ministry was symbolic rather than direct. The Jordan baptism opened up a whole new world for Jesus, and from that time on he began preaching the Kingdom of God.

This is not to say Jesus was totally unaware before this of some special mission the Father had in store for him. But what was clearly manifested to him now was that he was, in the Father's words, "my beloved Son, with thee I am well pleased."

Jesus knew his Scriptures well. He was aware that those words were from the book of Isaiah and were part of a poem that described, along with three other poems, a mysterious figure who was to come. And he knew that figure, called the "Suffering Servant," was to die like a slaughtered lamb for the sins of others.

What is most important, he now knew that he was the "Suffering Servant." He was aware that the coming of the Kingdom was connected not only with his preaching of the Kingdom of God, but also with his own death.

That Jesus associated his baptism with his awareness of the need to suffer and die is clear from another passage that would otherwise make no sense. When James and John asked Jesus if they could sit with him in his glory, he asked them if they could first be "baptized" with the "baptism" with which he is "baptized" (Mk 10:35-40).

The context of that statement shows that Jesus was referring to his coming death (giving "his life as a ransom for many" Mk 10:45) as a baptism. Thus, the shadow of the cross was cast over the public ministry of Jesus from the beginning.

Now we know why the apostles, when they later preached the Good News of Jesus, always began with the mention of his baptism by John. Peter does it in the second reading for this Sunday. Not even the dangers of a Baptizer movement could keep them from preaching Jesus' baptism by John.

The implications for us are enormous. It means that, when we are baptized in Christ's baptism, we are baptized into his death (Rm 6:3). All our suffering and our death have new meaning. The cross is part of the Christian "way." But it is the cross of the Kingdom, the cross of glory. It is an "Alleluia" cross.

First Sunday of Lent (C)
Deuteronomy 26:4-10; Romans 10:8-13; Luke 4:1-13

All three readings for this first Lenten Sunday are rich in meaning for the believer. The temptation account, in Luke's Gospel, is, of course, the most readily applicable to the season. Jesus' fasting and subsequent victory over evil are intended both to remind and to enable us to follow his example.

That Jesus was tempted, and tempted severely, tells us that temptation to evil is one of the most radical elements of human nature. The Word of God took on human flesh precisely so that he could experience the deepest realities that we experience. And to be human is to be tempted.

The author of Hebrews says that it was just because he was tempted, that Jesus "is able to help those who are tempted" (2:18). In fact, "he had to become like his brothers in every way, that he might be a merciful and faithful high priest before God on their behalf" (2:17). That is comforting. True, Jesus held out against evil, but he knows what we are going through. That is why he can be merciful.

Temptation is the measure of human freedom. That we can be tempted means that we can make a decision. We can say yes or no. Only the slave acts out of necessity. The free person has a choice. If there were no choice, there would be no responsibility. No wonder Jesus had to undergo temptation.

No wonder, too, that Luke makes the temptation account so dramatic. Twice in the opening verse he mentions the Spirit. Jesus was "full of the Holy Spirit" and he was "conducted by the Spirit into the desert. . . ." Luke is saying that the coming struggle was to be one of cosmic proportions, *the* power of good against *the* power of evil.

Also, the three replies of Jesus to the three temptations of the devil provide another key to the wider dimensions of the struggle. All three responses are from the book of Deuteronomy and refer to commands directed by God to Israel during the wandering in the desert. What is more, they are commands that she failed to heed during that experience.

Jesus did heed them. He is, then, the true Israel, the One we can confidently believe has been chosen by the Father to move into the true promised land. And we, part of that people of God, move with him. Where he goes, we go. He cannot desert us because we belong to him.

Now we can understand the reason for the first reading. It is from the same book that recorded the three commands made to Israel. Here it tells about the exodus of God's people from Egypt and the entrance into the promised land. It is the story of the movement of a people from slavery into freedom. And this is all done by the "strong hand and outstretched arm of God."

That is exactly what Jesus does for us by his victory over the tempter. He moves us from the reign of sin into the freedom of the children of God. His "strong hand and outstretched arm" against the tempter says how much he loves us and wants us to be free.

Every time, then, that we are tempted—to lose our patience, to ignore another in need, to judge on the basis of color or race, to envy or covet or hate—we must remember the pioneer of our salvation (Heb 2:10). "For we do not have a high priest who is unable to sympathize with our weakness, but one who was tempted in every way that we are, yet never sinned" (Heb 4:15).

How understandable that St. Paul, in the second reading, can speak of Jesus as the Lord who is "rich in mercy toward all who call upon him" (Rm 10:12).

Second Sunday of Lent (C)
Genesis 15:5-12, 17-18; Philippians 3:17—4:1; Luke 9:28-36

The fifteenth chapter of Genesis is a stunning piece of religious literature. The leanness of the prose, the vividness of the figures, and the depth of its theological insights all contribute to its power. The ancient readers, more appreciative than we, must have been fascinated by it.

First, the story itself. When God called Abram from the land of his fathers, he promised him a great name and many descendants (Gn 12:1-3). Now some years later Abram is still without an heir. Yet he "put his faith in the Lord," who then, in what we would call a bizarre ritual, initiated a covenant with the patriarch.

Let's consider those theological insights. First of all comes the divine initiative, an unvarying element in all of biblical religion. God always acts first, and always in a saving way, here in the form of a promise.

Abram believes in God. This is again, always the first and expected response of the human person. It is here an act of acceptance of, and surrender to the promising God. There is no compelling reason, no persuasive argument. It is sheer faith. St. Paul never ceased marveling at this faith of Abraham (Gal 3:6-9; Rm 4:1-25).

The bizarre ritual was actually a widely accepted form of treaty or covenant making in ancient times. The animals are split in two in order to signify the fate of those who break the covenant. The passing between the divided pieces by "a smoking brazier and a flaming torch" symbolizes God's acceptance and ratification of the covenant terms. God, as it were, puts his own life on the line for his servant Abram.

We also read that "a deep, terrifying darkness enveloped" Abram. It is the same Hebrew word that is translated "deep sleep" in Genesis 2:21, where it is said of Adam before God created woman out of his side. The idea expressed is that something awesome is about to happen and it is God's doing, not man's.

What all of this means for us is hard to express adequately. But it does say that God wills to inaugurate a deep relationship with a people. There is almost a divine loss of self-control in his eagerness to make human beings his friends. And on the human side there is simply the impossibility of comprehending this divine offer of friendship.

In reflecting on this we want to say with Job: "In my thoughts during visions of the night, when deep sleep (that same Hebrew word) falls on men, fear came upon me, and shuddering, that terrified me to the bones" (4:13-14). But we "put our faith in God" and let him act in our lives.

Reading the Gospel in the context of that Genesis passage, we see the same divine initiative and the same human incomprehension. It is the transfiguration of Jesus, at which the disciples fall into "a deep sleep." But the heart of the vision is the message of the voice from the cloud.

At the time of Jesus' baptism, Luke had noted a similar voice and a similar message. But there it was directed to Jesus himself, "You are my beloved Son" (3:22). Here it is directed to the disciples and to us, "This is my Son, my Chosen One. Listen to him."

Jesus is God's Son *for us*. He is our brother, our friend. The divine eagerness expressed in the Abram story spills over into a reckless giving of himself, his Son, to be with us. Only one question has meaning here: do we put our faith in him?

Third Sunday of Lent (C)
Exodus 3:1-8.13-15; 1 Corinthians 10:1-6, 10-12; Luke 13:1-9

"Reform your lives and believe in the gospel!" (Mk 1:15). With those words Mark introduces the public ministry of Jesus. The gospel, the good news of God's reign among his people, calls for a change in one's way of life. The Kingdom doesn't suffer mediocrity, much less evil. It always elicits the best from those who hear the Word and accept it.

The word "reform" has definite connotations for us. We think of the habitual drunkard who becomes a total abstainer, the prostitute who accepts a respectable job, the Mafia person who leaves the organization for good. In these cases reform means a complete turnabout.

When Jesus spoke of reform, he meant this kind of change. For him the Father's Kingdom was such an overwhelming reality that he could think of no other terms. Faced with the shattering presence of God in Jesus Christ, the hearer of the gospel must say either "yes" or "no." If it is "yes," reform will take place. If it is "no," then, in the words of our third reading, the tree must be destroyed; it bears no fruit.

There is some reason to believe, however, that, as the Church continued preaching the good news of Jesus Christ in history, she recognized that reform could be *gradual*. Those who heard the gospel would indeed accept the Lord and decide to live in accord with that acceptance. But a sudden and complete change didn't always take place. Rather, the Christian commitment now fostered a continuing growth in holiness.

Luke, especially, seems to have envisioned this possibility for the Christian. The Lord's second coming was delayed and the awesome imperative of "Reform!" in the radical sense intended by Jesus would be applicable only for the confirmed sinner. For the committed Christian reform meant constant growth.

Luke's recording of one of Jesus' sayings illustrated this. The saying is a familiar one. In Mark's Gospel it reads like this: "If a man wishes to come after me, he must deny his very self, take up his cross, and follow in my steps" (8:34). Jesus sees the taking up of the cross as a once-for-all act of his followers. Taking up the cross is the Christian expression of radical reform.

When Luke records that same saying, he makes a significant addition. Here Jesus says that his followers must "take up their cross *each day* . . . " (Lk 9:23). The saying now loses its once-for-all radical character. Now it has to do with the daily, continuing life of the Christian, a life that must be marked by a constant struggle, a steady effort to grow in Christ.

We're justified in reflecting in this way because without doubt reform is the message of the Gospel reading. And could it be that it was Luke who added the suggestion about waiting another year for the tree to grow and bear fruit? It would surely be in keeping with his concept of Christian holiness.

We do not make ourselves Christians. God's grace does that. Neither do we grow as Christians by our efforts alone. Again, it is God's love that empowers all growth. Maybe that explains why the first reading from Exodus, is given us this Sunday. It reminds us of the kind of God we have, a God whose name tells us of his presence in our midst, a presence that makes reform a joyful process.

Fourth Sunday of Lent (C)
Joshua 5:9, 10-12; 2 Corinthians 5:17-21; Luke 15:1-3, 11-32

To be reconciled to one's enemy is possibly the most difficult of human endeavors. A solid indication of this is the raging passion with which people seek vengeance on those who hurt them. Another indication is the difficulty that a person finds in making peace with someone who has spurned or slighted him. Almost instinctively he wants to "get even."

But "getting even" never really makes things even. Either the enemy is removed from the scene by foul play of some kind, or the animosity between the two is increased in the very process of "getting even." The chances for "healing" the relationship have become all the less likely.

The only effective way to "get even" is by reconciliation, difficult as it is. That is why reconciliation is one way in which the whole grand purpose of God is expressed in the Scriptures. He wills, above all, our reconciliation with himself and with one another. All three readings for this Sunday testify to this divine will.

The first and indispensable factor in the biblical notion of reconciliation is the divine initiative. God must act first. He must be present with his reconciling love before we can be reconciled with him or with one another. And what our readings tell us is that he is always present with that initiative. It only needs our acceptance.

The first reading begins with a statement about that divine initiative: "Then the Lord said to Joshua, 'Today I have removed the reproach of Egypt from you.' " There is some question as to the meaning of "the reproach of Egypt." Possibly it refers to Israel's state of slavery in Egypt.

In any case, it is a reconciling act of God's. He wants them to be free for himself. And the celebration of the Passover by the Israelites can readily be interpreted as their joyful acceptance of the Lord's reconciling act. They celebrate what he has done for them.

The theme of reconciliation is bursting out all over in the reading from Paul. He says that because of Jesus Christ we are "a new creation." The divine reconciling act in favor of us sinners is so thorough, so radical, so awesome that it is said to produce something out of nothing.

Paul goes on to speak quite explicitly of this divine reconciliation. Note, first of all, that it is properly the Father's work, acting through Jesus Christ. Note, too, that God considers this reconciling act of his in Christ so important that he makes human persons ministers of his reconciliation. Whenever the Word is preached or the sacraments celebrated, this ministry is being exercised.

Note, too, how distinctively Paul expresses the need for human acceptance of reconciliation. He says, "Be reconciled to God!" He doesn't say, "Reconcile yourselves to God." He can't say that because we can't do that. Rather, the passive imperative has to be interpreted, "Allow yourselves to be reconciled by God to himself."

And the parable of the reconciling father? It requires an article in itself. The only bad news about this good news is that we tend to imitate the older brother rather than the younger son. We need to accept the Father's forgiving love, for ourselves as well as for others.

A final note: when we find ourselves making peace with one who has hurt us, that is an infallible sign that God's reconciling love has broken through to us and that we have accepted it.

Fifth Sunday of Lent (C)
Isaiah 43:16-21; Philippians 3:8-14; John 8:1-11

"I wish to know Christ and the power flowing from his resurrection; likewise to know how to share in his sufferings by being formed into the pattern of his death." Paul is speaking, and those are the words either of a madman or of a saint. Whoever is familiar with the rest of Paul's writings knows that he is a saint who has reflected deeply on the mystery of Christ.

Most of us, finding ourselves in Paul's situation, would probably write something like, "I want to be released from this prison; I don't want to suffer and die." But Paul considers all such earthly concerns "rubbish" in comparison with his relationship to Christ.

Is it possible for us at least to understand Paul enough to say that, yes, he is a saint and not a madman? Is it possible for us to appreciate the values of a saint even if we haven't yet reached that level of holiness? This is, after all, a minimum requirement of being a Christian.

But what precisely *is* Paul saying in these words? We must realize, first of all, that he is writing from prison and that he is writing to a beloved community of Christians who had befriended him. He wants to allay any undue concerns they may have for him and, at the same time, encourage their own progress in holiness. The words we have quoted above, from the second reading, are at the heart of his message.

The meaning centers on the word "know." For Paul, as for the Scriptures generally, this doesn't mean simply intellectual knowledge, such as knowing the solution to a problem. It means, in this context especially, to experience within oneself, to absorb with all of one's being, to be totally permeated by something.

Three objects of this "knowing" are in Paul's statement: Christ, the power of his resurrection, the sharing in his sufferings. But we could better say that there is only one object, and that is Christ who has risen and who shares the power of his saving actions with those who believe in him and wish to be like him.

Always it is Christ. But it is Christ in his concrete existence, as he is and as he acts. It is Christ, suffering, risen, pouring out the love (the "power") to experience, to absorb, to be permeated by. The fact that he can call other concerns "rubbish" in comparison with this is evidence that he already knows Christ in this way.

All this has made Paul something entirely new, "a new creation," as he put it in the second reading from last Sunday (2 Cor 5:17). In the first reading from this Sunday the prophet has God saying, "See, I am doing something new!" The prophet was thinking of a new exodus. The Church understands it as a reference to the new creation in Christ. That is the newness that Paul "knows."

The Gospel reading, too, speaks of something new. An adulteress, by Jewish law, should be stoned to death. That's the old way of coping with sin, an eye for an eye and a tooth for a tooth. It sounds so just and proper.

But a new way is possible, the way of forgiveness. This way produces a new creation, something beyond justice. The adulteress "knows" Jesus. She is now what she was not.

Are we able now to repeat Paul's words with meaning? Are we at least able to *want* to make them our own?

Passion Sunday (C)
Isaiah 50:4-7; Philippians 2:6-11; Luke 22:14—23:56

It's an amazing irony. The one religious question that proved the most difficult for the biblical authors of the Old Testament to resolve provided the solution to the salvation of the human race.

The question, of course, involves human suffering. Why does a good and loving God allow us to suffer as much as we do? The question reached its climactical expression in the book of Job. There the questioner goes so far as to call on God to give an account of himself: "This is my final plea; let the Almighty answer me!" (Jb 31:37).

The people of the Old Testament believed that suffering was in some way associated with sin. Indeed, the opening chapters of Genesis say clearly it was the sin of the first couple that introduced pain, suffering, and death into the world.

At times the association of sin and suffering was almost reduced to a mathematical formula. The suffering undergone by any person was thought to be directly proportioned to the number and gravity of the sins that person committed. One of the great merits of the book of Job was that it demolished this thesis.

But the book of Job, classic that it is, did not come up with a final solution. What it does do is to show that once we experience the reality of God, we recognize that the mystery of suffering is swallowed up in the much greater mystery of God himself.

The Christian faith only intensifies the mystery; it doesn't resolve it. It offers an astonishing number of insights into the manner in which God makes use of human suffering to bring about his saving will. Above all, it tells us that he willed the suffering of his own Son as the way to our salvation. That is what our liturgy celebrates on this Sunday. But the mystery remains.

Even the evangelists, who record for us the story of Jesus' suffering and death, do not resolve the mystery, even while they proclaim its saving effects. For Mark it is the moment of Jesus' death that evokes the centurion's confession that he is "the Son of God" (15:39). Matthew sees the resurrection anticipated in Jesus' death (27:52-53). John identifies the moment of his death with the giving of the Spirit (19:30).

In his Gospel, which provides the third reading for this Sunday, Luke drives home the absolute necessity of Jesus' suffering and death. He uses a Greek word which, for him, spells out a divine "must." It is the Father's will and there is no evading it. What is written in Scripture, Jesus tells his disciples, "must come to be fulfilled in me" (22:37).

One of the most powerful presentations of this self-giving suffering of the Savior is offered us by Paul in the second reading. These ancient words have been called the "kenotic hymn" because of its use of the Greek word "to empty," referring to the act whereby the Son empties himself of divine glory and even of human dignity, accepting death, even death, as Paul emphasizes, "on a cross." It is the epitome of human suffering.

But the hymn goes on to say that it was precisely through death that exaltation came. "*Because of this*, God highly exalted him. . . ." And his exaltation became our salvation.

All of this makes us realize that, while suffering is linked with human sin, it is also and even more mightily associated with divine love. We see suffering now as his self-giving surrender for us.

The mystery remains. But wasn't the author of Job right on the mark when he said that suffering loses its enfeebling effect when seen in the larger context of the mystery of God? And as Christians we would add, in the context of a divine love that chose suffering as its means to save.

Easter Sunday (C)
Acts 10:34, 37-43; Colossians 3:1-4; John 20:1-9

He is risen! Every line of the New Testament was written in the light of that conviction. Every statement is suffused with the belief that Jesus is the risen Lord.

In some few of the writings this belief may not seem too clearly present. For example, the letter of James, it is said, could almost have been written by a pious Jew. But, "almost." For, in the midst of his ethical exhortations he exclaims, "My brothers, your faith in our glorious Lord Jesus Christ must not allow of favoritism" (2:1). Only a committed Christian could have written that. It manifests a morality founded on the resurrection.

As we might expect on this resurrection feast, the three readings are most explicit in affirming this belief. The passage from Acts is beautifully illustrative. Peter's address is probably typical of the early Christian kerygma, or preaching form. Other apostolic sermons in Acts are very similar in content (v.g., 2:22-24; 3:12-15).

The address is a summary of Jesus' total experience, beginning with the baptism of John. Added are Jesus' own life of good works and healing, his inglorious death "on a tree," and his resurrection "on the third day." You can be sure that, if that final entry could not have been made, none of the rest would have been worth recounting.

This is not to say, by any means, that those other events of Jesus' earthly life have no meaning, or are merely introductory to the resurrection. But it is to say that these events have an added and even a transformed meaning in the light of the resurrection. "Jesus risen" does something to crucifixion.

The Gospel reading, on the empty tomb, says nothing explicit about the resurrection until the final verse. Still, that event looms large in the background, so large that it isn't even mentioned as an object of belief. All we read is, "the other disciple . . . saw and believed." He saw the empty tomb, but he believed in the risen Lord.

The evangelist knows that no one would interpret the disciple as believing in the empty tomb.

The resurrection event is stupendous. This has happened to no other person in the history of the human race. What is said of Enoch (Gn 5:24) and of Elijah (2 K 2:11) in the Old Testament and of Mary in the Church's tradition is not the same as Jesus' resurrection. That is unique.

An important aspect of that uniqueness is what Jesus' resurrection means for us. When he was raised from the dead, our lives were affected. We ourselves were transformed in anticipation. In other words, his resurrection is a continuing, dynamic reality that changes those who attach themselves to him in faith.

Isn't this what Paul means when he writes, ". . . you have been raised up in company with Christ. . . .Your life is hidden now with Christ in God." Paul is surely writing here to some who hadn't yet been born when Jesus rose from the dead. Still, his resurrection affects them.

And there is more. If we share now in his resurrection, we will necessarily share in his glorious coming at time's end. That is what Paul means when he writes, "When Christ our life appears, then you shall appear with him in glory."

We seem to have exhausted the profound riches of Jesus' resurrection. We have written of what God has done in Jesus. We have noted what that has meant for us. But one thing is lacking—our response. Again, from Paul, "Set your heart on what pertains to higher realms where Christ is seated at God's right hand. Be intent on things above rather than on things of earth." In other words, "Be what you are. Live as God has created you anew in his Son!"

Second Sunday of Easter (C)
Acts 5:12-16; Revelation 1:9-11a, 12-13, 17-19; John 20:19-31

When Jesus was raised, it was not just some overwhelming act of God to make us mortals stand in awe. It was not like a meteor flashing through the skies for a brief moment, then dying away without a trace. Jesus' resurrection opened doors of amazing grace, and even today continues to work its power in the Church, in the hearts of believers. That is what our readings say to us this Sunday.

The Gospel gets to the heart of the resurrection's secret. Jesus appears to the disciples in the upper room. Even his greeting to them has special significance. The "peace" he wished them is that grace-filled assurance of a loving relationship with the Lord and with one another. He can make that wish because he himself is now united with the Father, the giver of all good gifts.

Still more significantly, he can "send" them out as "apostles," a word meaning "one who is sent." Jesus himself is the Father's apostle (cf. Heb 3:1), sent on mission. The resurrection marks the completion of his mission, and so he can send forth his own apostles. It is a commissioning that he continues to exercise year after year in the Church. "As the Father has sent me, so I send you." These words of the risen Lord echo down the corridors of a two thousand year history.

Even closer to the heart of the resurrection's mystery are these words of Jesus: "Receive the Holy Spirit." In his final words to his disciples before his death, Jesus had told them that he must "go," that is, back to the Father, in order that he might send the Spirit in power upon them (Jn 16:7).

In his speech on Pentecost Sunday Peter makes the same connection between resurrection and the sending of the Spirit. There he says, "Exalted at God's right hand, he (Jesus) first received the promised Holy Spirit from the Father, then poured this Spirit out on us" (Ac 2:33). Jesus' reception of the Spirit here designates him as the channel of the same Spirit's outpouring on the faithful. For his own mission Jesus had already received the Spirit at his baptism (Lk 3:21-22).

It is the Father's own secret why he willed to bring about our salvation in precisely this way. For us it is an astonishing manifestation of love. God the Father, Son and Spirit love us with such intensity that they expend themselves totally for our sake. All this divine activity is directed to people. Jesus' resurrection is the key that opens the door to this flood of grace and love.

The reading from Acts is further proof of this. Luke makes no explicit mention of the resurrection here. But it is the necessary background and presupposition of what he is recording. He had, after all, just recounted the Pentecost scene where Peter had associated resurrection and the Spirit, as we saw above.

Now the effect of that resurrection and of the Spirit's sending is seen as building up the community of Christians. Moreover, not only are numbers added to the Church, but the physically deprived are restored to wholeness. It reminds us of the power of the earthly Jesus. But it is now that of the risen Jesus working through Peter, his "sent one." Jesus' resurrection makes it possible for Peter to imitate the earthly Savior.

The reading from Revelation is much too rich to explain fully here. We can but note these words of Jesus: "Once I was dead but now I live—forever and ever." He is not simply asserting his divine eternity. He means that he lives *for us*—forever and ever. He means that we who accept him in faith are caught up in that same "forever and ever." We accept his life if only we accept his love. *That* is what the resurrection does for us!.

Third Sunday of Easter (C)
Acts 5:27-32, 40-41; Revelation 5:11-14; John 21:1-19

The Gospel reading provides a puzzle. Its solution will give a deeper understanding and appreciation of what the author is saying.

The puzzle rests on the common conviction of scholars that the Gospel of John originally concluded with the preceding chapter. The telltale marks of such a conclusion are still present. The final verses of chapter 20 speaks of the reasons why the author wrote his book. He even suggests that he could have recorded other deeds of Jesus but feels that he has written enough to achieve his purpose, that is, to help people believe. Our present chapter, then, must be a later addition.

The puzzle is this. Why was the chapter added? We know that the addition was made by the person responsible for the final edition of the fourth Gospel. This means that he was fully acquainted with the Gospel's message. Yet he felt something more was needed to complete the message.

The reading records an appearance of Jesus at the lake of Galilee, the disciples' miraculous catch of fish at Jesus' direction, Peter's threefold protestation of love, and the Lord's commissioning of him to feed his lambs and sheep. Finally, there is an enigmatic prediction of Peter's martyrdom.

The message contained here is fairly obvious. The disciples must "catch fish" (the number 153 is certainly symbolic of a large number of converts). Peter will have a special role in caring for the people. He will also bear witness to the Lord by death.

Why the addition of this chapter, then? The reason is that faith in Jesus Christ, which was forcefully stated in the preceding chapter, must issue forth in ministry. That faith may even call for the supreme sacrifice, as it will for Peter. In other words, the history of the Church is vital and dynamic. That history is part of the Gospel, the "good news of salvation."

In the last two columns we noted that the resurrection of Jesus does not stand in isolation, as some mighty act of God to be marveled at from afar. No, the resurrection has a continuing effect. It makes the history of the Church eventful. That is precisely why our author added this chapter. It completes the Gospel by making it open to the future. The first reading, from Acts, is a commentary on the Gospel. At least it shows in part how Jesus' prediction was fulfilled. The apostles, including Peter, are brought before the great court and reprimanded for their preaching. They are then whipped and released.

Suffering for the Gospel is just what Jesus had foretold. The reading only suggests that this is due to their having made many converts. But the context, especially vv. 12-16, explicitly states that. In fact, we can say Luke's account in these verses more than fulfills the Gospel's symbolic "153 fish."

We can see that the Jesus story has taken strange and wondrous turns. Just when his disciples had come to believe in him as the wonder-working messiah, he tells them of his coming passion and death. Then, at the transfiguration, his resurrection is anticipated. But, once the resurrection takes place, there is word of suffering even death, for his followers.

But neither is that the end. The second reading, from the book of

Revelation, tells of final victory. The "thousands and tens of thousands" are those faithful witnesses to the Lamb of God who shares in his glory. That is our final destiny, yours and mine. So, when that author added a final chapter to John's Gospel, he was opening up the Gospel's message to a rich and glorious future.

Fourth Sunday of Easter (C)
Acts 13:14, 43-52; Revelation 7:9, 14-17; John 10:27-30

"In this, thy bitter passion, Good Shepherd, think of me." The words are from a well-known Passion chorale often sung during the Lenten season. It is better known by its opening words, "O Sacred Head Surrounded."

But why quote a Lenten hymn in the midst of the Easter season? The most obvious reason and the one that first occurred to me is the reference to Jesus as "Good Shepherd." Our third reading for this Sunday is taken from the "Good Shepherd" discourse in John's Gospel.

On reflection, however, I became aware of a much more profound reason, the one that led me to use the words as the opening sentence. Briefly, the reason is that Jesus' passion and death are an active reality in our struggle for holiness, just as much as his resurrection. As Paul reminds us, every time we celebrate the Eucharist, we "proclaim the death of the Lord until he comes" (1 Cor 11:26).

An insidious error is abroad in our land. It says in effect that Jesus doesn't hurt any more, no matter how much we sin. His suffering and death are a thing of the past. They have been annulled, blotted out by his resurrection. They had meaning only inasmuch as they highlighted the greatness and the glory of the risen Lord. They can now be forgotten.

As Jim Stentzel expressed it in an issue of *Sojourners*, many "think of Holy Week in terms of the ribbons on our bonnets, rather than the nails through Christ's limbs." They "like neatness, and the crucifixion is messy. . . . The journey, the struggle, is over. They've found it."

The Gospel truth is that the cross constantly intrudes into our lives and reminds us that, while God's grace is free, absolutely free, it is not cheap. It makes demands on us even in the midst of our Alleluias. It is why Jesus' "bitter passion" must never be overlooked and why, when we celebrate it, we ask him earnestly to think of us.

A living proof of this is the book of the Acts of the Apostles; our reading from that book is but one illustration from many. While the young Christian Church rejoices in the risen Lord, while "the disciples could not but be filled with joy and the Holy Spirit," they still suffer "violent abuse" and "persecution."

Those who suffer in this way are not less convinced of God's love for them. Rather, their spirit of gratefulness, their constant joy, their eagerness to spread the Word in the face of opposition are infallible signs of that love working its way in them. They have really "found" his love and cannot keep from responding to it.

Is there, then, *only* the cross, *only* the struggle? That, of course, would be the opposite error. We could hardly be an Easter people if we did not believe that the resurrection does mean, ultimately, total victory. While God's love in us now brings happiness with it, it will bring unmarred happiness in glory.

That is the clear message of the reading from Revelation. Who are all those people "from every nation and race, people and tongue"? "These are the ones who have survived the great period of trial. . . .It was this that brought them before God's throne."

They are you and I, and all those whom God's shepherding love has guided safely through our worldly pilgrimage. We sing our Alleluias now, even if a bit off key. But then we will sing them on key and in harmony with unfettered joy.

Fifth Sunday of Easter (C)
Acts 14:21-27; Revelation 21:1-5; John 13:31-33, 34-35

"This is God's dwelling among men." The theme, a familiar one, is found frequently in the Scriptures. But this is one of its more compelling expressions.

Already at the time of Israel's formation as God's people at Mount Sinai, they began to think of him as dwelling in some way in their midst. The ark of the covenant was the symbol of his presence. God was said to be "enthroned upon the cherubims" (1 S 4:4), the angelical figures associated with the ark.

When David had captured Jerusalem and made it his capital, one of his first projects was to build a temple for the Lord, a place where he could dwell among his people. As David observed to the prophet Nathan, "Here I am living in a house of Cedar, while the ark of God dwells in a tent" (2 S 7:2).

The biblical authors had no crass conception of God's dwelling with Israel. The Deuteronomist, in fact, deliberately avoids any such understanding by referring to the temple as the place which God chose "as the dwelling place for his *name*" (Dt 12:11). While God's "name" is a reference to his person and thus indicates the reality of the divine presence, it is a way of denying that the temple *contains* the Lord as in a box.

The most singular and awesome form of God's presence was, of course, in Jesus Christ. John put that most starkly when he wrote, "The Word became flesh and made his dwelling among us. . ." (1:14). Almost surely, in choosing the Greek word that means literally "pitched his tent," John was thinking of the ark of old. That divine presence was now realized "in the flesh."

Since Jesus' return to the Father, the Lord's presence among us is realized in a number of ways. He is present in the Word when it is read or proclaimed. He is present when two or more of his followers are gathered in his name. And he is present, most strikingly, in the sacrament of the Eucharist.

The author of Revelation was thinking of an even more awesome presence of God when he wrote the words with which we began this column. And he was thinking of an end-time presence, a time when, as he notes so movingly, God "shall wipe every tear from their eyes, and there shall be no more death or mourning, crying out or pain, for the former world has passed away."

We, however, are still in that "former world." It is, for that reason, up to us to witness to God's presence in the midst of tears, pain, and death. We must witness to his presence for those who do not experience it. And this is what our first and third readings are about.

The reading from Acts tells us that God's presence is witnessed to in ministry. Tirelessly Paul and Barnabas go from town to town, preaching and encouraging believers to "persevere in the faith." It is through such ministry that God "opened the door" to many, and they recognized his presence in faith.

The Gospel reading, as we might expect, says it most simply and yet most profoundly. "This is how all will know you for my disciples: your love for one another." Those words of Jesus tell us that when we love others as he loves us, we make him present, for, as we read in 1 John 4:11-12, our love is really his love at work in us. If we truly love one another, then we know that the Lord is present since his love is there.

Sixth Sunday of Easter (C)
Acts 15:1-2, 22-29; Revelation 21:10-14,22-23; John 14:23-29

Love, Spirit, peace, and return to the Father. This is a dazzling array of rich biblical terms. And all of them are found, in that order, in the Gospel reading for this Sunday. Since the Bible is inspired, this is what we would expect it to produce.

The reading is part of Jesus' farewell discourse to his disciples. He reminds them of past lessons and promises them even greater goods to come. He speaks first of love, the pivotal Christian virtue. Here Jesus links it with being true to his word, because love *is* his word, just as he, the Word, is love.

But the specifically Christian dimension of love is the mutual relationship of Father and Son with the disciple. Jesus connects this with his return to the Father in glory. In other words, then the disciples will experience a communion with God that is, literally, out of this world. There is no possible way of expressing all that it means. It is a communion of love that all Christians enjoy.

This perfected communion of love, however, is only possible when the Holy Spirit comes into the hearts of God's people. That is why Jesus immediately speaks of the Spirit's coming. He calls him "the Paraclete," a legal term meaning intercessor, and also comforter.

In a sense the biblical authors portray the three Persons acting in chronological order in the salvation process. The Father, always acting first and initiating saving love, sends the Son, who then carries out the Father's will in loving obedience. Finally, the Spirit comes on the occasion of the Son's fulfillment of his work in resurrection (cf. Ac 2:33).

That is why John could make the almost outrageous statement that "there was no Spirit as yet" (7:39). His vivifying work in Christian hearts begins with Jesus' resurrection. But then it is an indispensable role that he plays, as instructor and reminder, and above all, as enabler of love.

In v. 16 the Holy Spirit was referred to as "another Paraclete." This suggests, of course, that Jesus was also a Paraclete and that the Spirit represents the continued presence of Jesus on earth. But it is precisely as Paraclete of the *risen Lord*, not the earthly Jesus, that he is able to do what he does.

From the resurrection scene in John's Gospel (20:19), part of the reading for the second Sunday of Easter, we learned that "peace" was associated with Jesus' glory and the Spirit's coming. Peace is the Spirit's gift as representative of the risen Lord.

We have written often of the biblical notion of peace, the richness of its meaning, the fullness of relationship that it implies. We can understand why Jesus adds that he does not give it as the world gives it. Too often the world's peace is the dove with broken wings, or more frighteningly, the eerily quiet battlefield with the smoke of blazing canons still hovering over corpse-strewn fields.

Christ's peace is the inner peace of the disciple who knows the Father's love and who loves in return. It is not the peace of quiet emptiness, but the peace of fullness of love and life. It is the peace the priest prays for at every Eucharist before the sharing of the sacred Bread.

And all of this comes as the result of Jesus' return to the Father. That return marks the completion of his saving activity as the God-man. The Father, who is "greater" in the sense that he initiated the whole of saving history, can now complete that history. And we are part of it. The love, the Spirit, and the peace that Jesus promised belong to us and are truly ours in the measure that we let them be.

Ascension (C)
Acts 1:1-11; Ephesians 1:17-23; Luke 24:46-53

Which of the New Testament authors contributed more writing than
anyone else to that magnificent anthology? Some might guess Paul—
and they would be wrong. With his Gospel account and his Acts of
the Apostles, Luke, a close friend of Paul, provides us with approxi-
mately one fourth of the New Testament. His writings give us vast and
penetrating understanding of the power and of the need of evangeli-
cal witness by the Church.

It is striking that Luke begins the Acts of the Apostles by recounting the same episode that concludes his Gospel. Obviously the
Ascension of the Lord is for Luke an unusually important event, and
that is the event we so joyfully celebrate today. Both Lukan passages
are used in our Liturgy of the Word.

In Acts, Luke tells us that Jesus departed from the apostles after
"appearing to them over the course of forty days and speaking to
them about the reign of God" (1:3). This is the only biblical reference
to the ascension as having occurred forty days after the resurrection.
Luke's Gospel does not mention this. And John understands the
resurrection-ascension as having occurred in the same moment
(20:17).

Apparently Luke is drawing a strict parallel between the apostles
and Jesus. Jesus had prepared for his public ministry by forty days of
prayer and fasting in the desert (Lk 4:1-2). The apostles were being
prepared by Jesus for forty days for their baptism "with the Holy
Spirit" (Ac 1:5). But it was not until the fourth century that Christians
began celebrating the Ascension forty days after Easter.

The apostles are held in high regard by Luke. They had been
"chosen" through the Holy Spirit. Jesus had personally selected the
twelve (Lk 6:12). In order to fill the vacancy due to Judas' defection,
the following criterion is given: the candidate (Matthias was chosen)
must have been associated with the apostles from the time of Jesus'
baptism by John until the ascension (Ac 1:21-22). It was important to
have been with the Lord from the beginning and to have been
instructed by him after the resurrection.

The word "witness" is used in both accounts of the ascension in today's readings. The faithful follower was to witness on Jesus' behalf. The message of that witness is spelled out in the Gospel (24:46-49): making known that Jesus the Messiah had to suffer and did rise from the dead on the third day; that in his name penance and the forgiveness of sins were to be preached to all; and that the power of the Holy Spirit, sent by the Father, would enable the faithful follower to accomplish this mission.

The task of bearing witness belongs to all who have experienced an encounter with the power of the risen Lord (cf. Ac 10:41). This is the theme of Acts of the Apostles; the deeds recounted are not merely the deeds of the twelve apostles, but of all persons sent by God to bear witness to the saving event of the life and works of Jesus Christ. That witness is borne by many individuals: Peter, Philip, and Stephen (cc. 1-12), and Paul, Barnabas, and James (cc. 13-28).

The disciples are called to be witnesses to "the ends of the earth" (Ac 1:8). The plan of Acts carries out the theme of the spread of Christianity to the Gentiles. Hardship falls upon those who spread the Good News. The witnesses suffer imprisonment, shipwreck, stoning, hunger, poverty, and even death. Yet with the strength of the ascended Christ who sent the Spirit upon his followers, their mission was fulfilled.

Acts concludes by picturing Paul's ministry in his confinement at Rome. He preached the kingdom of God and taught about the Lord Jesus Christ (Ac 28:31). Yes, even "the ends of the earth" have been witnessed to by a faithful follower of Jesus Christ.

Can we of the twentieth century do less?

P.J.S.

Seventh Sunday of Easter (C)
Acts 7:55-60; Revelation 22:12-14, 16-17, 20; John 17:20-26

"That all may be one." This prayer of Jesus, taken from Sunday's Gospel, has been the prayer of Christians in an intensified way since the close of the Second Vatican Council. That the prayer has been heard in part is evident in the eradication of so much religious prejudice and in the working together in common causes of so many religious groups. The prayer, of course, must continue, for so much remains to be done.

Our three readings offer us some insights into this unity. The most important is that we are speaking, ulitmately, of *religious* unity. We are speaking of our unity with one another in God. While unity in other causes, such as social or economic, is rightly pursued, that is subservient to our higher unity in the Lord. So do our biblical authors tell us.

The first reading, the story of Stephen's martyrdom, seems to contradict the essence of religious unity. Here a man is put to death because of his religious convictions. After recounting that death, Luke adds, "That day saw the beginning of a great persecution of the church in Jerusalem."

But we know that one of the overriding themes of Luke's writings is that of unity. He tells us of the coming of the Spirit upon the young church and of the great unity of tongues that followed. The ignoble story of the tower of Babel was reversed. Moreover, several times he speaks of the believers being "of one mind." Without doubt he sees this as the ideal for all peoples.

What Stephen's story tells us with respect to this final unity is that it will not be achieved without suffering. We are not to pray for persecution, of course, but we must be able to see in suffering for religious convictions the seedbed of future unity. That was surely Luke's conviction.

But he adds another important insight. He tells us that before Stephen died he cried out, "Lord, do not hold this sin against them." Forgiveness of one's enemies is an indispensable factor in religious unity. Without forgiveness, reconciliation cannot take place. Without reconciliation, there is no oneness in the Lord. And forgiveness, like peace, must begin with *me*.

The reading from the book of Revelation, which brings that book to a close, pictures the end-time when all the faithful will be gathered together in the Lord's city and in the presence of the Lord. And that presence clearly makes them one.

What the reading says is that we, too, must share the author's eager longing for the Lord's coming. Our "Come, Lord Jesus!" should be as passionate as his. If we yearn for that coming, then we know we are seeking unity, for where he is, all believers will be with him.

The Gospel reading says it all most fully. It is Jesus' own prayer for the unity of those who call themselves his disciples. And he prays, not just for those of his day, but also for us who believe in him "through their word." He prays, too, for the world, that it might come to believe and be one with him.

The unity Jesus prays for is likened to the unity of the Father and the Son, a unity that makes ours possible. This intercommunion of Father, Son, and faithful is beyond imagining. We can only say, as he says, that our life is theirs and theirs is ours.

As with suffering for unity, forgiving for unity, and longing for unity, so here we are asked to witness to unity so that the world may believe the Father has "sent" the Son. The oneness the Lord has already given us in himself should speak to others "that *all may be one.*"

Vigil of Pentecost (ABC)
See page 46

Pentecost (ABC)
See page 47

Trinity Sunday (C)
Proverbs 8:22-31; Romans 5:1-5; John 16:12-15

God is on *our* side. That could be an expression of self-righteous jingoism, or it could be an act of profound faith in a saving God.

It depends on what "sides" are involved. If it is America against Russia, or our baseball team against yours, or Catholics against Lutherans, then it's pretty sure to be jingoism. But if it is our frail spirits against sin and the mighty forces of evil, then it is, indeed, faith and trust in a loving Lord.

What has this to do with the Holy Trinity? We could write about the manner in which we understand this greatest of all mysteries, about the inner relationship of Father, Son, and Holy Spirit in one Godhead. That could evoke a burst of solemn praise and worship. We choose, instead, to see our readings as evidence that the holy Three are in fact on *our* side.

The first reading sets the tone beautifully for our argument. It is a description of Wisdom. For ancient Israel Wisdom was one of the most important attributes of God. So profoundly did Israel conceive this divine Wisdom that she personified it, as our reading attests. Wisdom is described as a Person who does the bidding of God in all of creation.

After portraying the magnificence of the heavens, the skies, the earth, the waters, Wisdom speaks in these words, "Then was I beside him as his craftsman. . . ." Wisdom had guided the Lord's hand, as it were, in all his works, providing the grand plan for nature's stunning beauty.

But, then, at the end of the passage we read, ". . . and I found delight in the sons of men." It is as though Wisdom were saying to us, "While all these other works are truly great and worthy of praise, what I really want is to be with you. I am on your side!"

Both St. Paul and the Church see Wisdom here as a prefiguring of Jesus Christ. In his letter to the Colossians Paul describes the Christ in much the same way as Wisdom is described (1:15-20). It is a hymn to the cosmic Lord in whom and for whom all things are created. And this cosmic Lord is ultimately, like Wisdom, *for us*. He is on *our* side.

That is what Paul says quite explicitly in the second reading.

Through Christ "we have gained access by faith to the grace in which we now stand. . . ." Because of him we can "hope for the glory of God" and "even boast of our afflictions!" A mighty Savior is our Lord!

The same reading speaks also of the Holy Spirit. And there is no doubt about whose side the Spirit is on. Paul says that ". . . the love of God has been poured out in our hearts through the Holy Spirit who has been given to us." The Spirit is a gift of God's love to us.

In the Gospel Jesus speaks of the gift of truth that is for us. For John truth is not an abstract proposition or philosophical conclusion. It is, rather, God's revelation of himself in the Son and in the Spirit. This truth has a saving power that leads to fullness of life. That is why Jesus can say elsewhere, "I am the way, the truth and the life" (Jn 14:6). There is no separating truth from the way and the life. All are *for us*.

Jesus says that the Spirit, too, is "the Spirit of truth." What Jesus was and did in his earthly life, the Spirit continues in our history and our times. And what that is, of course, is saving power, divine love bountifully poured out, God's glory shining in our lives.

When we reflect on our own weaknesses in the face of evil, our frailty before sin, we have reason to shout out our thanks to this triune God who is on *our* side.

The Body and Blood of Christ (C)
Genesis 14:18-20; 1 Corinthians 11:23-26; Luke 9:11-17

"I myself am the bread of life." These startling words of Jesus are found in John's Gospel (6:35). "Startling" is no exaggeration here. The only reason why they might not startle someone is because they have been heard so often they no longer make an impression. Listen to them anew!

How is Jesus the bread of life? The prophet Amos had spoken long ago of a famine of God's word (8:11). He was comparing it to bread that nourishes the body. God's word is spirit-nourishing bread.

The immediate context shows that Jesus was speaking of himself in this sense. He is the revelation of the Father, God's Word. That is why he goes on to say that no one who comes to him and believes in him will ever be hungry or thirsty (6:35). Just to know who Jesus is and to accept him proves to be rich fare.

But he says even more. The same startling words are spoken later in the context of his own body and blood. "If anyone eats this bread he shall live forever; the bread I will give is my flesh, for the life of the world" (6:51). Now "startling" appears a weak word. This is momentous!

In his Gospel John does not tell us how this can be. All he does here is to assure his readers of the awesome realism of Jesus' words, in part by noting that many of his disciples left him because they could not accept his words literally. And Jesus did not stop them!

Scholars have generally argued that John does not record the institution of the Eucharist at the Last Supper, as the other evangelists do, because it was so well known by his readers. In his Gospel he is providing deeper reflections on realities already accepted. The whole of chapter six, in fact, can be seen as a meditation on the Eucharist.

The celebration of the Eucharist was the most commonly practiced rite in the early Church. So common was it that we might wonder why any mention of its institution would be recorded in the New Testament at all.

When we do, then, find accounts of the Eucharist in the New Testament, we can suspect a special reason for them. The best proof of this is our second reading, from Paul's letter to the Corinthians. It is the oldest account of Jesus' words of institution that we have.

Still, even this account was given by Paul, not to instruct his readers in something they hadn't learned yet, but to warn them against abusing a precious part of their Christian heritage. And they were doing just that. They were celebrating the Lord's Supper with flagrant violations of Christian love (11:17-22).

Paul, then, recalls Jesus' words instituting the Eucharist in order to bring home to these Corinthians the awesomeness of the mystery they were celebrating. What he is really saying to them is this, "Listen anew to those words: 'This is my body. This is my blood.' Do you know what that means and still behave as you do"?

The story of the multiplication of the loaves, our Gospel reading is still more evidence that the Eucharist was part of the very tissue of Christianity. Long before Luke took over the account, it had taken on Eucharistic overtones. It had become a Eucharistic account. The food that fills thousands is Jesus, "the bread of life." This was so commonly accepted that, unlike many of the parables, the story didn't even need an explanation.

We're still hearing those same startling words from the altar. But do we understand? What does it mean to us that Jesus is himself the bread of life?

Second Sunday in Ordinary Time (C)
Isaiah 62:1-5; 1 Corinthians 12:4-11; John 2:1-12

"Thus did he reveal his glory. . . ." Those words were carefully chosen by John. He had just recorded the first act of Jesus in his public ministry, the Cana miracle. He equates it with the whole purpose of Jesus' coming, the revelation of his, or his Father's (for John it is the same thing) glory.

In a sense John could have laid down his pen. The reason for Jesus' coming had been achieved. That is confirmed by the words immediately following that statement, ". . . and his disciples believed in him." At the end of his Gospel John says that he wrote his story in order that people might believe in Jesus (20:30-31). That goal was attained at Cana.

This introduces us to a special characteristic of John's Gospel. Scholars call it "realized eschatology." The phrase means that, in his public ministry, Jesus already anticipated what the whole course of his life, including his death and resurrection, would bring about. Because he is who he is, the Word of God made flesh, every single act was an act of "glory revealed."

John, of course, knew that Jesus' first act did not reveal all the glory and power of his final act of exaltation. It was only in that final act that the Spirit was given (cf. 20:22). And even in this Cana scene Jesus tells his mother, after she requested his aid, "My hour has not yet come."

In John's Gospel Jesus' "hour" has special meaning. It is the "hour" of his exaltation on the cross and in resurrection. It is the "hour" when he would "draw all men to myself" (12:32). It is, in sum, the "hour" when he would "pass from this world to the Father" (13:1).

Still, in someway, that hour had come in Cana. At least some indication of the hour's presence was manifested. Jesus had just performed "the first of his signs." In biblical thought a sign is not an abstract concept; it is the initial manifestation of the reality to which it points.

That, too, is why Jesus here calls Mary "woman" instead of the expected title of "mother." The reference intended by John is to the "woman" of Genesis 3:15. There God speaks to the serpent in these terms, "I will put enmity between you and the woman, between your seed and her seed; he shall crush your head, and you shall lie in wait for his heel." Mary is the woman whose seed, Jesus, crushes the serpent's head.

The Cana scene, then, as described by John, captures both the beauty of an event in Jesus' earthly existence and the glory of his whole life, death, and exaltation. At Cana Jesus revealed his glory. At Cana his disciples believed in him. At Cana Mary became the woman of victory over evil.

This is not without its meaning for us. We, too, share in this "realized eschatology" of Jesus. Even here on earth we bask in his glory. From the moment of our baptism we already enjoy eternal life. Heaven is but the culmination of reality begun on earth.

We have spoken often enough in these columns of the necessity of the cross in Christianity. We do not take back those words in any way. But what we say—or better, what John tells us—is that we take up the cross as an "alleluia people," who are destined for glory, as coheirs with him who invites us *now* to the feast of Cana.

Third Sunday in Ordinary Time (C)
Nehemiah 8:2-4, 5-6,8-10; 1 Corinthians 12:12-30;
Luke 1:1-4; 4:14-21

The first reading, from the book of Nehemiah, is one of the earlier witnesses to the belief in biblical inspiration. When Ezra, the scribe, reads from the book of the law "which the Lord had given to Israel," the people weep in the sheer emotion of hearing God's Word.

The other major Old Testament witness to that belief is found in 2 Kings 22-23. "The book of the law" is discovered in the temple when renovation work is taking place after a long period of apostasy. The reaction to hearing the book read is similar to that in the Nehemiah reading.

Not only is their recognition of the Word's special character significant, however. Equally as important is the effect that it produced. In both cases a reform of the people's lives begins. This is the divine purpose of inspiration. This is why God wanted to associate himself in a special way with human words.

By the time of Jesus, belief in the sacred character of the Hebrew Bible was common to the Jews. They referred to it simply as "Scriptures, " meaning *the* writing par excellence. And the synagogue service involved an elaborate system of readings from the Law and the Prophets.

This brings us to the Gospel reading from Luke. A member of the community, or someone known to be versed in the Scriptures, would choose a reading and comment on it. In this instance Jesus, who would have been recognized as a native of Nazareth, was given the book of Isaiah for a reading.

The Gospel passage suggests that Jesus had a particular text in mind that he wanted to read. We are told that "he unrolled the scroll and *found* the passage where it was written. . . ." He was not engaging in some kind of "magic text" game, letting the Spirit guide his finger to an appropriate place.

The passage he found is an excellent summary of who Jesus is and of his messianic work. He is "the anointed" of the Spirit. Those acquainted with the Old Testament would have known that kings, priests, prophets, and the "suffering servant" were all spoken of as being anointed. While Jesus shared all of these offices in some way, the readers of Luke's Gospel would have remembered the anointing by the Spirit at Jesus' baptism, recorded in the preceding chapter (3:21-22). There he is identified further as God's beloved Son.

Also, the works that Jesus would do in his earthly life and in his death and resurrection are precisely those mentioned in the Isaian text. Good news to the poor, release to the captives, sight to the blind, liberty to the oppressed—these are the signs of the messianic age, of the jubilee year in its fullness.

The Gospel reading concludes with Jesus returning to his place, with the eyes of all fixed on him, and with his statement that "Today this scripture has been fulfilled in your hearing." The reference is, of course, to himself.

Perhaps the Church deliberately ended the reading here, not continuing with Luke's report of the people's reaction. Perhaps she ends it with this bold statement of Jesus to let us hear the fullness of the Word and express our own reaction, not influenced by that of others. What will it be? Rejection and continuing in the same rut? Or acceptance and change? It must be one or the other; that's the nature of the Word.

Fourth Sunday in Ordinary Time (C)
Jeremiah 1:4-5, 17-19; 1 Corinthians 12:31—13:13; Luke 4:21-30

Jeremiah is like Jesus. The comparison limps, of course, since Jesus is unique. But if any historical figure of the Old Testament reminds one of Jesus, that figure is Jeremiah. The Church suggests that, by the combination of the first and third readings for this Sunday.

Not long after Jeremiah's time an anonymous prophet of the exile described in a series of poems, now found in the book of Isaiah, a mysterious figure called the "suffering servant of Yahweh." A number of scholars think that Jeremiah's life prompted the poems. And Christians unanimously see Jesus as fulfilling the description. Jeremiah and Jesus.

The similarities are striking. Both were called to be prophets. Both were to suffer the agony of desolation. Both were to proclaim a message that would be repudiated. And both were to be persecuted. But the Father's presence would insure the ultimate vindication of both.

In the first reading the Lord tells Jeremiah that his election as "a prophet to the nations" was an appointment "from his mother's womb." It is a way of assuring the young man of the rightness of his calling despite the many misgivings he would later have.

The remainder of the reading is a concerted effort on God's part to assure the prophet also of the rightness of his message and of God's intent to deliver him in the end. If it is God who made Jeremiah "a fortified city, a pillar of iron, a wall of brass against the whole land," then, to be sure, it is God who would make him prevail.

Many scholars think Jeremiah wrote this account of his call toward the end of his life. He would then have seen his earlier experience of vocation in the light of a full life as a prophet. How much more clearly would he have understood what the Lord had had in mind for him!

Our Gospel reading, too, is a later account of an earlier experience. But there is no reason to doubt that Jesus experienced a rejection by his own people early in his ministry. What Luke wants to emphasize is that such a rejection was to be a dominant factor in his whole ministry. Again, Jeremiah and Jesus.

An interesting feature of the reading is the remarkable change in the attitude of the audience. Their first reaction to what Jesus had read (last Sunday's reading contained that part) and to how he interpreted it was to speak "favorably of him" and to marvel "at the appealing discourse." But then, "the whole audience . . . was filled with indignation. They rose up and expelled him from the town. . . ."

Scholars suggest that Luke sees this as an anticipation of Jesus' crucifixion outside the city walls. At any rate, the note of rejection is introduced from the beginning. Because Jesus, like Elijah and Elisha, must minister to all peoples, he is rejected by his own. Jeremiah and Jesus.

Now the crunch comes. Would we also be able to say, in the light of our reflections, "Jeff and Jesus?" Or, "Judy and Jesus?" Is there *something* in each one of us that someone could compare favorably with Jesus? An acceptance of suffering and, especially, misunderstanding as part of God's plan? A special concern for the outcast, the sinner? A genuine love for the poor?

We can't marvel at the similarities between Jeremiah and Jesus in a vacuum. They must have meaning for us. And, unlike Jeremiah, we call ourselves Christians. Our very vocation is to be like Jesus in someway.

Fifth Sunday in Ordinary Time (C)
Isaiah 6:1-2, 3-8; 1 Corinthians 15:1-11; Luke 5:1-11

Accounts of two of the most profound religious experiences ever recorded are in this Sunday's first and third readings. They involve cases of human confrontation with the divine and a consequent awareness of mission. While only relatively few persons have so intense an experience, most believers are probably conscious, sometime, of God acting in their lives. At the least, vocation means the conviction of God's call, however it may be experienced.

In our first case, that of Isaiah, the religious phenomena are many and richly symbolic. God is pictured as a majestic king seated high on a throne. Seraphim, winged creatures representing the royal court, act out their worshipful reverence.

With two wings they cover their eyes, lest the vision of the divine glory overwhelm them. With two wings they cover their feet, a euphemism for the lower body. It is the gesture often attributed in pictures to Adam and Eve in God's presence after their sin. It is awareness of creaturehood. With two wings they fly about, perhaps to prepare to escape the awesome presence.

The triple "holy," familiar to us from the Eucharist, is the only way in which thy can give utterance to God's absolute goodness, his transcendence, his otherness. No wonder foundations shake and earth takes on his glory.

In the second case, that of Peter, none of this happens. One asks where the similarity is. At first there is only a fruitless night of toil for fishermen. Then at the Master's word, nets break with their load and boats sink. These events said to Peter all that those other phenomena said to Isaiah. The Lord is here! He wants you!

Let's look now at Isaiah's reaction. It is one of sin-consciousness; not any particular sin, but the sin-prone condition of the human person when aware of the divine majesty and holiness. Unless that holiness somehow sears my lips, my heart, my soul, I can do nothing. I am lost.

With Peter the reaction is the same. That is why we know we are dealing with the same kind of religious experience. He falls down at Jesus' feet and begs him to depart. The holy Lord can have nothing to do with sin. Holiness means separation.

In each case, however, holiness cleanses and makes a partner in mission. With Isaiah the cleansing rite is, as expected, elaborate. A winged creature with burning coal touches the sinner's lips with the message, "Your guilt is taken away, and your sin forgiven."

Isaiah recognizes and accepts the forgiveness. When the call to mission comes, there is no hesitation. "Here am I! Send me!" With Peter, again, there is no ritual. Just the assuring words, "Do not be afraid; henceforth you will be catching men." And the counterpart to Isaiah's request for mission is Peter's "leaving all and following him."

Three basic elements are present in both cases. First is the experience of the holy, the awareness of God's presence and call. The second is the human reaction—awareness of unworthiness. And the third is the acceptance of mission on the conviction of forgiveness.

That second element is the stumbling block, isn't it? It doesn't tally with being "number one." But that's the secret of biblical faith. Once you are aware of your unworthiness in God's sight, you know you are number one. If you can say, in all honesty, what Isaiah and Peter said, you're called. You have met the biblical God and it's his work from now on.

Sixth Sunday in Ordinary Time (C)
Jeremiah 17:5-8; 1 Corinthians 15:12, 16-20; Luke 6:17, 20-26

"Blest are you poor!" "But woe to you rich!" These strong words could have been uttered only by someone with strong convictions. If these statements are an essential part of the Christian message (and it would be easy to show that Luke at least thought they were), then we Christians have to ask some hard questions.

Like any homilist, I think of some of my friends who are wealthy and ask myself whether I'll compromise the Gospel in order not to offend them. I must be aware of that temptation if I'm going to be honest. On the other hand, I cannot suppose that any modifying of the statements is necessarily a compromise.

If the statements are to be understood absolutely, without any modification, then I would have to conclude this column here. The words are all monosyllabic and intelligible even to the barely literate. The only question might be how much material goods one must possess to be considered rich or poor.

Since I'm continuing, it is obvious that I am convinced the statements must be understood in context. Part of that context would

be Jesus' consciousness of the Kingdom present. So powerfully present was it to him that it said to him, "The end-time is now." "The
Father reigns." "Nothing material counts, or is even an obstacle."

If that is the context of the statements as originally intended, then
we do have to understand them for us in a special way. While we
believe that Jesus has inaugurated the end-time, the Father's reign,
we realize, too, that the world and its history continue. In that
continuing history material goods can have a relative, but never an
absolute, value. They are even necessary for sustaining progress in
the world. Even Luke speaks, with apparent approval, of a great
dinner given for Jesus by the wealthy Levi (5:29).

Also, whenever the word "rich" is used elsewhere in the New
Testament in a disapproving manner, the author assumes one of two
things. Either the riches have been unjustly acquired, in which case
the rich are warned to "weep and wail" over impending doom (Jm
5:1-6), or they are seen as a powerful temptation, as the source of
one's trust in place of God (Lk 12:16-20; especially 1 Tm 6:17).

In the same way poverty is seen as something good, not in an
absolute way as a value in itself, but as one of the most powerful
means for trusting in God alone. So powerful a means is it, in fact, that
poverty is almost presented as a synonym for trust in God. To be poor
is to be dependent on the Lord.

We can interpret the first reading, from Jeremiah, in this way. The
prophet says that the one who trusts in anything but God is cursed.
On the other hand, "Blessed is the man who trusts in the Lord, whose
hope is the Lord." He doesn't speak explicitly of wealth or poverty
here, but the fact that the Church proposes this to be read along with
the Gospel shows clearly enough how she understands it.

It is true enough that we do not live in the consciousness of the
Kingdom present as Jesus did. Yet Luke has preserved the very tone of
his message on wealth and poverty in order to make us think of that
Kingdom as the only ultimate value. When we do, we are bound to
see wealth only as a relative value, even as a temptation. It is why
Religious take the vow of poverty and why all of us must take
seriously these words of the Lord.

Seventh Sunday in Ordinary Time (C)
1 Samuel 26, 2, 7-9, 12-13, 22-23; 1 Corinthians 15:45-49;
Luke 6:27-38

The long history of Christianity contains constant shifts between an emphasis on orthodoxy (right doctrine) and orthopraxy (right conduct). Does being a Christian mean basically acknowledging Jesus as Lord? Or does it mean loving our neighbor as ourselves?

At times the New Testament seems to favor orthodoxy. Paul tells the Corinthians, " . . . no one can say, 'Jesus is Lord,' except in the Holy Spirit" (1 Cor 12:3). And in 1 John we read, "Everyone who believes that Jesus is the Christ has been begotten of God" (5:1). Or, "Who, then, is conqueror of the world? The one who believes that Jesus is the Son of God" (5:5).

On the other hand, the famous parable in Matthew seems to favor orthopraxy. Jesus is pictured as king-judge at the end of the world. He judges the sheep and the goats solely on the basis of their having helped others, *whether* they recognize Jesus in the others or not (25:31-46).

Actually, theologians would admit that an intimate connection links the two. While the Matthean parable would suggest that the non-Christian can be saved by reason of his love for others, that Christian, *as Christian*, does these things *in the name of Jesus*.

All through the New Testament are references to the conviction that faith or belief is the foundation for loving concern for others. At the same time, the Christian must prove his faith by his actions, as James insists. Without orthopraxy, orthodoxy is meaningless.

The reading from Luke's Gospel clearly emphasizes orthopraxy. Jesus tells his disciples over and over that they are to love their enemies, do good to those who hate them, turn the cheek, and give the shirt as well as the coat. Love, compassion, and pardon are the marks of discipleship.

But the nature of these demands, extravagant as they are, point to the extraordinary character of the One who made them. Luke was surely convinced that they could be followed only because the One who made them was such as could provide the strength. Had not his own mentor, St. Paul, said, "In him who is the source of my strength I have strength for everything" (Ph 4:13)? Paul knew the Lord Jesus and so could be confident of victory. Orthopraxy flows from orthodoxy.

The first reading, from the book of Samuel, corroborates this interpretation. The scene is from Davids' life of exile in the hills of Judah. After having been brought into King Saul's court, he had begun to attract followers by his victories over the enemy. This aroused the jealousy of Saul and forced David to flee for his life.

In the story at hand Saul is searching for the fugitive with the intent of doing away with him. During the night David came upon Saul as he lay sleeping. One of his followers urged the young warrior to take advantage of the opportunity and have the king slain. David's answer, repeated twice, was that he could not harm the "Lord's anointed."

In other words, a religious motive is adduced as the reason for David's refusal to do injury. His conduct was motivated by his religious conviction. Here, clearly, orthopraxy flowed from orthodoxy.

Without question the New Testament sets great store on orthodoxy, on the acknowledgment of the Father and of Jesus Christ as his Son. John says that all he wrote was in order "to help you believe that Jesus is the Messiah, the Son of God . . ." (20:31). But the same evangelist records these words of Jesus, "This is how all will know you for my disciples: your love for one another" (13:35).

Eighth Sunday in Ordinary Time (C)
Sirach 27:4-7; 1 Corinthians 15:54-58; Luke 6:39-45

Our three readings for this Sunday celebration are examples of wisdom literature. The wisdom movement as such goes back many centuries before Christ. In Israel, although it was present in early times, it came to full flower during the period of the Babylonian Exile (586-538 B.C.). Written by the scribes and sages, wisdom literature was reflective, treating of the significance of living. Those who lived what the wisdom literature taught were said to be living according to proverbial religion.

A proverb is a short, forceful saying. Proverbial religion treats in a succinct way of the ordinary things in life: relationships with God, family members, friends, neighbors, and nature.

The book of Sirach, an example of wisdom literature, was written at the beginning of the second century before Christ in Jerusalem by a respected scribe and teacher. At the end of the second century this man's grandson moved to Egypt. It was here that he translated his grandfather's work from Hebrew into Greek. He tells us in the prologue of the work that the Jews of Egypt no longer understood Hebrew; thus, he was a proponent of the "vernacular movement" long before it became popular in the twentieth century.

Today's passage contains four proverbs dealing with man's thought and speech. It falls within a wider collection (26:19—27:21) treating of the dangers to a person's integrity and hindrances to friendship. A religion based upon one person's relationship to another is what is being stressed.

In the second reading Paul refers obliquely to the wisdom of God. He places great emphasis upon the resurrection of the body. Apparently some Corinthians were denying this teaching. Throughout this epistle Paul emphasizes the importance of the body (viz. 12:12-27). The whole of chapter 15 is an exposition of the theme that just as Christ died and was raised from the dead, so the Christian after human death will be gloriously raised in a new spiritual body (15:44). Death has no real power over the follower of Jesus.

In today's passage there appear to be two separate statements freely quoted from the Old Testament to show that they have been fulfilled by Christ's victory (vv. 54:55). The first comes from Isaiah 25:8, "he will destroy death forever." The second seems to be a paraphrase of Hosea 13:14, "Where are your plagues, O death! where is your sting, O nether world!" This is the wisdom of God brought to fulfillment in Jesus Christ. 1 Corinthians dwells upon the wisdom of God, which is so different from human wisdom (2:6ff.). It is not the wisdom of this world.

"To miss the mark" is a definition for sin. Paul refers to the law as empowering sin because the law could not save; it missed the mark of measuring up to God's demands of love (1 Cor 13). Thus the law with sin could not liberate human beings from the bondage of everlasting death. Jesus Christ has vanquished the sin, law, and death; immortal and incorruptible life has been bestowed upon us.

In the setting of the Gospel, Jesus has just chosen his faithful twelve (6:12-16). Now, on the plain in their presence he begins to teach those who come to hear him. His teaching is in parables, wisdom teachings based on similarities between two things or persons. It is another form of the wisdom motif. It was important for him to teach in the presence of the twelve because they were to be the ones who were faithfully to transmit his message after his departure (24:46-48).

The Gospel reminds us that we cannot help others as we should unless we have been converted. Personal integrity before God is necessary if we are to live according to his wisdom. Each of us must be a person wise in the ways of our Savior Jesus Christ. The Christian life is to be lived simply, concentrating upon relationships with God, family members, friends, neighbors, and nature.

P.J.S.

Ninth Sunday in Ordinary Time (C)
1 Kings 8:41-43; Galatians 1:1-2, 6-10; Luke 7:1-10

Among Paul's epistles, Galatians stands out for its unusually serious tone; the atmosphere is tense and sombre. Paul must defend his apostleship and the integrity of the gospel message. Apparently some Galatians were twisting and deserting the "gospel of Christ"; a perversion of the Good News was in progress in Galatia. And so Paul insists that the Mosaic Law is no longer to be a stumbling block for Gentile Christians (2:9), since "it was for liberty that Christ freed us" (5:1).

Paul also insists upon the need for maintaining the traditional gospel (1:9). At the same time he vindicates his own authority for he was "sent, not by men nor by any man, but by Jesus Christ and God his Father" (1:1). He infers that those who are preaching a twisted gospel have come from men. There is no place for false teachers who claim that the Mosaic Law is still needed to gain salvation.

Paul's main concern is an openness to the Gentiles that no one is to limit. The Gentiles, too, were to be justified through faith (3:8).

The first and third readings speak explicitly about salvation coming to the Gentiles. In 1 Kings we have Solomon, who had built the Temple unto the Lord, entreating the God of Israel to listen to the "foreigner." He makes the appeal that salvation might come to all Gentiles who pray to God at the Temple. It was typical of the Jews during their sojourn in Babylon (586-538 B.C.) to attempt to proselytize. 1 Kings may be a first effort of the Jews to do so in recorded Bible history. The emphasis in the reading is that salvation comes through the Jews to anyone who will believe and worship the one true God.

The centurion of the Gospel episode is presented as a foreigner who sends some of the Jewish elders of Capernaum to intercede in his behalf. He is preoccupied with the illness of a faithful servant. Before Jesus arrives at Capernaum, other friends of the centurion come forward with a message that Jesus can use his authority over illness even before arriving in the town. The centurion has a strong belief that Jesus has the power to heal—and the servant *is* healed. A parallel account is given in Matthew's Gospel (8:5-13) and a similar one in John (4:46-54).

With the exception of this event and the healing of the Syrophoenician's daughter in Matthew and Mark, no other healing at a distance is recounted by the Synoptics.

Jesus praises this centurion's faith. He had come to realize that God had delegated his authority to Jesus just as the official had been delegated by the king. The importance of Luke is that the centurion was not one who was looking for signs, but rather one who recognized power when he came across it. Among his own people Jesus did not find so great a faith.

Earlier in the Gospel, upon receiving the infant into his arms, Simeon had cried out that Jesus was "A revealing light to the Gentiles, the glory of your people Israel" (2:32). The centurion recognized Jesus as the revealing light.

In the liturgy the Church takes a verse from today's reading and paraphrases it (7:6-7). "Lord, I am not worthy to receive you, but only say the word and I shall be healed" is always recited by the faithful before receiving the Eucharist. We are reminded of the fact that Jesus has all authority and that we cannot merit salvation. Salvation and grace are free gifts from the Father through Jesus Christ.

The centurion had friends among the Jews, and they came to intercede for the foreigner. We have a friend before the throne of the Father—Jesus Christ, our Lord and brother. He shares his authority with us, and he beckons us into the heavenly city; we are mindful that "here we have no lasting city; we are seeking one which is to come" (Heb 13:14). All things do work unto good for those who allow him to enter their life and give it meaning.

P.J.S.

Tenth Sunday in Ordinary Time (C)
1 Kings 17:17-24; Galatians 1:11-19; Luke 7:11-17

On any spring day the fields of Galilee are alive with color, radiant and joyous in tone. The lilies of the field, anemones, blanket the hillsides and meadows. Outside of Naim today are glorious fields filled with these multicolored, buttercup-like flowers that speak so vividly of life. Naim is the scene of one of today's readings, and all of them deal with life that only God can bring.

Elijah, the hero of our first reading, was active in the ninth century B.C., prophesying in the name of God and fleeing from the wrath of Ahab and Jezebel. During a time of drought when the rains of heaven were held back, the Lord led Elijah to the town of Zarephath, nine miles south of Sidon on the Mediterranean coast. There he lodged with a widow and her son; the three did not want for food during the famine (1 K 17:15-16).

The reading for today begins with the sudden death of the widow's son. Through breathing upon the young man, Elijah brings the boy back to life. The miracle convinces the woman that Elijah is a true prophet, a man of God (17:24). This passage is one of several that recounts the marvelous happenings associated with Elijah.

Unlike other mortals, Elijah's death is depicted in a marvelous way; he was taken up into heaven in a flaming chariot (2 K 2:11). Prophets predicted that he would one day return (Ml 3:1.23). In Jesus' day, the Jews saw in Elijah a Messianic figure. The expectation of Elijah's return at the time of Christ was very intense; many felt that

Elijah had appeared in Christ (Lk 9:8). With Moses, Elijah is present at the transfiguration of Jesus (Lk 9:30). Jesus is misunderstood by the bystanders to be invoking Elijah as he dies upon the cross (Mt 27:47).

Liturgists have chosen our Old Testament reading to accompany the Gospel, because Luke presents Jesus as one who has the power of Elijah. One can imagine the scene outside of Naim: two crowds meet each other; Jesus and his disciples encounter the woman, the litter, and the mourners. This Lucan episode demonstrates Jesus' concern for women; he has compassion and understanding for this mother and her only son. For the first time in the Gospel Luke calls Jesus "Lord"; this is the name that the Greek translation of the Hebrew Old Testament reserved for God alone. God is the giver of life. Jesus restored life to the dead man and then "gave him back to his mother" (7:15); the same words are used in our first reading (17:23).

The gospel Paul preaches is not man's. The gospel is Good News. It is the proclamation that Christ has died, Christ is risen, Christ will come again. Such a gospel cannot be man's; a human gospel would never have entailed a death in order that there be life, nor would it have needed a cross. Paul insists that he has encountered the Good News "through a revelation of Jesus Christ."

Acts of the Apostles presents a triple recounting of Paul's initial encounter with the Lord (Ac 9:1-19; 22:3-16; 26:2-18); Luke is insistent upon this meeting so that no one will have any ammunition against Paul's apostleship.

His meeting of the Lord on the road to Damascus totally transformed Paul. This is what he recounts in today's reading from Galatians. God had chosen Paul to spread good tidings of Jesus among the Gentiles (v. 16). He came to understand that Christ's death was for life; it led to salvation for all believers. In his own conversion he went from a form of death as a persecutor into the Spirit-filled life of the believer.

Only God can bring life. Through God's power, Elijah raised a young boy to life. Through that same power, Jesus the Lord raised up the widow's son at Naim. And through that power, Paul was raised to Christian life. That power can work in us too—now.

P.J.S.

Eleventh Sunday in Ordinary Time (C)
2 Samuel 12:7-10, 13; Galatians 2:16, 19-21; Luke 7:36—8:3

To love is to be forgiven. That unfamiliar statement may seem difficult to understand. I hope in this column to show that it is a profound and consoling insight fully based on the Scriptures and, in a special way, on this Sunday's Word.

Let's begin, however, with a more familiar adage. To err is human, to forgive divine. Numerous texts throughout the Bible could be adduced as evidence for both parts of the statement. Here we'll content ourselves only with the second part.

In the first reading the prophet Nathan is pictured as pointing a stern, accusing finger at David and saying, "You are the man!" What he is referring to is intelligible only in the larger context. Nathan had just presented a judicial case to the king. A wealthy man, wishing to entertain a visitor, took from a poor man "one little ewe lamb," all that he had. The rich man slaughtered that lamb rather than one from his own abundant flocks.

On hearing this, David became angry and said the man deserved to die for such injustice. Then Nathan pointed his finger and identified David himself as the guilty one. For he had taken the wife of one of his soldiers, committed adultery with her, and then compounded his crime by having the soldier placed in the thick of a battle where he was sure to die and did.

We can fully understand Nathan's righteous indignation. And we can fully understand the Lord's decision to bring evil upon David out of his own house. What would happen to David would be, in a sense, the fruit of his own misdeeds. That would be punishment enough.

But notice the final verse. David confesses his sin against the Lord, and *immediately* Nathan pronounces the divine forgiveness. It is as though, all through the prophet's harangue against the king, the Lord was just waiting for a sign of repentance. When it was given, the response was already there. Forgiveness!

The reason for this, of course, is that God is a merciful God, kind and forgiving. He never wills the death of a sinner. If "his mercy endures forever," as the psalmist repeats endlessly (Ps 136), then it can never fail. Nor did it fail here. Because of this conviction, we are right in repeating that to forgive is divine.

The Gospel reading takes us a bit more deeply into the mystery of divine forgiveness. Our interpretation involves a reading of the Greek text that is different from that of the New American Bible. But the reading is fully justified.

Jesus is at a Pharisee's home for a meal. A woman, known to be a sinner, wipes his feet with her tears and anoints them with oil. The Pharisee is shocked that Jesus would allow this. He interprets Jesus' silence as a condoning of her sins. But Jesus tells him (following now the translation in the Good News Bible), "I tell you, then, the great love she has shown proves that her many sins have been forgiven." The woman's love flows from divine forgiveness. To love is to be forgiven.

The short parable given by Jesus previously in the account clearly indicates this understanding. The gratitude, or, more correctly, the love of the one man for his master is greater because his debt, ten times as much as the other's, is totally forgiven. To love is to be forgiven.

What consoling truth is found here! Not only can I be sure that God's forgiveness is always present and that it really enables me to love in turn. Still more, if I find myself showing love to another then I know the divine forgiveness has been at work. For me to love means for God to have forgiven.

Twelfth Sunday in Ordinary Time (C)
Zechariah 12:10-11; Galatians 3:26-29; Luke 9:18-24

To one point at least all the New Testament authors bear unanimous witness. Jesus is the Christ. He is the Messiah, the "anointed" of God, sent by God as the fullest revelation of his plan.

So common was this recognition that in time "Christ" became the second name of Jesus, rather than a title. That is why we refer to him as Jesus Christ rather than as Jesus the Christ, the earliest designation of him in the young Church.

To acknowledge someone as a messiah is not something lightly done. It means you recognize that person as a special courier of God's, as one intended by God from all eternity for a very special task. It is an act of faith.

Similarly, to claim to be a messiah is not something lightly done. If falsely done, it can have horrendous results. The Jonestown tragedy is witness to the possibilities of false messianic claims. The messianic complex is an awesome reality in an unstable personality.

We mention all of this in order to deepen the appreciation of Peter's confession in today's Gospel reading. The concept of messiah was an intimate part of the Jewish faith in Jesus' time. Encouraged by a number of texts in the Old Testament prophets, the Jewish people looked forward to an end-time figure who would usher in God's Kingdom.

Since the Jews' condition at the time was one of subjection to Roman rule, one of their principal hopes was that the messiah would bring that subjection to an end. A political or military messiah was what many expected. And some passages in the Hebrew Scriptures could be interpreted that way.

Let us take a look now at our Gospel passage. Jesus asks his disciples who the people thought he was. After several responses, Peter, speaking for the others, exclaims, "You are the Christ of God!" The exclamation point is deliberate. This was not a valid statement of fact; it was a strong profession of faith.

We must, first of all, applaud Peter for this act of faith. He was saying that this humble carpenter from the little known village of Nazareth was, in fact, the long-awaited Messiah. This poor Jesus was the one God had appointed for his own work. Would any of us have been able to profess that kind of faith at that time?

We must go on to say that Peter's faith, great as it was, needed refining. Jesus had no "messianic complex." He had no intention of overthrowing Roman power, nor did he want acclamation as a national leader. That is why he apparently made no messianic claims for himself.

Quite the contrary. After Peter's confession he charged them to say nothing to anyone else about it. Moreover, he told them he must soon undergo suffering and death. Now that is all that the people would have to hear about this "messiah" to make them change their minds. They wanted no crucified savior.

But that thought doesn't stop Jesus. He tells those who are still willing to listen to him that if they do want to go on following him they have to imitate him in suffering. The daily cross is his messianic gift. Losing your life—for him—means saving it.

If Jesus had accepted the popular notion of messiah of his day, there would have been no Christianity. If he had accepted that title of messiah or Christ, there would never have been a Jesus Christ. The title would never have become a second name.

Even more, if Jesus had been that kind of messiah, Paul could never have written what he did in our second reading. Because he was not, Paul could say that all of us, no matter what our differences, are one in Jesus Christ. Now all our prayers can be directed to God the Father "through Jesus Christ our Lord."

Thirteenth Sunday in Ordinary Time (C)
1 Kings 19:16, 19-21; Galatians 5:1, 13-18; Luke 9:51-62

One of the most common convictions of biblical scholars is that the Gospels are not biographies of Jesus. The evangelists were not concerned to recover and put down in writing the very words that Jesus said and the things that he did and in the precise order that he said and did them. That is why these writings never were called "lives of Jesus," but "gospels," and "gospel" means "good news."

This does mean that we cannot always be sure of the precise words and deeds of Jesus during his earthly mission. But it also means that we have a much more profound understanding of and a much richer insight into the meaning of Jesus for us. For the evangelists have taken the words and deeds of Jesus and put them in writing in a way that makes them relevant to contemporary Christians. The Gospels, in other words, are interpretations of the whole mission of Jesus, developed within the Church and for the Church.

An excellent illustration of what this means is found in today's Gospel reading. Most modern translations mark this off as the beginning of a new section in Luke's Gospel. And that is indicated by the solemn form in which Jesus is said to have "firmly resolved to proceed toward Jerusalem." It is a formal introduction to a journey that Jesus is making to Jerusalem.

Just where the section ends is not altogether certain. A good guess is 19:27, just before he enters the sacred city. What is important, however, is that Luke has inserted all the material in these chapters (and most of it is instruction to the disciples) within the framework of a journey. That the journey is artificially constructed can be shown by the geographical references. We conclude therefore that the journey is a literary device intended to tell us something about Jesus Christ.

The most obvious interpretation is that Jesus' journey is symbolic of the journey of all Christians. We are all pilgrims on the road to the heavenly Jerusalem. But we are pilgrims *with Jesus*. And all the instructions found in the section are meant to guide us *on the way*. They are pilgrim instructions to help us reach the goal. All ten chapters might be called a manual of Christian discipleship; it tells us how to follow Jesus on the road.

That Luke had this in mind is suggested also by the latter part of today's reading, which presents the requirements of discipleship. Luke has put these right at the beginning of the journey narrative to point up the precise religious nature of the narrative.

The requirements are radical indeed. But they can be summed up as absolute commitment to Jesus Christ. Such a commitment will entail hardships and heartbreaks, the impairment of friendships and relationships. But the commitment also brings an inner peace and security. The disciple knows that he or she is on a journey to a goal that Jesus himself has already attained.

In a sense, I suppose the entire Bible could be called a journey narrative. It tells of mankind's journey to wholeness of being, to *shalom*, to salvation. And many individual passages could be shown to illustrate this more concretely.

One such passage would surely be the first reading. It is the account of Elijah's call to Elisha to follow him. The latter was to take on the prophetic mantle and lead Israel as Elijah had done. The similarity between this and the Gospel reading is the reason for their being given on the same Sunday.

So, we are on a journey. But the important point is that it is initiated by the Lord and directed by the Lord. And the Lord is its true goal. Assured of this by our commitment, we embrace the perils of the journey.

Fourteenth Sunday in Ordinary Time (C)
Isaiah 66:10-14; Galatians 6:14-18; Luke 10:1-12.17-20

One of the themes of Luke's Gospel is universal salvation. Jesus came to save all people, Jew and Gentile alike. Thus, unlike Matthew, who traces Jesus' lineage back to Abraham in order to show that he fulfills all the promises made to the patriarch (Mt 1:1-17), Luke traces it back to Adam (3:23-38) to depict Jesus as the initiator of a whole new race of children of God.

The Gospel reading for this Sunday contains several indications of this universality of salvation. First, there is the number of disciples sent out by Jesus. Seventy-two was thought by the Jewish people of the time to be the number of all the nations. The number, then, is symbolic of all the people affected by the Christian missionaries.

Also, the context of our passage (cf. 9:51-56) suggests that our missionary discourse took place in a Samaritan town. For Luke Samaria, since it is not Jewish, symbolizes the Gentiles. They are seen here, then, as the object of missionary concern.

Again, in v. 8 we read that the missionaries are told to "eat what they set before you. . . ." The allusion would appear to be to non-kosher food eaten by non-Jewish peoples. Luke has the Gentiles in mind.

The whole tone of the discourse as well as the tone of the account of the disciples' return is filled with glorious sounds of universality. "The harvest is rich," which must mean, in Luke's time at least, peoples of the whole world.

Note that the disciples are to "travel light." This is not to be taken literally. It means that they are not to be preoccupied with minor matters. Their attention and concern are to be wholly on the gospel. This is the meaning, too, of the admonition to "greet no one along the way." Can you imagine Jesus meaning that literally?

And "peace" is that concrete and dynamic *shalom* of the Hebrew Scriptures. It is given "to this house," suggesting that all the blessings and closeness that *shalom* is will pervade the home and those who dwell in it.

All that is needed for the greeting to be effective is openness to its power. The passage says this, "If there is a peaceable man there, your peace will rest on him." The Greek has, literally, "a son of peace," that is, one who knows what true peace is and ardently desires it.

The heart of the missionaries' message is God's reign. Twice does Jesus state the nearness of that reign as the power behind whatever else they say or do. In the case of those who welcome them it is a power for salvation; in the case of those who do not, it is the power of judgment.

The "jubilation" of the disciples on their return is really Luke's special word for end-time joy, the fullest kind. Jesus confirms their report of success by adding that he himself witnessed the power of evil being cast down from the heavens.

Luke has already suggested that it is the saving power of God in Jesus Christ that makes all this possible. The presence of God's reign in the person and message of Jesus says this. The disciples' report that these things happened "in your name" is a similar testimony. (This is where the first reading comes in so beautifully. All these great and glorious things happen because of the Lord.)

Still, the missionaries deserve their honor. They are God's hands and arms. In the present dispensation—the way things are by God's will—there would be no universal salvation without missionaries. Even God's own miracles take second place to them. That is the meaning of the final verse, which ends, ". . . your names are inscribed in heaven."

Fifteenth Sunday in Ordinary Time (C)
Deuteronomy 30:10-14; Colossians 1:15-20; Luke 10:25-37

The Lord *asks* much of us. But he *gives* us so much more. And the "more" that he gives makes the "much" that he asks seem so little. That is the thought that struck me while reflecting on this Sunday's Word. Let's see how we can find it in the three readings.

The first, from the book of Deuteronomy, is an eloquent appeal to the people to turn to the Lord and to keep his law. But the law, which had been spelled out in the preceding part of the book, wasn't all that easy. So, at least, it would seem to one reading the book for the first time.

But our author, who sums up the whole law as a "command" or as a "word" (so in the Revised Standard Version, v. 14), says that it isn't something mysterious or remote. It isn't something that one has to climb to the skies or cross over the seas in order to fulfill. No, it's something very close to all, a "near word." It is "already in your mouths and in your hearts."

Why does he say that? He is convinced that the Lord is close to them, that he loves them with an undying love, and that he will make it all seem easy. He has so built them up as his people that doing his "word" is doing what comes naturally, if only they accept him. The "much" that God asks is so little in comparison with the "more" that he gives.

The second reading, from Colossians is an overpowering expression of God's "more." And the "more" is Christ. This hymn to Jesus Christ is one of the most articulate presentations of his preeminence over all creation.

All things "in heaven and on earth" (that is called a term of polarity; it means "everything") were created in him, through him, and for him. Those phrases mean that Christ is the center, the model, and the goal of everything created.

What makes all of it God's "more" to us is, of course, that this Jesus Christ is *for us*. He is what he is solely for our sakes. He is "the firstborn of the dead," which means that, because of him, we too will be raised from the dead. He "reconciles everything in his person" and "makes peace through the blood of his cross," which means that our sins are forgiven and we are brought back to the Father.

We learn nothing here of the "much" that God asks of us. But that's alright; that is spelled out elsewhere. Besides, Paul prefers to speak of God's "more" than of our "much." If we can accept that "more," he is convinced, then the "much" will be a near word that is already in our mouths and in our hearts.

The Gospel reading does spell out the "much" that God asks of us. On hearing it, I think all will agree, "Is that all, in return for so much?"

A lawyer asks Jesus to sum up the whole law. Like a man accustomed to precise terms, he wants to know what is expected of him in as concise a way as possible. Jesus prods him to answer himself. He does it in the form of the twofold law of love: love God with all that we are and have; love our neighbor as ourselves.

We say it's easy, and we can do it. But the Good Samaritan parable shows that even good people have difficulties with this. The priest and the Levite are good intentioned men and want to keep the law. They see this man in the ditch and would like to help. But maybe he's dead. If they touch a corpse, they will be unclean for seven days. There are so many "good things" they want to do in the coming week. They can't, or won't, take a chance.

How often do we not act in the same way? We don't want to get involved because it will take up too much of our time. We don't want to get our lives enmeshed in others' lives. It can get complicated.

Then we must think back to God's "more" and ask whether this "much" is really that much after all. We're not being asked to be nailed to a cross, just to help someone in need. Maybe God's "more" will prove the difference in our decision.

Sixteenth Sunday in Ordinary Time (C)
Genesis 18:1-10; Colossians 1:24-28; Luke 10:38-42

An anthropomorphism is an important literary device found especially in the Old Testament. It means literally "human form." The biblical authors use it when they depict God acting as a human being. Thus, to say that God is a shepherd is an anthropomorphism. To say that he saved Israel "with a strong hand and an outstretched arm" is also an anthropomorphism.

The use of this literary device is not the only way to express divine action in the world. One could use abstract language, such as a philosopher or a theologian would use. One could speak of God's salvific will being exercised in favor of his people, or of his prior and determinative love for us.

The value of the anthropomorphism, as merges from these examples, is that it expresses a religious conviction vividly and in down-to-earth terms. Everyone understands what is being said. The one difficulty with it, and it is a major stumbling block for many, is that the anthropomorphism is often understood literally. The external activity is emphasized and not the underlying religious conviction, which is the whole point of the anthropomorphism.

In our first reading, from Genesis, we have an excellent example of an anthropomorphism. The whole chapter, of which our reading is a part, is one of the most extended anthropomorphisms in the Old Testament. The Lord God is depicted in "human form" along with two angels, conversing with Abraham, having a meal with him, and later on, even engaging in a bargaining session with the patriarch.

What is the author telling us in this literary device? The most profound truth he conveys is that the omnipotent God has a very special concern for this man and his wife. The Lord loves them and wants to communicate that love to them. He promises them a child in fulfillment of an earlier promise that Abraham would be the father of a great nation (Gn 12:1-3).

As far as the whole book of Genesis is concerned, this chapter is intended as one more confirmation of God's will to form a special people. That will had been expressed at the very beginning of Abraham's story. The following chapters show how the divine will was put in jeopardy by some misadventure or other. But always, somehow, the danger was overcome and the promise secured. Here we have one more assurance of its fulfillment.

The Church, however, in giving us this reading in its isolated form, wants to expose the great love God has for his friends. She finds the most blatant expression of it that she can. The Lord God walks and talks and dines with those he loves. It is, indeed, a beautiful anthropomorphism.

In the Gospel reading the anthropomorphism becomes a literal fact. The Lord does, in reality, come to those he loves and speaks and dines with them. The Genesis reading, as powerful as it is, is completely overshadowed now by the Jesus story.

In the account Jesus comes to the home of Mary and Martha (John tells us the home is in Bethany—11:1). While Martha's role in serving the meal is not disparaged (it is her undue anxiety that needs moderating), Mary is without doubt the better example of the true disciple. The disciple is one who feasts on the word of the Lord.

These two readings are unsurpassed in the intensity of their feeling. To be with the Lord, to reflect on his word, to know his love, to accept him unreservedly into our lives—that is the beauty and power of our biblical faith. The wonder is that it's all possible because of what he has done. That is not an anthropomorphism.

Seventeenth Sunday in Ordinary Time (C)
Genesis 18:20-32; Colossians 2:12-14; Luke 11:1-13

Last week we spoke of the anthropomorphism, a literary device depicting God in human form or engaging in human activity. Its purpose is to convey some underlying conviction about God's saving activity in the world.

Our Genesis reading for this Sunday is a continuation of the anthropomorphism in last Sunday's reading. There we read that the Lord, with two angels, visited Abraham's tent, had a meal with him, and promised that Sarah would have a child within a year. The underlying conviction was God's special love for these friends and his intention to make the patriarch the father of a great nation.

On this Sunday we learn of God's intention to see if the sins of Sodom and Gomorrah are as bad as claimed. Then Abraham engages the Lord in dialog and bargains with him. Would the Lord spare the cities if fifty innocent people are found? He would. What if forty-five are found? Or forty? Or thirty? Or ten? In every case the Lord agrees to withold his punishment.

What can possibly be behind this bold anthropomorphism where the Lord is depicted as a desert sheik dealing with a canny merchant? What the Church sees here especially, in view of the Gospel reading, is not only the possiblility but also the efficacy of prayer. Deal with the Lord in everyway that you can. He's all you have, ultimately, to depend on. And he'll listen.

Prayer's efficacy (which means that it works!) is shown in the

Lord's willingness to withhold his punishing hand at the patriarch's request. It also reveals the divine mercy. He wants to save; he is only awaiting the desire for salvation, even if it comes from another!

Why does the "bargaining" cease after the mention of ten innocent people? Perhaps the author felt that he had gone as far as he possibly could. More likely he did not want to put limits on the divine mercy. The extent of his mercy still remains open to all possibilities.

In ancient Semitic thinking, the crimes of a few could merit the punishment of many. Israel was defeated in battle because one man had violated the ban (Jos 7). Here we have the reverse. A few just people could win the salvation of many, a conviction needing no later nuancing in revelation.

One last thought on this reading. In v. 27 Abraham says that he speaks so boldly to the Lord "though I am but dust and ashes!" It is a fascinating note. Right in the midst of a long passage on the "humanness" of God, the author emphasizes his transcendence, his otherness, his mysteriousness. Before him we are all "dust and ashes." And yet we pray without inhibitions.

The Gospel reading, from Luke, continues the theme of prayer. It is one of Luke's favorite themes, especially prayer's efficacy. The Genesis author established the principle that prayer works. Jesus more than confirms it with two stories and two sayings about prayer. The "Lord's Prayer" is an added bonus.

If someone doesn't know how to pray, that person doesn't need teaching; he or she needs conversion. What Jesus offers here is for his disciples, for believers who may have grown weak in their faith. They need to be reminded that it is a loving Father whom they address in prayer. Would such a father give a snake if asked for a fish? The other story, about the man who doesn't want to be disturbed but who gets up and helps the begging friend anyway because he's so persistent, is almost as bold as the Abraham story. So, the consoling lesson in all of this is that prayer of intercession is fruitful. The philosopher has problems figuring out how an infinite Being can be moved by human prayer. But long before that philosopher reaches a conclusion, the person of faith is already there—and praying.

Eighteenth Sunday in Ordinary Time (C)
Ecclesiastes 1:2; 2:21-23; Colossians 3:1-5, 9-11; Luke 12:13-21

What in the world is that first reading doing as part of Sunday's Word? It says life is an illusion, nothingness, total frustration. What good does it do to work your fingers to the bone, build up a fortune, and then have to leave it to some shiftless oaf who never did a day's work in his life?

Bubbles in the air! That's all life is, our author seems to be saying. One prick of a pin and poof!—it's all over. If "vanity" means emptiness, "vanity of vanities" means the "fullness" of emptiness. Don't bother yourself, the author tells us, I've tried everything under the sun and nothing lasts. A moment or two of pleasure, of satisfaction may occur, but in the end it all goes down the drain.

Two considerations temper the harshness of that view. The first is that the author lived before Israel had been graced with faith in the afterlife. Only in later books does she come to the conviction of resurrection from the dead (Daniel) and of immortality (Wisdom). We can be fairly sure that our author's realistic probings of the true dimensions of this life contributed to the later development.

The second consideration is that he offered his reflections outside the context of his own faith. This was the general practice in wisdom literature. Its purpose was to examine the values of secular reality independently of God's covenant love for his people. The book of Proverbs, for example, suggests any number of such values. Our author says, yes, but in the total picture where do they bring us?

We can be truly grateful to the author. He makes us evermore conscious of the richness of a life of faith, a life that sees the real depths of secular reality and recognizes the finger of God at work. This faith rejoices in the goodness of things because it knows there is an unseen and eternal dimension to them, an everlasting beauty guaranteed by the presence of the Lord.

Qoheleth (that is the Hebrew title of our author) came almost to the brink of seeing this. He wrote that God "has put the timeless into men's hearts, without their ever discovering . . . the work which God has done" (3:11). He knew there was something deeper there; his heart, as Pascal once put it, had "its reasons of which the reason knew not." But his faith was not yet perfected.

How appropriate, then, are our two other readings. The Gospel could almost be a commentary on the thoughts of Qoheleth. "A man may be wealthy," Jesus says, "but his possessions do not guarantee him life." To that Qoheleth would have said, "Amen!"

There follows the story of the rich man whom God calls "this very night." His treasure goes to another. "Exactly what I said," we can hear Qoheleth muttering. But Jesus says that life can be rich in another way, in a way that not even death can touch. This is life with God.

Paul spells it out more clearly. "Your life is hidden now with Christ in God. Put on a new man, one who grows in knowledge as he is formed anew in the image of his creator." This is the life of faith that recognizes a Christ-element in all of reality, a life that doesn't end with death.

What Qoheleth says, then, makes us realize the richness of this faith we have. We can see that without that faith life does indeed lose its meaning. It's just what Qoheleth said. So we should say "Thanks, Qoheleth, we needed that!"

Nineteenth Sunday in Ordinary Time (C)
Wisdom 18:6-9; Hebrews 11:1-2, 8-19; Luke 12:32-48

"Do not live in fear, little flock." These words of Jesus to his disciples open our Gospel reading. While the Greek reads literally, "Fear not, little flock," the translation given above conveys the meaning more forcefully. Our lives as Christians should be marked by the knowledge that the kingdom is ours. That knowledge excludes an oppressive fear.

This does not mean I can have an irresponsible attitude to life. It doesn't mean God will take care of me no matter what I do or how I act. Nor does it mean that, having accepted Jesus as Lord and Savior, I can say, "I've found it" and then go my merry way.

Anyone who thinks like that has to read the rest of the Gospel passage. "Let your belts be fastened around your waists and your lamps be burning ready." "That servant is fortunate whom his master finds busy when he returns." "When much has been given a man, much will be required of him."

What Jesus combines here is the peace of the kingdom and the responsibility of the kingdom. Responsibility will never induce fear in the mature heart. That is why Jesus can so serenely exclude fear from those who follow him even while they gird their loins and light their lamps.

Jesus presupposes that all that is asked of his followers is but the response to a mighty love the Father has shown them. To be responsible is, in fact, to respond. And the Christian gospel makes clear that is a response to love.

When we read the passage from Hebrews that forms our second reading, we see a beautiful illustration of this response. The author calls it the response of faith. The entire chapter of the latter recounts this phenomenon of faith manifested in the lives of Old Testament personalities. Our reading centers on the faith of Abraham and Sarah. It is important that we appreciate the depth of that faith. Then, when Jesus tells us to live without fear, we'll understand what he means.

Chapter 12 of Genesis opens up with a solemn divine charge to Abraham to leave his father's house and to go to the land that God would show him. God would bless him, make his name great, and, above all, make him the father of a great nation (12:1-3). Abraham believed and went.

The chapters of Genesis that follow might be compared with "the perils of Pauline." Time after time something occurs in the life of the patriarch and his wife that seems to put God's promise in jeopardy. But Abraham retains his faith and the danger is overcome.

The most severe test of faith (and it is mentioned in the longer form of our reading) came when Abraham was told by God to offer up his son, Isaac, in sacrifice. Consider the demands that faith makes. Isaac was the fulfillment of a promise God had made to the patriarch and his wife. The child was the apparent basis of Abraham's faith. If he should die, how could a nation emerge from the patriarch's loins?

Abraham's faith, however, was in God. So Abraham did not murmur nor question why. He went as the Lord commanded. He lived in peace and without fear because his trust was in the Lord.

Now, perhaps, we can understand how Jesus can tell his disciples not to live their lives in fear. If their faith is strong enough, nothing can bother them. No matter what is asked of them, they believe in the Lord who promised them the kingdom, and they respond. They know he will be faithful, for he is the Lord.

Twentieth Sunday in Ordinary Time (C)
Jeremiah 38:4-6, 8-10; Hebrews 12:1-4; Luke 12:49-53

Brace yourselves. Our readings this Sunday do not readily lend themselves to the description of "good news." We read of Jeremiah being thrown into a cistern where he "sank into the mud" and almost starved to death. We are told that we "have not yet resisted (sin) to the point of shedding blood." And Jesus himself tells us that he causes divisions in the family. How do we make "good news" out of all that?

Let's consider them in order. Jeremiah really never had a chance to be popular if he was to tell the truth, for the truth was that Judah was doomed. The Babylonians were infinitely more powerful. Judah's only hope for some kind of survival was surrender.

That is what Jeremiah told the people over and over again. But to talk surrender was to be disloyal. So thought the royal princes who no doubt represented the popular opinion. And the king let them have their way with the prophet. Their way was confining him in a cistern. That would keep him from spreading his treachery and maybe teach him to be their kind of prophet, not God's kind.

Jeremiah was no masochist. He didn't enjoy being treated harshly, as his "confessions" abundantly prove (cf. 15:10-18). Nor did he *want* to prophesy doom for his country. God was allowing this to happen to them because of the people's faithlessness. This was his Word to Jeremiah and that Word was like a fire burning within him that he could not restrain (cf. 20:7-9).

Did Jeremiah find fulfillment? The problem with that question is that for so many people fulfillment means "doing one's own thing," "looking out for number one," gratification of surface desires. In this sense we must answer no, Jeremiah was not fulfilled. But in the end he was fulfilled in a much more profound way than self-seekers could ever imagine. Read 1:19 and reflect on it for a moment. Would you like to share that conviction?

The second reading, from Hebrews, talks about resisting to the point of shedding blood. The author is writing to Christians undergoing a crisis of faith. In a time of persecution, or at least of harassment, defection is a great temptation.

The author had just listed, with joyful enthusiasm, the many saints of old from Abel on down. They had suffered for their faith. And now this "cloud of witnesses" surrounds today's Christians as a powerful reminder to persevere in the faith.

He points above all to Jesus, who had "endured the cross, heedless of its shame." But the cross brought him to glory. And so, the author reminds us, "let us keep our eyes fixed on Jesus, who inspires and perfects our faith." We must, in other words, have a deep personal attachment to him who has shown us what true fulfillment is and who offers it to us.

But when we accept this real fulfillment, when we accept the way of Jesus, we encounter opposition. That is what Jesus means in the Gospel reading. When he says that he came "for division," that is a Semitic expression meaning his coming will inevitably result in division for many. The way of Jesus is not a way that all accept. In fact, it is actively opposed by some, and that is what brings division.

"Good news" is the presupposition of all these readings. Simply put, God loves us with a saving love that reaches its height in Jesus Christ. Accept that love and you will know fulfillment, regardless of the sacrifice. Ask Jeremiah. Ask the author of Hebrews. Ask Jesus.

EDITOR'S NOTE: This was the last column Father Maly wrote and published. It appeared on August 17, 1980. The following columns of his were written earlier.

Twenty-first Sunday in Ordinary Time (C)
Isaiah 66:18-21; Hebrews 12:5-7.11-13; Luke 13:22-30

In the opening verses of the twelfth chapter of Genesis we read of the beginning of a plan that God had in mind for the salvation of the whole world. The preceding chapters had told of the incursion of sin and its phenomenal growth until it led to the scattering of peoples over the face of the earth; no one could understand anyone else's speech.

Now was the time for the reversal of that tragedy. God chose Abram (later to be named Abraham) to be the bearer of the promise and the medium for the ingathering of the nations. The climax of God's message to Abram was that all the nations of the earth would find a blessing in him (12:3).

The Bible is the record of the unfolding and the fulfillment of this plan. Through the people of Israel and her incredible history over more than a thousand years, God revealed himself, gradually and patiently, until they could come to know what he had in mind.

That history was not a peaceful one of uninterrupted progress. It was one of victory and defeat, of glory and humiliation, of joy and sorrow. For it was through suffering as much as through anything else that Israel grew in her knowledge of the Lord. Indeed, crisis was more often than not the springboard of revelation.

Our first reading for this Sunday is a witness to that. Although now a part of the book of Isaiah, it was appended to that book only at a later period. It was written after the return from exile when the Jewish people were frustrated and despondent. They were not experiencing the glory of a full life that they had so eagerly anticipated. Through suffering God was revealing himself.

His revelation was remarkable. He would bring together all the nations and tongues. It was not just Israel that he wanted to share in his blessings. It was all peoples. The story of Babel and the promise to Abram must have been recalled.

This universalism of salvation had not been stressed much before this. Israel was powerfully caught up in the wonder of her own election by God and understandably so. But she had to learn that it was an election of service for others, not an election based on merit for self-fulfillment. It was suffering that brought her to that awareness.

Jesus is altogether in accord with that message of universalism. The Gospel reading contains his statement that people will come from all the ends of the earth to partake of the messianic banquet in the kingdom of God. The reading had begun with the question of one who had asked whether salvation was for the few. It concludes with the statement of universal salvation.

But we must recall the larger context of Luke's Gospel in which this reading is found. It is part of his "journey narrative" in which Jesus is presented as on his way to Jerusalem. The opening verse reminds us of that when it states that he went through towns and villages on his way to Jerusalem.

Jerusalem, of course, was to be the scene of Jesus' glorification when he was taken up to heaven (Lk 24:51). But that glorification was necessarily preceded by suffering and death. He had first to suffer and be rejected by his own generation (Lk 17:25).

Just as Jesus' personal glory was attained through suffering, so was God's whole plan to be realized in the same way, as Israel had discovered. Jesus was well aware of this when he spoke of all the nations sharing in the Kingdom. The realization of that plan would not be automatically achieved.

And so we have the history of the Church. It is marked by the presence of Christ, by the sacraments, by all the noble efforts of sainted men and women. But it is also marked by struggle and persecution, by misunderstanding and rejection. It is a history that leads, however, to the salvation of all nations.

Twenty-second Sunday in Ordinary Time (C)
Sirach 3:17-18, 20, 28-29; Hebrews 12:18-19, 22-24;
Luke 14:1, 7-14

In a Horatio Alger society, such as is America, where human endeavor and personal initiative are the presupposition of success, our first and third readings sound a strange, even unwelcome, note. Humility is their theme. We are advised not to strive for that which is beyond us, not to seek the higher place. Does our faith, then, forbid us to "dream the impossible dream"?

The second century B.C. sage, Sirach, is probably addressing the wealthy and influential of his society. He counsels them to carry out their transactions with humility, which includes proper respect for those with whom they are dealing. This is all the more important for those who are more powerful. Moreover, uncontrolled ambition is contrary to true wisdom.

Two factors modify somewhat the wise men's observations. First, in the preceding section (3:1-16) he had given advice about children's conduct toward their parents. In the concluding verse he had spoken of the unruly child who forsakes his father and angers his mother. It was this attitude that doubtless sparked his comments on the conduct of all of God's children.

Second, in a later passage (10:27) he shows that he is not counselling indolence or the abdication of human effort. There he writes that the one who works and has an abundance is better than the one who always boasts but has nothing. Sirach does not reject the common biblical conviction of the value of human labor.

Still, that is not the full resolution of the problem. Sirach himself would have admitted that there is a deeper truth that makes his counsel of humility valid for all times, regardless of the context. It was so much a part of his religious heritage that he felt no need to express it here.

Even the Gospel passage does not expose the truth in a way that is obvious from a cursory reading. But it is evident to the one who recognizes the faith context of Luke's Gospel.

Jesus begins by giving what would appear to his hearers to be common sense advice, even "face saving" advice. One who comes early to a banquet takes a place of honor. But then a higher dignitary arrives and he is asked to make room for him. Because he was not humble, he is humiliated. Conversely, the one who takes the lowest place may well be invited to a higher place.

All of this would have been known to Jesus' hearers, and most of them would probably have acted in accord with this advice. But Jesus is not concerned with ordinary social etiquette. He has more in mind than that.

At the conclusion of the anecdote he says, "For everyone who exalts himself shall be humbled and he who humbles himself shall be exalted." This is no longer an observation of social etiquette. This is Kingdom talk. This is the way it is in the Kingdom of God.

A presupposition of the saying is that God issues the invitation to the Kingdom banquet. And he issues it to the lowly, the humble,

those who recognize their total dependence on God's salvation.
These are the ones who will be exalted. But those who say, "Look at
me, Lord! See my strength, my wealth, my influence," are the ones
who will be humbled.

This humility, this total openness to the strength of God, leads to
greatness. And this humility before God expresses itself in humility
before my neighbor, in openness to the other, in a recognition that
the other may be far more precious in God's sight than I am.

No Horatio Algers live in the Kingdom. The full-fledged citizens
are those who achieve great things in the Lord because they recognize that they achieve them in God's strength. This radical humility
makes a saint, whether canonized or not. And a saint not only dreams
the impossible dream but also makes it a reality.

Twenty-third Sunday in Ordinary Time (C)
Wisdom 9:13-18; Philemon 9-10,12-17; Luke 14:25-33

In the Gospel reading Jesus presents two fascinating parables. Their
fascination lies, however, not so much in the stories themselves as in
their application. Jesus uses them to illustrate what it means to be a
follower of his. How they *do* illustrate that is the heart of the problem.

The first parable concerns one who wishes to build a tower. A
prudent person will carefully estimate his resources beforehand to be
sure that he is able to complete the work. In much the same way a
king will ask whether he has sufficient manpower before engaging
another in battle.

In all the parables of Jesus, as he first enunciated them, he was not
concerned to give a meaning for all the details. Thus we need not ask
whom the king represents or what the tower refers to. Later, Church
writers did concern themselves with such details, but, in general,
Jesus did not.

Rather, he normally had one point in mind. And the point of these
parables seems obvious enough. Be sure you can complete the task
you undertake. Check your resources. That sounds sensible enough.
The question is how it applies to being a follower of Jesus.

A helpful insight here is provided by a comparison with the

disciples of other Jewish rabbis. These young men would go about from one rabbi to another, listen attentively to what they had to say, often initiate discussion with them, and then decide whose teaching they preferred. Such a disciple was called a *talmid hakam*, a learner of wisdom.

It is clear here what resources a disciple must have. He must be able to listen to what is said (the Hebrew word *shama'*, "to listen," was intimately associated with the disciple), to ask pertinent questions, to appropriate the wisdom of the rabbi to himself. All of this could be gauged pretty accurately.

Such a description would never do for a disciple of Jesus. That Jesus did have a message which he proclaimed, that many listened to the message and made it a part of themselves—all of this is true. But that doesn't come close to defining a disciple of Jesus.

Basically what defines a New Testament disciple, as our Gospel reading makes evident, is total self-giving to the Master. This doesn't require great intelligence, a keen imagination, natural strength or beauty. These are not the resources that Jesus says you are to look for. Rather, can you say "yes" completely to Jesus Christ?

This is born out by what precedes and follows the two parables. In what precedes, Jesus says that a follower must "turn his back" on his family and his very self. (The Greek literally has "hate," but this is a Semitic way of saying "love less," as Matthew 10:37 makes clear.) Surely, no more radical a way can be found for expressing total self-surrender.

In the end, of course, this does not mean, necessarily, a complete rejection of family and self. It means putting Christ first. Then all other relationships are to be seen and evaluated in the light of that one fundamental relationship.

The same idea is expressed in the verse following the parables. Jesus says that a disciple must "renounce" or "say goodbye to" all his possessions. On the analogy of what was said above, we can conclude that this does not necessarily mean completely stripping oneself of all material goods. It means that those goods are renounced as having any kind of power or influence over us. Jesus alone can have that.

In the parable of the tower Jesus had said that the builder must "calculate the outlay," or "count the cost" ahead of time. Maybe that puts the question to us as forcefully as possible. If we really want to be disciples of Jesus, we must first "count the cost" and ask if it is too much.

Twenty-fourth Sunday in Ordinary Time (C)
Exodus 32:7-11, 13-14; 1 Timothy 1:12-17; Luke 15:1-32

Lost and found. Strayed and returned. Sinned and forgiven. Estranged and reconciled. In one way or another the idea of separation from God and ultimate reunion with him is the theme of all three of our readings. A brief consideration of each will reveal the richness of the theology presented here.

The first reading is a section from a familiar Old Testament story, that of the golden calf. The Israelites become impatient with the prolonged absence of Moses on Mount Sinai and somehow blame God. They ask Aaron to make them another god. The golden calf is the result.

Our reading depicts God's reaction to the event, his determination to destroy the people because of their sin, Moses' plea for forgiveness, and finally God's relenting in his judgment. That brief summary hardly does justice to the intensity with which the feelings of both God and Moses are presented. Sin is abhorrent to God. Yet he can be moved to forgive.

A number of scholars think that this whole story tells about something that happened over three hundred years later. When the northern kingdom separated from Judah after Solomon's death, King Jeroboam set up two golden calves at Dan and Bethel. He did not want his people to be going to Jerusalem to worship, lest they develop a desire for reunion with Judah (1 Kings 12:26-30).

This action of Jeroboam was considered so radical a break from true Yahwism that the religious authors put it in our present story form and placed it there at the beginning of Israel's history as a chosen people. By doing this they not only suggested that idolatry was a "typical" sin of Israel throughout her history (an "original sin"), but also emphasized its grossness in contrast to God's saving actions and merciful forgiveness.

The second reading presents Paul thanking Jesus Christ for the favors bestowed on him. He then goes on to say how great a sinner he was before his conversion. He was "a blasphemer, a persecutor, a man filled with arrogance. . . ." He even says that he was the worst of the sinners whom Christ came to save.

The emphasis on Paul's earlier condition is made only to bring out by contrast the mercy of the Lord. His grace was poured out "in overflowing measure." So, while the reality of the original separation is painted almost as darkly as that of the golden calf story, the Lord's mercy is given much more extended treatment. The final doxology is an outburst of praise occasioned by that mercy.

Still another scholarly opinion serves to enrich this religious conviction. It is commonly thought that the present letter was written, not by Paul himself, but by one of his later disciples who was fully acquainted with the apostle's life and theology. If this is true, it means we have here a much more deliberate picture of man's sinfulness and of God's forgiveness. Rather than a spontaneous confession, it becomes a formal, and so more solemn and convincing, statement.

The Gospel presents three parables: the lost sheep, the lost coin, the prodigal son. The last was already considered on the Fourth Sunday of Lent. The interesting point about the first two parables is that there is no hint of sin, of deliberate separation. The sheep simply strays; the coin is lost. Both are recovered.

From the conjunction of these two parables with that of the prodigal son, and of this reading with the first two, we have to conclude that the Church wants, ultimately, to proclaim salvation. Sin is real and cannot be denied. It is why there is salvation. But found, returned, forgiven, reconciled—this is the heart of the gospel of Jesus Christ.

Twenty-fifth Sunday in Ordinary Time (C)
Amos 8:4-7; 1 Timothy 2:1-8; Luke 16:1-13

In reading the earlier parts of the Old Testament, one has the definite impression that earthly goods are to be eagerly sought. In fact, they are looked upon as a blessing from a bounteous Lord, a kind of reward for virtuous living.

While Abraham was told to leave his own country, he was still promised a great land for himself and his descendants. The Hebrew people, struggling through the wilderness, looked forward to the possession of that land, "flowing with milk and honey." Even the priestly author of a later date saw human dominion over all the earth and its inhabitants as willed by God from the beginning (Gn 1:28).

This positive relationship of the human person to the world and its goods underlies all of biblical revelation, including that of the New Testament. But it has been historically conditioned by another factor, sin, the abuse and misuse of those same goods. This factor colors much of the Scriptures.

It is clearly present in the reading from Amos. As "a shepherd and a dresser of sycamores" (7:14), Amos would hardly have disdained earthly goods. But he was overwhelmed by his experience of greed and rapaciousness on the part of the wealthy.

Their desire for more goods was so gross that it led them to scorn religious holidays whose restrictions on human labor limited their profits (v. 5). They would sell almost worthless husks of wheat to those who could not afford more (v. 6c). In these cases, Amos is denouncing greed, pure and simple.

But the prophet is even more outraged by the injustices brought on the poor by the rich. The former are often forced into slavery to pay their debts. It is not difficult to understand, in the light of such experience, why the possession in itself of earthly goods would assume the guise of evil. If they can lead to that kind of depravity, perhaps they should be shunned altogether.

The Gospel reading also has to do with earthly goods, but several different points are made concerning them. First, there is the parable of the wily manager (vv. 1-8). Then there follow originally distinct sayings of Jesus (vv. 9-13). They really do not hang together very well; Luke put them here because they all have to do with possessions.

In the parable the manager, about to be dismissed, calls in the master's debtors and reduces their bills (probably by renouncing part or all of his own commission) in order to gain their good will for the future. The lesson intended by Jesus is simply that we should be as enterprising about our future in the Kingdom as was the manager about his future. No judgment, good or bad, is made on the possession of goods.

The saying in v. 9, about making friends through the use of earthly goods, is difficult to understand fully. In general we can say that it at least inculcates prudent use of these goods and that they are to be evaluated in the light of the Kingdom.

The sayings in vv.10-12 have to do with trustworthiness in the disposition of earthly goods, whether one's own or another's. The Kingdom orientation is only implicit here.

Finally, in v.13, the clearest Christian statement on earthly goods is presented. They must never stand in the ways of one's relationship to God, which is primary. "You cannot give yourselves to (literally 'serve') God and money." The means (earthly goods) and the end (God's reign) must never be confused.

Fundamentally Amos and Jesus do not differ in this matter. Only, in Jesus the Kingdom has been revealed. Thus are Christians more powerfully motivated to use their earthly goods for the sake of others and, ultimately, for God's glory.

Twenty-sixth Sunday in Ordinary Time (C)
Amos 6:1, 4-7; 1 Timothy 6:11-16; Luke 16:19-31

What ever happened to hell? Is it just another piece of mythological furniture of the ancient mind that has been chopped up and destroyed by the inexorable process of secularization? How can we square the notion of hell with faith in a good God whose nature is to save? The readings for this Sunday warrant our asking the questions.

The parable in Luke's Gospel is the familiar one of Lazarus and the rich man. One intriguing aspect of the story is that it is the only one of Jesus' parables in which one of the characters is named. Leaving the characters nameless would, of course, be a help in universalizing the lesson. Some scholars suggest that the poor man in the parable, as Jesus told it, was also nameless. He may have been given the name of Lazarus later after the story of the raising of Lazarus from the dead had begun to circulate (cf. Jn 11:1-44).

The main point of the story, however, is the fate of the two men after death. Lazarus is taken to "the bosom of Abraham," an expression found in ancient Jewish literature. It probably suggests association with the one to whom the biblical promise of divine blessing was first made (Gn 12:1-3). Here the blessing is seen in the form of "resting."

The rich man, on the other hand, is pictured as being in "the abode of the dead," literally, Hades, a term that does not necessarily imply a place of punishment. In the context, however, that is precisely what it is. The rich man is "in torment" and seeks relief from the pain. A clear connection is made between his and Lazarus' present situation and their earthly condition (v. 25).

What is more important for our consideration is that Abraham speaks of "a great abyss" between the two that cannot be crossed. This is quite picturesque language, but the underlying conviction is that the only kind of communication possible between the saved and the damned is the confirmation of the irrevocable judgment. Their conditions are stable; they cannot be reversed.

Admittedly an awful lot of mythological dressing is present in the story. The bosom of Abraham, the flames, the cooling of the tongue with fresh water, the great abyss—all are literary figures, as is the entire conversation between Abraham and the rich man.

But this says something very real. For some life after death will mean the absence of any divine blessing. It will mean isolation, aloneness. Perhaps the clearest way to express it is with the concept of "distance." The unrepentant sinner is distant from God and from others. And that distance is the sinner's free choice. Because it is, God himself must respect it.

Throughout most of the Old Testament period the biblical authors had no convictions about an afterlife, either for the just or for the sinners. Yet, they too were convinced that the just were close to God while the sinners distanced themselves from him.

The reading from Amos, whose major stress is the sinfulness of the people, expresses the distancing in the form of exile. They will be removed from their land, from the place where God had made himself known to them. Amos suggests that exile—or distancing—is the necessary consequence of their will to live as they did. It is the result of their free choice.

Hell—the irreversible distancing of sinner from God—is the inevitable result of the former's total rejection of the latter. That is how radical human freedom is. Hell, then, in a real sense is not God's creation, but the sinner's. God could not destroy it without destroying human freedom.

Twenty-seventh Sunday in Ordinary Time (C)
Habakkuk 1:2-3; 2:2-4; 2 Timothy 1:6-8, 13-14; Luke 17:5-10

One of the fascinating characteristics of the Scriptures is the constancy with which they come up with provocative statements. The reader, on reflection, has to ask hard questions. Is this really what God is saying? How can he allow the inspired author to make that statement? How can I possibly make this a part of my own life?

We have especially good examples of provocative statements in our first and third readings for this Sunday. The second reading contains a more sober observation that can serve as a summary response to the other two.

The prophet Habakkuk lives at a precarious time in Judah's history. The mighty Assyrian empire had collapsed before the Babylonians in 609 B.C., and a new enemy had arisen to threaten God's desperate people (the "Chaldea" of 1:6 refers to Babylon). The prophet was writing at a time when this threat loomed large. The first part of the reading reflects his anguish.

What is most provocative in these verses is the manner in which the prophet challenges God. "How long, O Lord? I cry for help but you do not listen!" Our traditional notion of piety would hardly recommend this kind of prayer. But there it is in the sacred Scriptures, an accusation against God!

We do find examples of this kind of human questioning of divine wisdom in other books of the Bible. The most notable, of course is the book of Job where the human protagonist challenges God to appear in a court of law with him. As far as we know, Habakkuk was the first to utter words of this kind to the God of Israel. Shortly we shall consider the "reasoning" behind such complaints.

But first let us consider the Gospel reading. The saying about the power of faith is clearly provocative. While Jesus does not expect us to go around commanding sycamore trees to drown themselves in the ocean, one has to admit that it is a striking illustration.

Even more provocative but in a subtler way, is the parable about the servants. They are expected to go about their ordinary tasks in an unostentatious way. They are not to expect a handsome reward every time they pour their master a cup of coffee. Jesus' disciples are to serve him in the same way: "We have done no more than our duty."

This is provocative because, in a sense, serving Jesus is quite extraordinary. The total dedication to him, the acceptance of the cross, the serving of others in his name—these have always caught the attention of the world. How can they be said to be no more than duty?

The answer is faith. When one makes that total surrender to the Lord, then all else follows "naturally." The extraordinary becomes ordinary. The unexpected becomes the completely expected. Saying "of course" to the difficult is the mark of the Christian disciple, the person of faith. Thus the joining of the saying of faith's power to the parable of the servant-disciples is no accident.

The same explanation applies to the first reading. The person of faith becomes so much a part of the world of God that even God is one of the family, a Person whom one can address in perfect familiarity, even to the point of complaining. In faith, this is the expected, the ordinary, the "natural."

The Pauline author of the second reading had this kind of faith in mind when he tells Timothy to "stir into flame the gift of God. . . ." We are to recognize our rich heritage whereby we can address God as our Father in a familiar way and can serve Jesus as easily and as readily as children of light.

Twenty-eighth Sunday in Ordinary Time (C)
2 Kings 5:14-17; 2 Timothy 2:8-13; Luke 17:11-19

A good story always has a point that the ordinary audience will be able readily to grasp. A really good story also has certain subtleties that will be missed by some. It is necessary to know something of the cultural or religious background of the storyteller to understand all he is saying.

The editor of the two books of Kings has gathered together a number of stories that had been passed down among his people over the years. His main purpose was to provide a religious history of the monarchy, whence the title of the books. Above all, he wanted to show how Yahweh, the God of Israel, revealed his will in history.

Our first reading captures only a small part of a much longer story. But it is the heart of the story and tells us what major religious truth the author wants to convey.

Naaman, a pagan army commander afflicted with a skin disease, washes in the Jordan River at the prophets Elisha's command. He is cured and acknowledges Israel's God. He then offers Elisha a gift, but the prophet refuses it. Next the cured man asks if he can take some soil from Israel back to his home in Syria. He would build an altar on it and offer sacrifice to Yahweh.

Our reading ends here. The story continues with a sub-plot concerning Elisha's servant, Gehazi. After Naaman leaves, Gehazi follows and tells him that his master really could use some money and clothing for some friends of his. The deceived commander willingly gives him more than he requested. When Elisha, by unknown means, learns of his servant's deception, he curses him with the same disease that had afflicted the pagan officer.

God's power to cure people is clearly a point of the story. This point is consistently made in the Bible, and is one of which we must always remind ourselves. Even more significantly, in the context of Israel's history, is that God cures a pagan, an outsider, one of Israel's enemies.

A large number of stories in the Old Testament betray Israel's less than friendly attitude toward the pagans. Frequently enough Israel prays that they might be exterminated. That fairly pervasive attitude makes the story of Naaman the exceptional one it is. One wonders whether the editor had any difficulty in including the story. It surely would have been hard reading for many Israelites. And the point is even intensified when Gehazi, an Israelite, is cursed with the pagan's disease!

No doubt the editor was somewhat assuaged when he could report that at least the pagan office acknowledged Yahweh as the only God. He also recognizes the holiness of the promised land by taking some of it back to Syria with him. Yahweh is the God of all lands.

The less than friendly attitude toward the pagans still existed in Jesus' time. Even the first Jewish Christians had a difficulty in recognizing Gentiles as possible candidates for Christianity. Paul's work among them, though officially ratified and encouraged in time, was not appreciated by all.

Luke, writing some 25 years after Paul's death, was well aware of this attitude. He wanted to make it clear that Jesus came for *all* people. His Gospel is called the Gospel of universal salvation. The story of the cured Samaritan who, like Naaman, also returns to give thanks is one of the evangelist's arguments. Luke, the only New Testament writer to refer to the Naaman story (4:27), probably had that incident in mind as he wrote our Gospel story.

This bitterness to other groups, whether racial, ethnic, or religious, is obviously a problem not peculiar to Israel. We see it alive in our own day. The readings for this Sunday are as relevant now as they were 2500 and 1900 years ago.

Twenty-ninth Sunday in Ordinary Time (C)
Exodus 17:8-13; 2 Timothy 3:14—4:2; Luke 18:1-8

The young boy bounced his body, gently but repeatedly, against the locked gym door. He knew well enough that he could not crash through, cop-like, with one powerful leap. But he also knew that if he struck the door often enough, the lock would weaken and give way.

The lad was quickly persuaded to practice his gymnastics elsewhere, but the observer was impressed with the lesson. Persistent, persevering action can accomplish what, on first consideration, seems impossible. Our readings from Exodus and Luke present the same lesson. As we shall see, aspects of these readings qualify the lesson, but do not deny it.

In the Exodus story we learn of a battle between Israel, who had just escaped from Egypt, and the Amalekites, a nomadic tribe that dwelt in the southern part of Palestine. As long as Moses, who is on a hilltop, holds his hands in the air, the battle goes in Israel's favor; when he drops them, Amalek has the better of the flight. Finally, Aaron and Hur come to Moses' aid and support his hands until victory is won.

Early Jewish and Christian scholars saw in the story a lesson on the power of persistent prayer. The Church gives it this meaning by combining it with the Gospel parable of the persevering widow. And indeed this may very well have been the meaning intended by the final editor of the book of Exodus.

Modern scholars see in Moses' gesture a prophetic action rather than an attitude of prayer. By his raised hands he is indicating victory. This is not to be understood psychologically, as simply an encouragement to the troops, but religiously, as symbolizing God's saving presence. This is clear from the later statement, not included in our reading, that Moses built a commemorative altar that he called "Yahweh-nissi," meaning "Yahweh is my banner." In other words, the Lord gained the victory.

Even if the original text did refer to a prophetic act rather than to a prayer of petition, the important lesson is there. Persistence in a religious action, if motivated by faith, will find a favorable response. The Lord who grants the victory is always there.

Perseverance in prayer is clearly the lesson of the Gospel parable. Luke even interprets it beforehand by saying that it has to do with "the necessity of praying always and not losing heart." The parable concerns a widow who persistently beseeches a corrupt judge. Although he has no interest in her, she is so persistent that he grants her request in order to be rid of her.

As we have pointed out before, details in the parables are not to be stressed. Thus, we should not think that Jesus is comparing God with the corrupt judge and suggesting that he answers prayers to avoid being bothered so much. In fact, Jesus *contrasts* God with the judge, suggesting that, if a wicked man acts in this positive way, *all the more* will God, our Father.

The final verse, mentioning the (second) coming of the Son of man (a title referring to Jesus), indicates that Luke, at least, was applying the parable to persevering prayer for the parousia. And the Church does pray persistently for that, as the Eucharistic Prayers show. We do also when, in the "Our Father," we pray, "Thy kingdom come."

But the broader lesson surely emerges. If our faith is strong enough to move us to perform religious actions for any proper goal and not to become discouraged, the divine response will ultimately be made. God's saving arm is always there. Our faith, not his arm, needs the testing.

Thirtieth Sunday in Ordinary Time (C)
Sirach 35:12-14, 16-18; 2 Timothy 4:6-8, 16-18; Luke 18:9-14

We Americans like to count our assets. We want to know what we have on hand in order to do effective business with others. And the greater our assets, the greater will be the results of our transactions.

One of the characteristic features of biblical religion is that, between God and the human person, that approach is meaningless. We do not bargain with the Lord in our own behalf. We do not list our virtues in the expectation of a generous divine response.

That is what the parable in today's Gospel reading tells us. The Pharisee is depicted, subtly, as an arrogant man who is quite proud of all his accomplishments. His "prayer" is a listing of his supposed assets. While he does begin with an expression of thanks to God, the impression is given that the man really considers himself ultimately responsible for his goodness.

Interestingly, the *New American Bible* makes this a bit more explicit in its translation. It says the Pharisee prayed "with head unbowed." The Greek reads simply that he prayed "standing (off) by himself." That Luke intended, by this phrase, an attitude of arrogance is almost certain. Our English translation, therefore, is justified.

The translation is even more surely justified when we read that the publican, or tax-collector, did not even dare "to raise his eyes to heaven." In the light of that phrase, we can say that the phrase about the Pharisee was intended to express an attitude, as the translators assumed. Luke is contrasting the personalities, as he often does in his Gospel.

The tax-collector does not list his assets. Probably he doesn't have any, at least the kind that would be acceptable to the Lord. His major assets were likely material ones and were frequently gained by unjust means, if he acted as the majority of tax-collectors in the Roman Empire did at that time.

But his attitude now is clearly one of humility and sorrow. He begs, not for divine approval as the Pharisee did, but for divine forgiveness. Sorry for his sins, he is determined, with God's grace, to amend his life. Therefore is this man justified (made right before God) while the other is not.

Human life, in the context of relationship with God, is not a state fair contest where we display our wares or talents before the divine Official to see who gets the prize of best in class. There is a prize, to be sure, as the second reading indicates. Paul awaits the "crown" that will be awarded to him. But note how he insists that the Lord is the source of his strength and of his perseverance.

The race of life is not just like an athletic contest. The reason is that the divine Judge is himself the ultimate source of all goodness, of all talents. The religious athlete can indeed run a good race, but not without an openness to him who is the source of grace.

That is why our first approach to God has to be one of recognition of our poverty, of our need for his strength, of sorrow for our offenses. True sorrow necessarily involves an opening of the heart to the One offended. That is why our Eucharistic liturgy always begins with the confession of sins and request for God's mercy.

Recall that this is exactly the way Isaiah the prophet reacted when he experienced God's call. "I am a man of unclean lips . . . (Is 6:5). Because of that he was cleansèd and sent forth on mission.

What our readings tell us is that, in God's eyes, our best assets are openness to this Spirit, sorrow for our sins, and acceptance of his love. Then we can say with Isaiah, "Here I am, Lord; send me!"

Thirty-first Sunday in Ordinary Time (C)
Wisdom 11:22—12:1; 2 Thessalonians 1:11—2:2; Luke 19:1-10

BANKER REMITS ONE MILLION DOLLAR DEBT! A headline such as that would doubtless be greeted with much surprise by many readers

and with skepticism by the rest. Human mercy of such magnitude is
rare.

In a religious column, as this is, it is obvious that a contrast is
being initiated between human and divine mercy. And this is, in part,
true. This writer is not the first to make such a contrast in just those
terms. Jesus told a parable about a king who forgave his official a
huge debt (Mt 18:21-24), and he told it for the same purpose.

But in that parable, if our readers will recall, the official did not
really understand the meaning of the king's act of mercy. It made no
difference in him or in his way of life. He immediately went out and
forced a fellow servant to pay back a much smaller sum that he owed
the official.

In a real sense that official did not *accept* the king's act of mercy.
True, he accepted the remission of the debt and that gladly. But for
him it was a purely mechanical operation, a transaction that a
computer would register, uncomprehending and unmoved. The loving mercy of the forgiving king was, for him, meaningless; it did not
reach his heart.

The attitude of this official offers an excellent contrast to that of
Zacchaeus in today's Gospel reading. But let us first consider some of
the details of the story. When the incident first occurred, it must have
aroused much interest and surprise among the people. The
characters and circumstances make for a great story that Luke uses to
his advantage.

Zacchaeus is a tax collector and a short man, an interesting
combination as the story reveals. The sycamore tree (really a kind of
fig tree and not the same as our sycamore trees) has a squatty shape,
ideal for climbing and for comfortable observation. And a crowd
surrounds Jesus.

The imagination has no difficulty picturing the diminutive publican scurrying out in front and climbing the handy tree. Zacchaeus,
being what he was, would have been known to everyone in the
district. We can suppose he would have been pointed out to Jesus by
any number of those crowding around him.

Jesus' command to the man to come down is not surprising; he
was known to deal with the "odd" person. Nor should his intent to
spend the night in the man's house be surprising. Luke had already

told of Jesus having dinner at the presumably wealthy Levi's house (5:27-32). But it is always difficult for the self-righteous to understand this.

The climax of the whole story appears to be the announcement by Jesus that "Today salvation has come to this house. . . ." The divine mercy has been manifested. This meant that Zacchaeus' sins had been forgiven, for, even though they had not been specified, the supposition throughout is that he was a sinner.

But, unlike the official in Matthew's parable, Zacchaeus accepted Jesus' saving love and mercy. This is clear from Jesus' statement about "salvation." His grant of mercy reached the heart. Just when in the incident the conversion happened is hard to say. Zacchaeus' statements about his generosity could be simple boasting, similar to the Pharisee's in 18:11-12. But, no matter; Zacchaeus accepted the divine love and was saved (v.10).

Divine mercy is all through the Bible. It is one of the themes of the first reading, probably the reason why it was chosen. But the acceptance of that love and mercy, the recognition of what it really is, that is where the miracle lies. That God loves and forgives should need no headlines. That we accept it does.

Thirty-second Sunday in Ordinary Time (C)
Maccabees 7:1-2, 9-14; 2 Thessalonians 2:16—3:5; Luke 20:27-38

"A man dies. Those who worked or lived with him gather together. Why should there be a ceremony? Why not simply leave this deserted body alone? . . . Birth, life and death are all part of the same blind necessity. Man, who creates meaning, has only one link with nature: he fights it" (G. Mury).

These words of a leading French Communist represent the views of a large segment of mankind. As such, they provide a powerful background against which we can see the richness and the depth of the biblical view of life and death. They can help us to appreciate the beauty of the convictions expressed in our first and third readings.

For a long time Israel of the Old Testament period had no positive conviction of a life after death. True, they thought that the deceased went to Sheol. But Sheol was a shadowy place of shadowy existence. Israel had no conviction of a fullness of life after death.

But Israel had a hope. It was in a God who willed that fullness of life and would somehow bring it about. "I will give full comfort to them and to those who mourn for them, I, the Creator, who gave them life" (Is 57:18). "For with you is the fountain of life, and in your light we see light" (Ps 36:10).

The real breakthrough in the expression of this hope came in the second century B.C. In the book of Daniel we read, "Many of those who sleep in the dust of the earth shall awake; some shall live forever . . ." (12:2). It is no accident that this revelation was realized at a time of persecution of the just.

The book of Second Maccabees was written as a theological reflection on that same persecution. Our reading is part of a story of a Jewish mother and her seven sons who were put to death for their faith. And we read of their affirmations of the resurrection of the body, powerful statements that need no commentary of themselves.

It is not surprising that the conviction of life after death should take the form of resurrection of the body. Israel always had a holistic view of the human person, that is, a view that conceived of the person not so much as a sum of distinct parts but as a totality in itself.

For this reason, whenever the terms that are translated as "body," "soul," "spirit" and so forth were used, they were not intended as designations of "parts" of the person, but as different ways of expressing aspects of the *whole* person. Thus, when they were brought to the recognition of life after death, it was only natural that they should think of resurrection of the body.

The resurrection of the dead became part of the tradition of the Jewish people, but not of all of them. The party of the Sadducees, for example, did not accept this development in revelation. That is why they are the ones who question Jesus about the subject in the Gospel reading. And the manner in which they formulate the question (a woman married successively to seven men) indicated their difficulty with the issue.

It is obvious that Jesus did accept the development in revelation. His answer to the Sadducees ("They become like angels. . . .") necessarily presupposes his belief in the resurrection. And his basic reason is that "God is not the God of the dead but of the living." If he is the God of Abraham, Isaac, and Jacob, they too must live.

Radically, it is the living God who makes the resurrection possible and even necessary. He wills life. And his will is not fulfilled in a "deserted body." If we believe in God, we must believe in the fullness of life after death.

Thirty-third Sunday in Ordinary Time (C)
Malachi 3:19-20; 2 Thessalonians 3:7-12; Luke 21:5-19

REPENT! THE END IS NEAR! The figure of the bearded man wearing a flowing white gown and carrying such a sign is familiar to most of us, at least in cartoon form. He's been around a long time, almost as long as Christianity itself.

Behind the figure is the conviction, shared by many, that the second coming of Christ in glory is soon to take place. As a Christian denomination, the Adventist movement (which has this conviction as a major point of doctrine) began in 1831 in Dresden, New York. At that time the date of the second coming was set at 1843-44. When that year passed uneventfully, other years were proposed from time to time, but all the predictions proved false. Today, the Seventh Day Adventists, the major branch of the movement, do not set a specific date.

All such attempts to date the *parousia* (second coming) of the Lord are based on an overly literal interpretation of the Scriptures. It rests on a failure to understand the underlying meaning of the Bible, what the sacred authors intended by the figures they used.

From early in the second century B.C. to the second century A.D., a strong apocalyptic spirit was present in Judaism. This spirit, nourished by persecution, expressed itself in special "revelations" (the meaning of "apocalypse") in which world history was seen in a kind of completely condensed form. It might be compared to looking through the wrong end of a telescope.

In this view the past was seen as unfolding according to a distinct pattern and leading up to the present. But its major concern was with the end of world history, which it depicted in highly symbolic figures, and which would witness the ultimate victory of God over all the forces of evil. Vivid imagery, taken from the contemporary world of the author, marks the literature.

The underlying conviction of the apocalyptic authors was not that the end was coming now, but that the end would witness God's victory. Some of them may have been so hard pressed by persecution that they actually did think the end was imminent, but this was not a necessary part of the movement. Words that may have suggested imminence were intended primarily to convey certainty. There is a great difference between the end that is certainly coming and the end that is coming soon.

It is understandable that Jesus should have been touched by this spirit. We have an expression of it in what has been called his apocalyptic discourse. The reading from today's Gospel is a part of it.

The passage speaks of wars and insurrections, of all kinds of natural calamities, and of persecution of Christians. It concludes with the assurance that the Lord will be with his own. In the following section of the discourse (not included in the reading) Jesus also speaks of the end when the Son of Man will come "on a cloud with great power and glory."

We must repeat that it is the absolute assurance of the Lord's control of history and of his ultimate victory at the end that is the heart of apocalyptic. Despite all the evil that can be imagined he will emerge victorious.

In retrospect we can see that this spirit emerged from prophecy, although the prophets did not attempt to depict the future in such detailed form. But with the prophets, too, as our first reading manifests, there is the conviction of "the Lord's day" that will come.

Several times in the Eucharistic Prayer of the Mass, as at the memorial acclamation after the consecration, we look forward to the second coming of the Lord. The certainty of that coming is a prominent part of the Christian faith. The assurance of it is to brighten our lives and encourage us to labor mightily for the Kingdom of God.

Christh the King
2 Samuel 5:1-3; Colossians 1:12-20; Luke 23:35-43

One of the most tension-filled moments in the history of ancient Israel occurred when a decision had to be made, about 1020 B.C., whether the Hebrew tribes should become a monarchy. The Bible records the feelings of two groups. One favored the monarchy in the hope that it would bring unity and political strength to the somewhat disunited tribes. The other feared that the kingship of Yahweh would be threatened if a human king was appointed.

The royal party prevailed, and Saul became the first king. Both the hope and the fear were, in a sense, realized. Political unity was achieved, especially under Saul's successor, David. But the history of Israel's kingship shows a frequent disregard for God's sovereignty, a disregard that the prophets continuously denounced.

But even the bitter experience of human kingship was not without value. It brought home to the more religious persons of Israel the unparalleled character of Yahweh's kingship. He was all that they were not. And because of him the people could look forward to an end-time king who would fulfill all the promise that those ancient tribes hoped for in seeking a king.

That end-time king is described in the Old Testament in what are called the royal messianic prophecies. He is presented as a descendant of David, the one king who was thought to have realized in someway the hope of ancient Israel.

Isaiah describes this future king: "Wonder-Counselor, God-Hero, Father-Forever, Prince of Peace. His dominion is vast and forever peaceful . . . both now and forever. The zeal of the Lord of hosts will do this" (9:5-6).

In Jesus' time the hope for the coming of just such a king burned brightly. And in that time of political subjection, the Jewish people yearned for the independence and greatness they associated with David's reign a thousand years earlier.

It is true that Jesus is given the title of "king of the Jews" in Matthew's Gospel (2:2). But the evangelist understood this in a religious, not a political sense, since the angel had earlier described Jesus as one who "will save his people from their sins" (1:21).

The evidence is conclusive that Jesus avoided the title of king during his ministry because he did not wish to be understood as fulfilling a political role. Rather, he spoke openly and often of the Kingdom, or reign, of his Father to which he was bearing witness and which he was inaugurating. That Kingdom was, above all, a spiritual one, but affecting the whole of human society.

The post-Easter Church did not emphasize the kingship of Jesus, probably for the same reasons that Jesus avoided the title. Paul refers to Christ's Kingdom (1 Cor 15:24-25), but it is clearly in a spiritual sense. Much more often, however, the Church preferred titles such as Savior, Son of God, and above all, Lord.

Only in the passion narratives of the Gospels do we find an open reference to Jesus as king. And no doubt this reflects the conviction of some of Jesus' contemporaries that he claimed to be a king. It was at least one of the major charges made against him, as the sign on the cross indicates.

But when, in this Sunday's reading, the criminal asks to be remembered in Jesus' Kingdom, he answers with the assurance of his being in paradise. This is no earthly kingdom.

What Jesus' kingship really means is brought out in forceful terms in the letter to the Colossians, our second reading. He is the Lord of all things, of principalities and powers, of all creation.

This is the kind of king we praise and glorify and to whom we give ourselves in the complete surrender of faith. This kingship is something far greater than those ancient Hebrew tribes could possibly have anticipated.

THE WORD ALIVE

Solemnities, Major Feasts, and Holydays

With the exception of the Solemnity of
the Sacred Heart, the following liturgical
celebrations usually replace the
Sunday Mass when they fall on Sunday.

The Presentation of the Lord (ABC), February 2
Malachi 3:1-4; Hebrews 2:14-18; Luke 2:22-40

This feast day commemorates both the purification of the Virgin Mary
and the presentation of the child Jesus in the temple of Jerusalem.
Luke is the only evangelist to record this event. Since the actions of
the Holy Family were in complete accord with the law of Moses, no
reason exists for doubting the historical nucleus of the scene.

According to Exodus 13:2, "every firstborn that opens the womb
among the Israelites" was to be consecrated to the Lord. He belonged
in a special way to God. And, according to Leviticus 12:1-4, the
woman who gave birth to a son was unclean for a period of 40 days,
when she was to present herself in the temple with the proper offering
for purification.

In the Western Church the blessing of candles came to be a
distinctive feature of this feast. The lighted candle symbolizes Christ
as the "light of the Gentiles," a title given him by the aged Simeon on
the occasion of the presentation.

According to Numbers 18:15-16 the firstborn male child could
.be redeemed or bought back for a certain amount of money. Luke

does not mention this ceremony, since Jesus remained possessed by the Father throughout his life. His presentation to God in the temple was a formal act of recognition of a reality already verified and never to be denied.

What is probably most significant for Luke in this episode is the first contact of Jesus with the temple of Jerusalem. Jerusalem plays a most important role in his Gospel. It is the focal point of his entire narrative. Both the opening and closing scenes, for example, take place, in Luke's Gospel, in Jerusalem.

Moreover, he has one whole section of his story of Jesus that tells of a journey to Jerusalem (9:51—19:27). It is there that Jesus is destined to die and to be taken up again in glory. ". . . no prophet can be allowed to die anywhere except in Jerusalem" (13:33). This holy city is secondary only to Christ in Luke's Gospel.

Jerusalem, of course, was of utmost importance to the Jewish people. Not only was it the capital of their kingdom in the periods when they had a king, but also its temple was the one place where God manifested his presence in a special way. Isaiah saw Jerusalem as the place where all the nations would come in the end-time to learn the law of God (2:1-5).

The first reading for the feast, from the book of Malachi, highlights this significance of the temple and the city. The opening verse speaks of both the Lord and his messenger coming to the temple. It is an eschatological or end-time coming of which the prophet speaks, and the Lord will have his precursor preparing the way.

It is uncertain whether the following verses speak of God or his messenger. But it is certain that it deals with a final purifying act of God whereby the temple and city would be given their fullest meaning and true sacrifice offered to the Lord.

We cannot be sure whether Luke had this passage from Malachi in mind as he described this first coming of Jesus to the temple. But almost certainly he would see it as appropriate to his intentions. Jesus is the one who gives the city and the temple their fullest meaning, and this first presentation anticipates a whole life centered on the spiritual significance of Jerusalem and its temple.

Jesus universalizes Jerusalem. Not only is he the glory of his people Israel but also "a revealing light to the Gentiles." He belongs to God as he has always belonged to God, as our feast suggests, but always this is *for us* and for the sake of our salvation.

Sacred Heart (A), Friday after the Second Sunday after Pentecost
Deuteronomy 7:6-11; 1 John 4:7-16; Matthew 11:25-30

In an age when the possibility of heart transplants is a reality, the human heart is better understood as a center of life. That is precisely the concept associated with "heart" in Scripture. The Bible does not emphasize the heart as the center of emotional life, but rather the center of human life as such. The heart related to the emotions is much more attributable to romanticism than to biblical theology. Thus we should think of the heart of Christ not in emotional terms but in life terms.

In the readings for today's liturgy as found in the *New American Bible*, the word, "heart," is found twice. Matthew 11:29 is the only citation in the New Testament where Christ's heart is explicitly mentioned. To paraphrase v. 29, "I am gentle and humble of heart," one could say, "I am a gentle and humble person." And Deuteronomy 7:7, "the Lord set his heart on you," is better translated, "the Lord has sent his love upon you," since the word, "heart," is not found in the Hebrew text.

The context of our first reading from Deuteronomy is that of the holy war (7:1-5) which Israel is asked to wage against seven pagan nations. Many thought that the Israelites would fall into the pagan practices of their neighbors and depart from authentic worship of the one true God if such a holy war was not waged. The Israelites were asked to remain obedient to God's laws and the demands that he had placed upon them.

The first reading recounts the great love God has shown his people. It is a love freely given on God's part through no merit of the people. They were neither a large nation nor a strong one. Nevertheless, God chose them, and he always remained faithful to his steadfast word. The response to God's love is that of the people's love for him.

In the Gospel reading a way of life is sketched. The words of Jesus are clear: "learn from me." We are not told what we should learn, but only that we should learn from him. Jesus is the teacher (Jn 3:2), and he is also the subject matter, for we are asked to learn about *him*. This reminds one of Sirach 6:24-28, which finds the author addressing his son on the nature of true wisdom: the son should seek her, learn from her, and carry her yoke. Wisdom is personified in Sirach. In the Gospel, Jesus is a person, a true teacher, and true wisdom.

On the feast dedicated to the Sacred Heart of Jesus, the second reading from 1 John tells us that God "has sent his Son as an offering for our sins"; this is how God shows his love for us. The word for "offering" is the same as that used for "expiation"; God the Father sent Jesus as our expiation through his blood (Rm 3:25).

Expiation, an offering for sins, is what God has done for us, not what we might have done for God. The Father put forward Jesus as an offering to be received by faith. This manifests the love for us of both the Father and the Son.

God's love for us is immense (Jn 3:16), and our response must be to manifest that love for one another (1 Jn 4:11). Through our love for one another, God's love can take root in our midst.

That divine love for us is compassionate and at the same time a willed love, not merely emotional. Paul says it best: "It is precisely in this that God proves his love for us: that while we were still sinners, Christ died for us" (Rm 5:8). God willed to love sinners. And so we must will to love those who appear unattractive: the sick, the imprisoned, the criminal, the enemy.

This feast day commemorates a heart divine and the Lord's willingness to love. Our response must be a human heart willing to love.

P.J.S.

Sacred Heart (B), Friday after the Second Sunday after Pentecost
Hosea 11:1, 3-4, 8c-9; Ephesians 3:8-12,14-19; John 19:31-37

"If you, with all your sins, know how to give your children what is good, how much more will your heavenly Father give good things to anyone who asks him!" (Mt 7:11). These words express the spirit of today's feast, which celebrates God's goodness. Our readings focus upon the Father's gifts to his people, and the supreme gift is Jesus Christ, who poured out his lifeblood on the cross (Jn 19:34).

Hosea, whose love had been rejected by his wife Gomer, develops an account of God's great love for his people. The Hebrew text of our passage is not as clear as we would like. Hosea lived in the northern kingdom, Israel, prophesying shortly before its destruction in 722 B.C. at the hands of Assyrians. This northern kindgom would never rise again; the offspring of the strangers imported into the land and marrying the remaining Israelites would result in the Samaritan race.

In the past, Hosea reminds us, God had intervened in behalf of his children; he had called Israel out of Egypt before it became a nation. Israel was like a son to him (11:1); the Father liberated, healed, and demonstrated compassion to his son. These were his good gifts. God would not destroy Ephraim (being a large tribe, a subtribe of Joseph, it was often identified with the whole northern kingdom). Nevertheless, because of its perfidy in setting up other cult centers and for allying itself with God's enemies, it eventually brought about its own demise at the hands of the Assyrians.

Although God is holy and separate, still he remains in the midst of his people. Even sin does not lessen God's love for those whom he calls his children. Paul says that God demonstrates his love for us in that while we were still sinners Christ died for us (Rm 5:8).

Ephesians carries on this same theme of God's loving gifts. Paul experienced Christ's love for him; it was a humbling experience for he goes down on his knees before God (the normal prayer position was to stand, not to kneel).

The knowledge Paul had of Jesus Christ is not the knowledge that comes from private revelation, a false knowledge as was that associated with the Gnostic error of the times. His knowledge came from a personal encounter with the saving Lord within the Church. The power of the Lord dwelled within him. The word, "strength," in v. 16 comes from the Greek word that gives us our English word *dynamite*. The power of the Lord was explosive; because of his faith in Christ Jesus, Paul had access to God the Father. Faith was the explosive good gift that he had received. His prayer is that the Church continue to make known God's wisdom, Jesus Christ.

Christ's good gift is his love poured out as blood coming from the sacred side. Blood is not death; it is life (Gn 9:4). In the surrendering of his blood Christ has given his life for us; on our behalf the Father has received Jesus as a pleasing sacrifice. In biblical anthropology blood is not considered part of the body as it is today; rather it is the life source that makes an individual alive. Our feast of the Sacred Heart is an expression of God's love in sending his Son as our good gift.

Exalted upon the glorious cross, Christ drew all people to himself (Jn 12:31-33). In the giving up of his life he has given his power to us to experience his compassion and love. He has given us his abiding presence. Elsewhere in the Gospel (Jn 6) we are reminded that we must eat Christ's flesh and drink his blood; this is the power-source in the life of the Christian. The Eucharist is Christ's great gift of compassion and love. It far surpasses what Hosea could have imagined; it fulfills Paul's ardent desire for Christ's perfect indwelling within the hearts of his faithful followers.

P.J.S.

Sacred Heart (C), Friday after the Second Sunday after Pentecost
Ezekiel 34:11-16; Romans 5:5-11; Luke 15:3-7

The reading from Paul's letter to the Romans sets the tone for today's celebration, the Sacred Heart. To many Christians the word, "justification," is a mystery. It sounds awesome, or vague, or unclear. For some it suggests juridical procedures or a courtroom.

Webster gives this definition for the word, "justify": "to prove or show to be just, right, or reasonable." And Paul tells us today that we have been justified by the blood of Christ (5:9).

God proved his love for us by justifying us through Christ's lifeblood (5:8). He reconciled us while we were still sinners (5:10). By the surrender of his life for us, Christ put us into the proper relationship with God; a change occurred, not in God, but within human beings, a change from being an enemy to being a friend of God.

Because of the environment of sin that pervaded the world through the disobedience of the first man and woman, humankind was in a state of enmity with God. Because of the healing grace that entered our earthly existence due to the obedience of the God-Man Jesus Christ, humankind became a friend of God. Christ's blood has put us into an ordered existence with the Father, Jesus, and our brothers and sisters in the Church. God has proved his love for us.

Christ's reconciling activity has saved us from God's wrath (5:9). God was not angry with his people; he constantly called humankind to repent and follow his ways. This was repeated throughout history. In rejecting God's love, however, human beings experienced rejection, which they called wrath. But God was not doing the rejecting; rather people refused to accept God's word.

Through Christ's saying yes to the Father, God's love was no longer resisted and no longer experienced as wrath. The Bible does not portray man as a sinner in the hands of an angry God; the Bible portrays man as a sinner whom God lovingly calls to repentance.

The readings from Ezekiel and Luke portray God's love for his people in vivid terms; it is a love similar to that of a shepherd for his sheep. In the Bible, words like *sheep, ram, and lamb* are used almost five hundred times. The New Testament employs the word *sheep* almost forty times and *shepherd* fifteen times.

Sheep are in constant need of care, defenseless, and fairly docile. They need the shepherd as a protector and leader. Ezekiel lamented the conduct of the priests and kings of Judah who had led the people astray, and who were held responsible for the Babylonian victory. They had been poor shepherds. God is the true shepherd; he shows great love for his sheep. He will bring justice and strength to the scattered flock in exile in Babylon. The flock was liberated in 538 B.C. and allowed to go home to Judah; God was their shepherd and leader.

In chapter 15 Luke recounts several stories about rejoicing: the woman who finds her lost coin, the father whose prodigal son returns home, the shepherd who searches out his lost sheep. God's love is ever searching. He is the *Hound of Heaven*, who will not allow those entrusted to him to perish. He rejoices over the repentant sinner just as a shepherd rejoices over finding his lost sheep. Jesus is the good shepherd (Jn 10:11), the great Shepherd of the sheep (Heb 13:20).

Jesus' love is joyful. The feast of the Sacred Heart reminds us that we have need of rejoicing; Christians are to be a joy-filled people. God's love is greater than ours, for he causes wrath to be turned into friendship, sorrow into joy. He defends the defenseless and searches out the stray. The love of his Heart fills the whole world.

P.J.S.

Birth of John the Baptizer (ABC), June 24
Isaiah 49:1-6; Acts 13:22-26; Luke 1:57-66, 80

Man proposes; God disposes. That maxim is an attempt to express our belief in divine providence. God is the sovereign Lord of history, and his will for human fulfillment will prevail. He disposes all things.

While we can rightly be edified by such a belief, the Scriptures really take that maxim one step further. God both proposes and disposes. Before we ask what that does to human responsibility, let's first see the evidence of the biblical maxim. The readings for our feast give all the evidence we need.

The first reading, from the book of Isaiah, provides the clearest argument for what we can call total providence. It is one of a series of poems depicting a mysterious figure whom the scholars have called "the suffering servant of Yahweh." Precisely whom the prophet had in mind when he wrote these poems is unknown, which is why we called him a mysterious figure.

The early Church from the beginning identified Jesus as the suffering servant and interpreted the poems as depicting him carrying out his mission of salvation to all the nations. A swift reading of our present poem shows how readily such an interpretation can be justified.

But the contemporary Church, for this feast only, applies the poem to John the Baptizer. The overriding reason is that the poem speaks of the Lord calling him "from birth" and giving him his name from his "mother's womb." How true this is of the Baptizer we see from Luke's Gospel where the angel tells Zechariah that his future son's name is to be John (1:13). Our Gospel reading tells the story of Zechariah's compliance with the angel's command, which is really an expression of God's will.

Here, then, in the case of John the Baptizer we have a striking illustration of total providence. From womb to tomb God has care for his own. You will find no discussion in the Bible about when the implanted seed becomes a human person. That's because the biblical authors see things always from God's side. His presence and his care are there from the beginning, and even before!

Doesn't this make puppets out of human persons? If God is always there "calling the shots," how can we be said to be free? Paradoxically, the one conviction that the Scriptures put on a par with that of divine sovereignty is that of human freedom. God proposes and disposes, but we are free.

There is a philosophical approach to the solution of that paradox, but we will adhere to the biblical evidence for its existence. And there the one incontestable argument for human freedom alongside divine sovereignty is sin. We can defy the divine will. That is precisely what sin means in the Bible.

No other literature in the history of mankind speaks so insistently of the possibility and reality of sin. In fact, it is precisely because of the conviction of total providence that sin takes on the grotesqueness that it does. Sin is human freedom run amok; but without freedom, sin would not be possible.

The Baptizer's story tells us about human freedom exercised in its finest form through acceptance of God's total providence. When we accept ourselves as God really intends us to be (and how well John knew who he was!), then we affirm both his providence and our freedom.

Only in looking back on John's life did the Church know it could apply that poem in Isaiah to him. John did not hear that call in his mother's womb. Only when he gave himself freely to God did he recognize the call. As with John, so it is with all of us. God is there calling us by name from our mother's womb. When we make the surrender of faith, we recognize it.

Sts. Peter and Paul, Apostles (ABC), June 29
Acts 12:1-11; 2 Timothy 4:6-8, 17-18; Matthew 16:13-19

In some religious circles structure is a bad word. To connect it with religion, these people claim, is to put God in a box. It institutionalizes the Spirit. And that, they argue, is not good.

The most radical of these "free-the-Spirit" buffs hold that any kind of limitation put on religious realities is a form of manipulation of the divine. Creedal formulas must go; they're only human attempts to express the inexpressible. All rituals must go; basically they're only magic, playing with the ghostly. Above all, hierarchy, or the ranking of religious persons in a gradation of command, is harmful to the free human spirit.

It sounds so right. Who is going to argue against untrammeled freedom? Who is going to say, "This is the way we express our faith?" Who would dare devise a rite guaranteed to channel divine grace? Who would lay hands on another and declare that person an official minister of religion?

The answer, of course, is that God does. He accepts the limits of humanity, the crutches of ritual, and the boundary lines of structure. The Scriptures give strong evidence of this kind of divine condescension.

When God called Abraham and made a promise to him, he began a series of self-limitations that would never cease. Israel became *his* people because *he chose them*; they did not choose him. His own unfettered love tied him irreversibly to this one nation.

When Samuel anointed the young David in anticipation of his future kingship, the Spirit of God came upon him "from that day on" (1 Samuel 16:15). What does that mean? It means that, for good or bad, God's Spirit had bound himself to David's house, the Davidic dynasty: "Your house and your kingdom shall endure forever before me . . . " (2 S 7:16). Now *that* is institutionalization of the Spirit if anything is! But the Spirit does it himself.

When Jesus came, did he do away with these self-limitations that the Father had opted for himself? Incarnation is the most obvious argument that he did not. Incarnation is *this* flesh, of *this* people, at *this* time and place, of *this* woman—it all says structure in no uncertain terms.

In the light of this kenotic activity ("kenotic" means self-emptying, a way of expressing God's willingness to abide by human structure), we should not be surprised to find in the New Testament Scriptures things like creedal formulas, ritual and sacraments, and yes, hierarchical structure.

Our feast today is, in fact, a celebration of God-willed structure in the Church. The Gospel reading says it clearly. The Church of Jesus Christ is built on *this* man, Peter. He is given keys to open and close doors. He is given authority to declare bound and loosed. It's difficult to imagine that Matthew was recording these grandiose words just for a short-lived community in some Syrian outpost.

Yes, Jesus willed structure. But just as clearly he willed it *for us*, not for it. Structure is not an end in itself, but a means to come closer to God and one another. When structure stifles the Spirit instead of providing the channel for its free and authentic expression, it doesn't serve its purpose.

A leading Lutheran theologian wrote recently, "No trial oppressed Luther's spirit more often in his later years than his recognition that structure was inevitable . . . " (J. Pelikan). But then, Luther knew the Scriptures well enough to realize that God had already come to that conclusion.

Transfiguration of the Lord (A), August 6
Daniel 7:9-10, 13-14; 2 Peter 1:16-19; Matthew 17:1-9

One hopes that visions help people live better, since there are so many recorded in the Scriptures. Scholars say, however, that in comparison with other religions, visions are relatively few in the Bible. Ordinarily revelation takes place through prophetic interpretation of history.

But visions are the subjects of these three readings. The first, from the book of Daniel, shows us the "Ancient One" and a "son of man." In the Gospel is the vision of Jesus transfigured witnessed by Peter, James, and John. The second reading contains a reference to the same vision. How can these accounts help us?

The "Ancient One" in Daniel is God himself. All the character-istics attributed to him are symbols of his eternity (white hair), his glory and power (fire), his role as judge (attendants, books opened up). The "son of man" represents the renewed people of God to whom the "Ancient One" confers the kingdom.

The book of Daniel was written in the early part of the second century B.C. The Jewish people were being severely persecuted for their faith. For many it was difficult to remain faithful. For them the book was written. It was an assurance that God was still in charge and that his will, his plan, would prevail. Kingship would be restored to his people. By 166 B.C. this happened; the vision proved true.

In this case the vision was a source of consolation in time of difficulty. It is a revelation of divine power that will be effective in time. The vision does not remove one from the sound and fury of actual history; it is not an escape from life. But it does offer hope and the courage to persevere.

The apostles' vision of Jesus transfigured has its own meaning, one not altogether different from that of Daniel's. But first, note the symbolism in order to appreciate the overall meaning. The trans-formed body reminds one of Paul's description of the resurrected body in 1 Corinthians 15:40-44. The dazzling face and radiant clothes suggest the divine glory manifested in the resurrection.

Moses and Elijah represent the two major portions of the Old Testament, the law and the prophets, which Jesus fulfills. The cloud is always a symbol of transcendence, the sphere to which no human has access. The voice is the Father's; he repeats the affirmation of Jesus' sonship made at the time of his baptism by John (3:17).

In all three Gospels, where the transfiguration is mentioned, it occurs shortly after Jesus' first prediction of his coming passion and death and of his followers' involvement in the cross of suffering. In other words, those involved are real flesh and blood people, Jesus and his own who belong to the kind of world we know, a world of frequent opportunities to bear the cross.

Like the vision in Daniel, so the transfiguration is a vision of victory, of resurrected glory. It is, therefore, an assurance to the traveler that the goal is there. We all need that assurance as a basis for our hope.

But perhaps the emphasis should be that *Jesus* was transfigured rather than that Jesus was *transfigured*. It is he who is our brother, who shared our sorrows and our sufferings, who knows our heartaches. He beckons us onward in the journey.

Transfiguration of the Lord (B), August 6
Daniel 7:9-10; 13-14; 2 Peter 1:16-19; Mark 9:2-10

"Metamorphosis" is a strange sounding Greek word. *Webster's New Collegiate Dictionary* defines it as "a change of physical form, structure, substance, esp. by supernatural means." The dictionary also mentions that the term is applicable to the process whereby a caterpillar turns into a butterfly and a tadpole into a frog.

The word, "transfigured," from Mark's Gospel is a translation of the Greek word for metamorphosis: literally, to change form. Mark underlines the marvelous change that occurred in Jesus and to which the apostles bore witness. "And his clothes became dazzling white— whiter than the work of any bleacher could make them."

In the New Testament the word, "bleacher," is found only here. A bleacher was a textile worker; the less common but still more precise word is "fuller." A part of the fuller's job was to shrinken and thicken newly carded wool and then to cleanse it. No soap was used in biblical times; borith or the ashes of borith, later on potash, was used for this purpose.

The disciples, Peter, James, and John, bear witness that no human bleacher's activity could have made Jesus' clothes so "dazzling white." Jesus was "transfigured." The word, "transfigured," is used but four times in the New Testament: Mark 9:2; Matthew 17:2; Romans 12:2; 2 Corinthians 3:18.

In Romans and 2 Corinthians the emphasis upon the change concerns the lives of the faithful followers of Jesus; they are being transformed by their living faith, being made into new persons, and in the process of achieving glory as a gift from God. Thus, transfiguration says something not only about Jesus, but also something about those who follow him. It has meaning for us today, for we are on the way to the enjoyment of that blossoming gift of glory.

In the transfiguration of Jesus Christ, the apostles witness the transformation of one who was in "the form of a slave" (Ph 2:7) into the glory of the one who was in "the form of a God (Ph 2:6). This section of Philippians is known as the kenotic passage (2:5-11); it treats of the preexisting state of the Son of God, his earthly existence, and his resurrected, glorified existence.

The Son exists before the incarnation, becomes incarnate, taking upon himself human form, and then as the God-Man is gloriously resurrected. In Mark the disciples are given a preview of the glory of Jesus Christ, the Son of God and the Son of Man. At this time they do not know what he meant when he spoke to them of the need of the Son of Man to rise from the dead (Mk 9:9-10). It is at the foot of the cross that Mark has the centurion publicly proclaim that the Son of Man "was the Son of God" (Mk 15:39).

The reading from Daniel has been chosen because of the reference to "one like a son of man" who comes to the Ancient of Days. His vehicle is the clouds of heaven. For Daniel, "son of man" is not a proper name. Rather it represents all the people of God; "son of man" is a corporate person who will vanquish God's enemies. In Daniel it refers to faithful Israel.

In the New Testament, however, Jesus uses this title to designate himself, thus making it a proper name, "Son of Man." In the Gospel it is used over 80 times. Jesus as Son of Man vanquishes the Father's enemies: sin, death, and the devil.

Peter emphasizes that the apostles are true witnesses to the events that have transpired; the apostles are those who preach "the prophetic message," which is a reliable one. The law (Moses) and the prophets (Elijah) had looked forward to the one who was to come. At the transfiguration Jesus demonstrates that he is the fulfillment. He is not "a son of man," but rather "the Son of Man."

P.J.S.

Transfiguration of the Lord (C), August 6
Daniel 7:9-10, 13-14; 2 Peter 1:16-19; Luke 9:28b-36

The first and third readings for today's feast introduce us to the theme of "journey" or "passage." Daniel speaks of the journeying "one like a son of man," who uses the clouds of heaven as his mode of transportation, going to meet the Ancient of Days. The Gospel presents a conversation, omitted by Matthew and Mark, of Jesus, Moses, and Elijah about Jesus' intended journey, his "passage."

Luke's twin works, the Gospel and Acts of the Apostles, concern themselves with various journeys. In Luke cc. 1 and 2 Mary and Joseph journey from Nazareth to Bethlehem and then back again; when Jesus was twelve years old, the Holy Family went to Jerusalem and then returned to Galilee. Beginning in 9:51 Jesus embarks on the journey of his public ministry from Galilee to Jerusalem. Upon reaching the holy city he weeps over it (19:41). In Acts several journeys occur; each concerns Church growth and the spread of the faith beginning in Jerusalem and finally ending up in the political center of the world, Rome.

According to popular Jewish tradition of the times, the people expected the return of Moses and Elijah in the end-times. In the context of Jesus' face being changed and his garments being made white, the two Old Testament personages are indicative of the marvelous "passage" that Jesus is to make through his death-resurrection-ascension event. They had been admitted to God's realm in marvelous ways.

The word, "transfiguration," does not appear in Luke's account; it does appear in Matthew's and Mark's. According to Luke, Jesus prepared for the important events in his life through special emphasis on prayer. Before his baptism (3:21), before his arrest in the Garden of Gethsemane (22:41), before choosing his apostles (6:12), and here in the "transfiguration" Jesus prays. His disciples accompany him, but their prayer turns into sleep; the same thing will occur in Gethsemane.

Because of their sleep, the disciples, upon being awakened, don't understand the significance of what is happening before their eyes. They do not realize that Jesus must leave them so that they can carry out the mission in his name. For this reason Luke records the conversation that concerns Jesus' "departure." Each of the three disciples present, and all disciples of every age, would have to undergo his own "passage"; this is the theme of Acts of the Apostles.

Jesus' passage entailed being delivered up (9:44), "to be taken from this world" (9:51). And yet he resolutely set his face toward Jerusalem and the journey began. In anticipation of the glory that belongs to the ascended Christ, his disciples were given a glimpse of what would one day be: a glorified leader.

The author of our second reading presents himself as Peter and is at pains to point out that he was an eyewitness to the transfiguration. Modern day scholarship discounts the Petrine authorship of this work; nevertheless, its canonicity and inspired character are universally maintained. It was common among people of old to ascribe their works to some well-known personage in order to be accepted. The message of 2 Peter is that of the necessity of the faithful follower of Jesus to remain true to his authentic teaching and to be wary of all who pervert the good news (2:1). It is necessary for each of us to keep "a lamp shining in a dark place until the first streaks of dawn appear" (1:19).

In our lives as Christians there is always the tension of joy and sadness, glory and shame. One lesson from this feast is: we must stay awake in prayer, watchful for the coming of the Lord, eager to read the signs of the times, ready to begin or to continue our "passage" of witnessing to the glorious Christ by preaching his name and living his life within us.

P.J.S

The Assumption of Mary (ABC), August 15
Revelation 11:19; 12:1-6, 10; 1 Corinthians 15:20-26;
Luke 1:39-56

The assumption of the Blessed Virgin Mary into heaven was solemnly defined by Pope Pius XII on November 1, 1950. The definition does not decide whether Mary died or not before her assumption, a point widely debated for centuries in the Church. Basically what the definition tells us is that Mary enjoys, to the fullest extent possible, eternal life with her Son, a goal that all of us hope to attain eventually.

There is no direct evidence of the assumption in the New Testament. Some texts, however, can be said to form the beginning of a trajectory that will continue to develop in succeeding ages. These texts say something, either directly or indirectly, about Mary. By reflecting on them over the centuries the Church sees more clearly a deeper meaning in them. The Spirit, always present in the Church, instructs her on what is to be taught.

The first of these texts is found in the book of Revelation. It presents the well-known sign of "a woman clothed with the sun, with the moon under her feet, and on her head a crown of twelve stars." It goes on to say that this woman gave birth to a child, "a boy destined to shepherd all the nations with an iron rod."

The identification of the child is clear; it is the Messiah, Jesus Christ. No one else could be described in those terms. Then his mother must be Mary, and the description given of her in the opening verse would be a powerful witness to what we believe with respect to the assumption.

Many scholars, however, feel that the author means the woman to refer to the Church, which can be said to have given birth to the Messiah. This interpretation also fits in better with what is said about the woman fleeing into the desert, "where a special place had been prepared for her by God."

Those last words, of course, can be applied beautifully to the assumption of Mary. But if it refers to the Church, then it means that God provides protection for his persecuted Church until the end of time. And so we are torn between the two interpretations. Indeed, some scholars think the author had *both* realities in mind, Mary and the Church.

The history of the interpretation of the passage is fascinating. We see how the Church throughout the ages has grown in her understanding. And there is no doubt that, in giving us this reading for the Solemnity of the Assumption, the Church is intending it for our reflection on Mary united with God forever.

The second reading, for Paul's letter to the Corinthians, does not mention Mary. But it does tell us how the assumption is possible. It is through the power of Christ's own resurrection. " . . . in Christ all will come to life again, but each one in proper order: Christ the first fruits and then, at his coming, all those who belong to him."

The Church believes that Mary, who belongs to Christ in a special way, has already achieved this life.

Of the three, the Gospel reading is the most direct text on Mary. In the famous *Magnificat* a solid foundation is had for all the honors that God, through his Church, would eventually heap on Mary. All ages have called her blessed.

We suggested at the beginning the meaning of the assumption for us. Mary points to where we, too, are destined. Eternal union with the Lord is our goal. Mary shares it already.

Triumph of the Cross (ABC), September 14
Numbers 21:4-9; Philippians 2:6-11; John 3:13-17

Sacred Scripture makes it clear that salvation comes to mankind in two complementary ways: through the cross and through the resurrection. "The message of the cross is complete absurdity to those who are headed for ruin, but to us who are experiencing salvation it is the power of God" (1 Cor 1:18). Jesus was "raised up for our justification" (Rm 4:25). The same Paul wrote both those sentences.

Salvation through the cross is referred to as a theology of the cross. Salvation through the resurrection is referred to as a theology of glory. Both are essential to God's plan. Both are part of the same movement of man back to God. On this day the emphasis is placed on the theology of the cross.

The earliest Christian confession of faith was most likely "Jesus is Lord!" This formula was a result of the experience of the resurrection. Jesus' victory was seen as constituted in being raised from the dead. Only by such a release could he exercise lordship over the whole world.

But the early Church had, almost immediately, to face the reality of Jesus' suffering and ignominious death. The truly remarkable thing is that she never tried to conceal it, to explain it away, or to apologize for it. From the beginning she recognized it as also contributing to man's salvation.

The many statements of Jesus in the Gospels about the necessity of taking up the cross are a witness to this recognition. "If a man wishes to come after me, he must deny his very self, take up his cross, and follow in my steps" (Mk 8:34). " . . . unless the grain of wheat falls to the earth and dies, it remains just a grain of wheat. But if it dies, it produces much fruit" (Jn 12:24).

The Church also saw the necessity of suffering and death presented in Old Testament passages. The suffering servant of Yahweh, described in the book of Isaiah, was one figure whom they saw fulfilled in Christ. The servant had been "crushed for our sins" (Is 53:5). Jesus, too, was "handed over to death for our offenses" (Rm 4:25).

The Bible sees the crucifixion of Jesus in two distinct ways. In the first it is the climax of a downward movement that will be paralleled by an upward movement of resurrection and glorification. This is the way it is seen in our second reading from Philippians. Notice that there are stages in the self-emptying of Christ, the final stage being that of death, even "death on a cross." The hymn then continues with the exaltation of Jesus, the parallel movement. Both movements are essential to the concluding affirmation of lordship.

John, on the other hand, sees the crucifixion as part of the upward movement. For him the downward movement climaxes in the incarnation, the taking on of human flesh at the time of Jesus' conception in Mary's womb. From that moment Jesus begins his return to the Father. And his being raised up on the cross is the first stage of his being raised up in resurrection and ascension. This the Gospel reading brings out.

That is the reason why the bronze serpent story, referred to in the Gospel, is given as the first reading. Whatever may have been the original meaning of the story, the Old Testament author sees it and uses it as a symbol of God's will to save his people. Salvation comes through the lifting up of a bronze serpent on a pole.

This is the meaning that John, too, sees present in the story. Jesus, like the serpent, must be lifted up on the pole of the cross, and whoever looks to him in faith will be saved. That is why the Church can speak, in all truth, of the triumph of the cross.

All Saints (ABC), November 1
Revelation 7:2-4, 9-14; 1 John 3:1-3; Matthew 5:1-12a

Happy Feast Day! This is a joyous celebration; the Church on earth and the Church suffering rejoice with the Church triumphant. Today we celebrate what we proclaim in each Sunday of the year: "We believe in the communion of saints."

In Matthew's Gospel Jesus is presented as the preacher of good news (11:5), the teacher of the kingdom (5:2), the one in whom the prophecies of the old dispensation have been fulfilled (8:17). It is of these things that our third reading speaks. Jesus preaches the good news of the Kingdom, for it is breaking into the lives of those who listen. Jesus is the one who has fulfilled the Old Testament promises and turned the world upside down. Through him, the poor in spirit, the hungry, the persecuted, the mourners, and the meek will be satisfied; through him the compassionate and the peacemakers will have their reward.

The second reading highlights the expectant hope the Christian must have while awaiting the manifestation of the Lord. 1 John points out that God loves us and has made us his children. Yet we await the coming of the Lord to see him face to face. We long not only for his coming at the end of time, but also and even more importantly for his coming at the end of our earthly existence when he will take us by the hand and lead us into that heavenly city.

It is primarily for the inhabitants of that city that we have this celebration today. Revelation 7 points out the final state for those who have gone before us to meet the Lord.

At the end of c. 6 the question had been asked: who can withstand the wrath of the Lamb? Those who have been sealed will not be harmed by the wrath of God. Note that the lectionary has omitted vv. 5-8, which mention the 12 tribes of Israel and the 12,000 sealed from each tribe. The 144,000 of v.4 is the result of the multiplication of these two numbers. In apocalyptic writing (Revelation is written in this literary style), numbers are significant. The people of old considered 7 a perfect number. Three and 4 shared in that perfection and were also considered perfect: thus 3 groups of 4s or 4 groups of 3s made 12 a perfect number as well. One hundred was an indefinite number—unlimited. Thus 144,000 means a perfect unlimited number. The seal that they receive is a protecting shield; it is the name of the living God (22:4). This seal protects them from the punishment that the messenger angels will wreak upon "the inhabitants of earth" (8:13). The inhabitants of the earth are those who are enemies of God and Christ the Lamb. They wage war upon the Lamb's followers.

The author is at pains to point out that among those destined for heaven and among those already in heaven are both Jewish and Gentile Christians. In vv. 9-12 we see the great multitude praising God and the Lamb in heaven. They now share in the victory of the Lamb and carry the palm of victory and wear the white robes of glory. Victory has been won. They sing to God employing 7 nouns in their acclamation: praise, glory, wisdom, thanksgiving, honor, power, and might.

In vv. 13-17, which follow our lectionary reading, we are told how the victory was won. It was not by words alone. They have gained a right to the victorious celebration because "they have washed their robes and made them white in the blood of the lamb" (v. 14).

On the Solemnity of All Saints, Matthew, 1 John, and Revelation remind us that this is our day. We are to be joyous as we celebrate the solemn festival here below. Our lifetime is a pilgrimage to the heavenly city above. Yet it is only in the total commitment of our personality to Christ that we can make our robes white in his lifeblood and have the fulfillment of our hopes. It is in him that we live—and hope to die. We are pilgrims on our way home. The path is found in the beatitudes, and the end is found in heaven. Happy Feast Day!

P.J.S.

All Souls (ABC), November 2
Wisdom 3:1-9; Romans 5:5-11; Matthew 11:25-30

The universal practice of commemorating the souls of the faithful departed on a special day of the year is almost a thousand years old in the Roman Catholic Church. The commemoration itself is as old as Christianity and even has its roots in the Old Testament. Throughout the centuries an ever enriching process in the revelation of this mystery has taken place.

Throughout most of Israel's history no clear recognition of personal immortality existed. The dead slept "with the fathers." They went to "Sheol," a place conceived to be underground, where they lived a kind of shadowy existence, but without any hope of a fuller life. They simply existed. They neither praised God nor looked forward to his help. God is even said not to remember the dead any longer (Ps 88:6).

Just why the revelation of an afterlife was not given to Israel at an earlier date is not clear. Other peoples, especially the Egyptians, Israel's neighbor, had an elaborate cult of the dead, but this had no apparent influence on official Israel. Perhaps they could not reconcile certain aspects of this pagan cult with their unique concept of God.

A couple of the Psalms reveal an incipient hope in a life after death. "With your counsel you guide me, and in the end you will receive me in glory" (Ps 73:24). But this seems to be the conviction of an individual psalmist rather than a firmly grounded doctrine. God, it seems, willed that Israel have a proper regard for the significance of this life before revealing the existence of another.

But that revelation came in due time. It is found in the books of Daniel, Maccabees, and Wisdom with equal clarity. (Any of these, or others, can be used as the first reading for this feast. The other readings also are a matter of choice.) None of these books is earlier than the second century B.C. It was then that belief in resurrection and immortality became widespread.

The first reading we have chosen is from the book of Wisdom. It is the clearest affirmation of an afterlife of union with God that is found in the Old Testament. There is no explicit mention of the resurrection of the body, a doctrine already proclaimed in Daniel. But the significant point is that life for the dead is envisioned.

The context of the passage indicates that the catalyst for the revelation was the suffering of the holy ones here below. "Chastised a little, they shall be greatly blessed because God tried them and found them worthy of himself." While their death seemed futile in the eyes of the foolish, they are in peace.

Union with God is the strongest element in this doctrine. The fear of complete separation from him had moved the psalmist to cries of hope. To be with God forever is the deepest longing that one who enjoys God's friendship on this earth can have. Heaven is a continuation of earth when earth is seen as life with God.

St. Paul was filled with the belief in immortality. But he sees it taking on new meaning because of Jesus Christ. It was his passion, death, and resurrection that makes possible the total transformation of the Christian dead.

The passage we have chosen from his letter to the Romans does not mention life after death. But it does refer to our salvation (which for Paul includes eternal salvation) and shows how God's love, manifested in Jesus, effected it. We have "received reconciliation"; we are reunited with our Creator and Redeemer.

The Gospel reading stresses that all revelation is perfected in Jesus, since he is the Son through whom the Father reveals himself. The conviction of this truth is closely tied to the rest that faithful souls will find in him. It is this eternal rest of the faithful departed that the Church recalls today and remembers in her prayers.

Dedication of St. John Lateran (ABC), November 9
Isaiah 56:1, 6-7; Ephesians 2:19-22; John 2:13-22

Today again a special feast replaces the Ordinary Sunday of the year. As on last Sunday, the feast of All Souls, the readings can be chosen by the celebrant from among several designated for the dedication of a Church. The above readings represent only this writer's choice.

St. John Lateran (named after St. John the Baptizer and the ancient family of Laterani on whose land the church is built) is the cathedral church of Rome and one of the four major Roman basilicas. For almost a thousand years the original building was the residence of the Popes. Thus, both because it is the cathedral church of Rome and because of its history, the church's dedication is celebrated in the universal Church. The readings give us an insight into the significance of such a feast.

In the Old Testament period Jerusalem was hailed as the religious center of Israel after David moved the ark of the covenant there about 1000 B.C. It took on even greater significance when his son Solomon built a temple there for the ark and for liturgical service.

The Jerusalem temple remained the focus of Israel's worship for a couple of centuries. It is true there were other shrines on the sur-

rounding hillsides, but often these were marked by the intrusion of
pagan worship in the services. In the reform of Josiah, about 620 B.C.,
these shrines were destroyed and sacrifice was permitted only in the
Jerusalem temple. This necessarily enhanced its meaning in the eyes
of all.

The central significance of the temple of this period is reflected in
the first reading. The anonymous prophet, writing after the return
from exile about 500 B.C., sees the restored temple as the place of
prayer and worship for all peoples. This is a remarkable development. Israel's role will be a missionary one to all nations, and the
temple will serve as their gathering place.

An even more radical development takes place in the New
Testament. Both the second and third readings illustrate it. In John's
Gospel we read of Jesus' cleansing of the Jerusalem temple and his
statement, "Destroy this temple and in three days I will raise it up."
St. John informs us that Jesus was referring to his own body as the
temple, raised in the resurrection.

What did John have in mind when he referred to Jesus' body as
the temple? Most likely he intended the risen Jesus as "the 'place'
where God is to be adored, the true 'house of God' " (R.
Schnackenburg). Thus, too, he would be the focus of the gathering of
all peoples as predicted in the first reading.

Before trying to understand this in the context of a material
church building, let us take a brief look at the second reading. Here
we read that the new temple or house of God is the Church. ". . . in
him (Christ) you are being built into this temple, to become a dwelling place for God in the Spirit."

Behind these rich images lies the conviction that the glorified
Body of Christ is the focal point of all worship of the Father. It is
through him, with him, and in him that all honor and glory are given
to the Father. He is the new temple and all who accept him as Lord
form a new temple since they are "in him."

The material church building, then, takes on new significance in
the Christian dispensation. It is the place where the Eucharistic Body
is most often made present and offered to the Father. It is the gathering place of the new temple that is the Church, the people of God. It is
a sign, therefore, of a deeper spiritual reality, of another temple not

made by hands. It is for this reason that we celebrate the dedication of the material church building.

Immaculate Conception (ABC), December 8
Genesis 3:9-15, 20; Ephesians 1:3-6, 11-12; Luke 1:26-38

With the decree, *Ineffabilis Deus*, Pope Pius IX solemnly declared the Immaculate Conception of Mary a doctrine of the Church. The dogma is this: from the first moment of her conception in the womb of her mother, Mary, by the special choice of God, was preserved from the existing situation of sin to which all other human beings are subject. Destined to be the mother of Jesus Christ, Son of God and Son of Mary, she was protected by God from all effects of original sin. Note that this doctrine does not deal with Mary's virginal conception of Jesus in her womb.

The scripture readings have been selected for this solemnity because they indirectly have something to tell us about the Immaculate Conception. Genesis recounts how sin entered God's created universe. Ephesians places emphasis upon the free choice of the Father in predestining us in Christ. Luke points out the unique role of Mary as mother of Jesus. None of these texts contains an explicit reference to the Immaculate Conception.

Genesis 3:15 has been called the *protoevangelium* (first Gospel) because a promise is given that one born of woman will eventually arise and he will put an end to the wiles of the serpent. In recorded bible history this is the first literary promise of an eventual liberator who will set humanity free. The Genesis reading for today's solemnity underlines the role of the woman called Eve in committing the first sin in the garden. This woman is in sharp contrast with Mary whose Son died for our sins (1 Cor 15:3). (The name, Eve, is not a proper name, but is derived from a popular etymology, mother of all the living. Adam also is not a proper name, but a word for man or mankind.) The woman of Genesis is similar to Mary for from her will eventually come forth an offspring to strike at the head of the serpent (Gn 3:15).

The second reading is a selection from a longer Trinitarian hymn that runs from 1:3 to 1:14; vv. 1-6 describe the activity of God the Father; vv. 7-13a recount the activity wrought by God the Son in redemption, and vv. 13b-14 speak of the activity of God the Holy Spirit. The lectionary's selection emphasizes that each of us has been chosen in Christ before the world began (v.4). In lieu of Christ's redeeming activity the Father freely chose and predestined us "through Christ Jesus to be his adopted sons" (v.5). This reading is a wise choice for our celebration; Mary was chosen for an extraordinary position, the mother of Jesus Christ. In a most special way did the Father predestine her from all eternity; she was immaculately conceived in the womb of her mother.

Luke presents us with a beloved passage from the Scriptures. A simple maiden in an obscure town in Galilee received an astounding message: "The Lord is with you" (1:28). Similar words are addressed to Gideon (Jg 6:12) to preannounce God's remarkable demonstration of his power. For Mary the remarkable demonstration of God's power is that Jesus will be virginally conceived within her womb. In Matthew's Gospel Jesus is called the "Emmanuel" (1:23), God who is with us. At the end of this Gospel, just before his ascension, Jesus promises to be with the disciples, with the Church always (Mt 28:20). In our Lukan Gospel today the author tells us Jesus' promises are already fulfilled in Mary: "The Lord is with you." Mary possesses that which was promised to the Church, the presence of the Lord. And that presence exists even before she conceives by the power of the Holy Spirit.

On this solemnity the Church rejoices with Mary, who was chosen to have a unique role in God's plan. She was greeted with the words, "Rejoice, O highly favored daughter" (Lk 1:28). Mary rejoiced and said yes to God's will. We, too, must rejoice and praise God for what he has accomplished in Mary.

P.J.S.